Mindful Leadership in Practice

Volker Schulte • Christoph Steinebach •
Klaske N. Veth
Editors

Mindful Leadership in Practice

Tradition Leads to the Future

Springer

Editors
Volker Schulte
University of Applied Sciences Northwest Switzerland
Windisch, Switzerland

Christoph Steinebach
ZHAW – School of Applied Psychology
Zürich, Switzerland

Klaske N. Veth
Hanze University of Applied Sciences Groningen
Groningen, The Netherlands

ISBN 978-3-030-97310-0 ISBN 978-3-030-97311-7 (eBook)
https://doi.org/10.1007/978-3-030-97311-7

This Springer imprint is published by the registered company Springer Nature Switzerland AG
The registered company address is: Gewerbestrasse 11, 6330 Cham, Switzerland

Foreword

Leadership in the 21st century

The three traditional leadership maxims of power, authority, and influence have a different meaning in today's leadership context than they did thirty years ago. At that time, a superior was still able to initiate a will-forming process solely through his or her social status and to check that the will was being secured through close monitoring. The employees simply had to implement the will of the superior without questioning. Power implies having power over someone. It further implies a strong hierarchy in an organization. It guarantees the assertiveness of the powerful by unilaterally defining implementation goals without duly accommodating the wishes or demands of employees. Such a culture of leadership has had its day. It no longer works. Power and authority have eroded.

Leadership now only works through the role model function of the leader, by setting a good example and setting cultural and ethical milestones. Leadership requires a will to shape things that can motivate people to do creative work by means of conviction, a human-centered attitude, and empathy. Leadership means providing orientation, integrating employees into processes and contexts, and thus convincing them of the meaningfulness of actions and activities.

This book opens up about what mindful leadership might look like. It is a foundational work that illuminates a mindful value system and compares it in different cultural contexts. It offers philosophical reflections, tips, and action guides that can be applied in a wide variety of industries and traditions. It is hoped that leaders of today will embrace mindful leadership so that they can educate, support, and mentor the leaders of tomorrow. After all, humanity and authentic collegiality are more important than ever in today's technologized, complex, and highly connected workplace.

Reha Rheinfelden, Rheinfelden, Switzerland — Thierry Ettlin

Contents

About the Editors

Marc Aeschbacher Dr. Phil., is a lecturer at the Institute for Corporate Management, School of Business, University of Applied Sciences Northwestern Switzerland, and lecturer and coach for organizational development.

Reyk Albrecht is trained in international management and applied ethics. He is the scientific director of the Ethics Center at the Friedrich Schiller University Jena, and holds teaching positions in the Social and Behavioral Sciences and Medical Faculty of the Friedrich Schiller University Jena. He is a certified trainer in Mindfulness-based stress reduction (MBSR), one of the co-founders of the German Network of Mindful Universities, Achtsame Hochschulen, and co-editor of the book series Achtsamkeit-Bildung-Medien/Mindfulness-Education-Media. He teaches, researches and co-develops mindfulness programs across a variety of disciplines including leadership, applied ethics, education, and medicine for students, teachers, staff and leaders. His key question is: How can mindfulness be made fruitful in the context of universities?

Sathiyaseelan Balasundaram Prof. Dr., is Director of the Institute of Management at Christ University, Bangalore. He has held senior management positions in human resource management in renowned companies such as Balmer Lawrie, Royal Sundaram, Nokia, and Renesas Corporation. His teaching interests include human resource management, performance management, compensation management, and international human resource management. His research interests are in the areas of work engagement, leadership, spirituality, and positive psychology.

Kristina Bodrozic-Brnic is sinologist, author, consultant, and coach in the fields of intercultural communication, languages, mindfulness, digital teaching, and digital working. She develops German and foreign language learning apps, and online procedures for knowledge transfer.

Jan Willem de Graaf Prof. Dr., is a lecturer in Brain & Technology at the Saxion University of Applied Sciences, the Netherlands. He received his master's degree from Radboud University in Nijmegen and wrote his thesis on the design of a melody generation machine and PhD at the University of Groningen on the theory of dynamical systems. He also worked for several years as a leading neuropsychologist in health care.

Martijn de Kiewit MSc, is a lecturer at the Erasmus University Rotterdam and teaches business ethics. He is currently the ethics and compliance officer for a multinational company. He has been working for more than 10 years as a consultant at KPMG Forensic. He started his career at PwC as a sustainability consultant. He works at the Rotterdam School of Management, Erasmus University, where he has been teaching for more than 10 years the course Business Ethics for master's students. In his lectures he combines academic research with practical examples and case studies.

Thierry Ettlin Prof. Dr. med., neurology FMH, specialized in behavioral neurology, physical medicine, and rehabilitation FMH. He is chief physician and medical director of "Reha Rheinfelden." He holds a titular professorship in neurology, specializing in behavioral neurology, delegated psychotherapy (FMPP), and psychosomatic and psychosocial medicine (SAPPM). Thierry Ettlin is a member of numerous professional societies and sits in several scientific and expert committees. He serves as president of the C. Barell Foundation.

Susanne Hübenthal is an HF nursing specialist and mindfulness trainer. She holds an Executive MBA from the University of Applied Sciences Northwestern Switzerland and a Bachelor's in Business Psychology from the same university. She works as a clinic manager in the city of Bern.

Paul Imhof Prof. Dr. theol. Dr. phil., is film producer and pastoral counselor, a specialist for systemic constellations, family, and management constellations. He studied at the School of Philosophy SJ in Pullach and Munich as well as at the Philosophical-Theological University of St. Georgen/Frankfurt am Main. In 1977, he received the ordination to the priesthood from Joseph Cardinal Ratzinger in Munich and became a member of the Societas Jesu SJ; from 1978, he continued his studies in philosophy and catholic theology at the University of Regensburg; and in 1982, he completed doctoral studies in philosophy, historical theology, and systematic theology. In 1990, he received his doctorate in theology in the subjects of dogmatics and pastoral theology at the University of Vienna. Paul Imhof was for many years assistant to Karl Rahner. In 1999, he changed from the Roman Catholic Church to the Lutheran Church of Hanover and was ordained as a pastor in honorary office. He has been a full professor of philosophy of religion and theology at the German University in Armenia since 2002.

Nikolaus Knoepffler heads the Department of Ethics in the Sciences and Humanities and the Ethics Center of Jena University as well as the Institute of History, Theory and Ethics of Medicine of the Medical School. He is member of various Commissions, e.g., the Bavarian Ethics Council, and president of the German Academy of Transplantation Medicine.

Álvaro I. Langer Prof. Dr., is a clinical psychologist and holds a Master's in Functional Analysis from the University of Almería (UAL), Spain, from which he also received his doctorate. He has received several postdoctoral fellowships and awards in Spain and in Chile. Currently, he is an associate professor and Director of Mind-Body Lab, the Institute of Psychological Studies of the Faculty of Medicine of the Universidad Austral de Chile (UACH), and deputy director of ANID, Millennium Science Initiative Program, the Millennium Nucleus to Improve the Mental Health of Adolescents and Young Adults (Imhay). He is also a member of the Millennium Institute for Research in Depression and Personality (MIDAP), Chile. His research interests include prevention and mental health promotion, psychosocial interventions based on mindfulness, and the study of social and cultural variables related to the health/illness process. In addition, he is a member of the academic faculty of the Doctor of Medical Sciences at UACH.

Valeria Legena is a lecturer at the School of Business at the University of Applied Sciences Northwestern Switzerland and a coach for cultural development in organizations.

Vanessa Nowak holds a state examination for the teaching profession at grammar schools and a Master of Arts in Romance Studies and Organizational Sociology from the Ludwig-Maximilians-University of Munich. In addition, she holds a Master of Business Administration (MBA) from the Universidad Austral de Chile. She is a lecturer in innovation, entrepreneurship, and business ethics at the German Chilean Competency Center for Development, Valdivia, Chile, and a member of the Faculty of Economics and Administration, Universidad Austral de Chile. For many years, she has worked as an innovation consultant in Germany, Chile, and Switzerland for international companies and for the United Nations. She is particularly interested in innovation management as well as digital transformation and the associated business models, entrepreneurship, corporate strategy, and the potential development of economic ecosystems.

Anuradha Sathiyaseelan Prof. Dr., is a psychologist and rehabilitation scientist. She received her doctorate in the field of psycho-oncology from the Medical University of Chennai, Tamil Nadu. She holds an MBA degree in human resources and management and has worked for about 25 years in the field of mental health in different institutions as well as a WHO Collaborating Center for mental health research in India. She is currently working at Christ University, Bangalore.

Volker Schulte Prof. Dr., is a lecturer in leadership, human resources, and health management at the School of Business, University of Applied Sciences Northwestern Switzerland. He is a mindfulness trainer and management consultant. Volker Schulte studied law, history, social sciences, and education at the Universities of Tubingen, Bochum, Gottingen, and New York (Fulbright Scholar). He has a diploma of postgraduate studies in nonprofit management at the University of Freiburg/Switzerland, and holds an MA in theology from the University of Salzburg. He worked for many years for the Swiss Federal Department of Foreign Affairs as well as for the Directorate of Health Education of the WHO in Geneva. He also served for several years as Vice Director of Health Promotion Switzerland and as a lecturer at the School of Applied Psychology ZHAW. In 2019 and 2020, he worked on an international research project for Mindful Leadership in Chile, financed by Swiss National Science Foundation SNF. He regularly teaches business ethics at Ho Chi Minh City University of Technology.

Christoph Steinebach Prof. Dr., is a developmental psychologist at the Zurich University of Applied Sciences. After working for several years at a social pediatric center, he took over the management of an early counseling center. In 1995, Christoph Steinebach became Professor of Special Education at the Catholic University of Applied Sciences in Freiburg/Germany, where he worked for several years as director of the Institute for Applied Research, and was active as president. Since 2006, he is dean of the School of Applied Psychology, ZHAW, and director of the Institute of Applied Psychology (IAP), ZHAW. In 2013, he was additionally appointed Adjunct Professor at Ryerson University, Toronto (CA). Christoph Steinebach is currently President of the European Federation of Psychologists' Associations (EFPA) and a member of the Board of the SPS Swiss Society of Psychology.

Thomas Thiessen Prof. Dr., is a communications and media scientist. He is the rector of the BSP Business School Berlin and head of the "Mittelstand 4.0 Communications Competence Center," which is active throughout Germany. For many years, he has been studying the behavioral and reception-psychological effects of digitization on organizations and their stakeholders.

Arie Hans Verkuil Prof. Dr., is a theologian and holds a doctorate in business ethics at the University of Zurich. He holds a postgraduate degree in nonprofit management from the Institute for Association, Foundation and Cooperative Management (VMI) at the University of Fribourg, and Swiss Postgraduate Studies in Human Resource Management (SNP). He is a lecturer in management, mindful leadership, and ethics at the School of Business, University of Applied Sciences Northwestern Switzerland, and heads the Institute for Corporate Management there. He was a strategic advisor to the Swiss Federal Administration for many years.

Klaske N. Veth Prof. Dr., is a professor in Sustainable HRM at the Hanze University of Applied Sciences, Groningen, and leading lecturer at AoG School of Management. She completed her doctorate at Radboud University in Nijmegen on the topic of Healthy Aging@Work. She has worked in various senior (management) HR positions. At the University of Utrecht, she completed the postgraduate program "Coaching and Consulting in Context." Within her professorship, Klaske N. Veth focuses on the research lines Well-being@Work (W@W), (Self)Leadership, and Inclusive work, comprising topics such as social psychological HRM, work engagement, healthy aging, and (personal) leadership.

Thomas Zimmer Prof. Dr., researches and teaches at the "Center for Sino-German Socio-Cultural Exchange" at Tongji University in Shanghai. He is a sinologist, and his research focuses on the literature and history of China. From 2003 to 2009, he was Vice Director of the Sino-German University College at Tongji University in Shanghai. Between 2012 and 2018, he worked as the Vice Dean of Sino German College and the Director of the German Cultural Center at the University of Shanghai for Science and Technology (USST) in Shanghai.

Michael Zirkler Prof. Dr., teaches at the Zurich University of Applied Psychology and is a management consultant. He studied psychology at the University of Hamburg. Under the heading of "New Work Design," his work focuses on the transformation and governance issues of social systems, currently primarily in self-directed organizational systems such as holacracy. He also works on the integration of complementary knowledge systems, such as the Indian Veda or a Hasidic psychology. This is accompanied by a growing teaching and consulting activity with a focus on India, Israel, Thailand, and other countries, mainly Asian.

Chapter 1
Introduction: Key Elements of Leadership in the Twenty-First Century

Volker Schulte, Christoph Steinebach, and Klaske N. Veth

1.1 Digitalization Under COVID 19 Conditions

The corporate world has changed rapidly in recent years. While generations Y and Z were already critical of traditional hierarchical models, the COVID 19 crisis has dramatically changed the interaction between management and employees yet again. A study published by the editors and authors of this book (Schulte et al., 2020) during the first wave of the pandemic in April 2020 asked about the conditions of well-being in the home office. This showed that *good leadership was the decisive factor for safe and motivating work at home. This was much more important than the* working conditions at home. Leadership that provides human orientation, empathy and trust will prevail across the board in this era.

In our consumer-centric digital societies, huge productivity steps have been taking place for years. Repetitive services in both front and back offices can be streamlined away through automation. By means of algorithms and fast data analyses, corporate decisions are increasingly being made by lower hierarchies in ever faster succession. Entire hierarchical levels are thus becoming superfluous. What sense does it make to convince the next hierarchical level of the necessity of an

V. Schulte (✉)
School of Business, University of Applied Sciences Northwestern Switzerland, Windisch, Switzerland
e-mail: volker.schulte@fhnw.ch

C. Steinebach
ZHAW School of Applied Psychology, Universities of Applied Sciences Zurich, Zurich, Switzerland
e-mail: seit@zhaw.ch

K. N. Veth
Hanze University of Applied Sciences Groningen, Groningen, The Netherlands
e-mail: k.n.veth@pl.hanze.nl

V. Schulte et al. (eds.), *Mindful Leadership in Practice*,
https://doi.org/10.1007/978-3-030-97311-7_1

acquisition or development investment if the project manager knows and can do it better than the boss? The focus on self-determined project management creates new autonomous work units, self-organizing teams, in which each individual employee bears and uses more responsibility. This worldwide pressure provokes a new mindful cooperation in companies.

The growing complexity of the world of work can no longer be managed with conventional instruments of control. Former life worlds that offered security and long-term stable relationships have given way to social fragmentation. Oswald von Nell-Breuning called this development "de-naivization" (Nell-Breuning, 1984, p. 27). On the other hand, there is an increasing need on the part of both employees and management to improve their own competencies with regard to leadership and self-leadership. Whereas in the past, both continuing education and health management programs primarily addressed the functional and efficiency-oriented side of leadership and the acquisition of soft skills, the new focus on empathic, appreciative communication as part of mindful leadership leads to a new dimension of human interaction.

But what does this mean for the qualifications of management? What does mindful leadership mean and, above all, are there differences in mindful leadership in the various cultural contexts in which it takes place? This is where this book aims to provide initial answers. The results compiled here are based, among other things, on a research project that the authors Aeschbacher, Langer, Schulte and Steinebach had worked out during the turn of the year 2019/2020 in Chile.

In this introductory chapter we will discuss the following questions: Why do people demand mindful leadership, what are its prerequisites? How can mindful leadership be learned and applied? What organizational cultures are necessary to embed mindful leadership in the system? How can mindful leadership be defined? Finally, the individual contributions of the authors are presented and contextualized with the imperative of authenticity.

1.2 The Search for the Self-Meaningful Work, Meaningful Life

In Western societies—and here we include South and East Asian societies of a capitalist and crypto-capitalist nature—we find an ambivalence of different attitudes and behaviour. While we find an omnipresent self-cultivation industry in the social networks, which feeds on self-portrayal clips, a culture of frivolity and a certain infantilization, the younger and middle generations are now seeking to rediscover a spiritual and mental compass in the world of work and in private life, which aims at rediscovering the meaning of life. People are asking themselves the question of meaning. The range of offers is manifold. There is a suitable offer for all concerns and religious as well as areligious attitudes. The intention for the willingness to attend a mindfulness training course is the search for the meaning of life in general, in which the seeker has usually already achieved a lot. The question of meaning arises, what really makes us happy and what is essential in life. Almost inevitably, this is joined by the search for life in general, for questions of transcendence and the ethical treatment of each other and of our creation. Especially in the second half of life, many people become aware that with the slogan more and more and more varied, the limit of what is still meaningful is reached relatively soon. In other words, we increasingly recognize that we are going down a path of de-disciplining in society, once toward ourselves, but then also in our lack of service to our neighbour. By becoming aware of our one-sided balances of altruism, we recognize the need to resume more civilizing tasks towards ourselves and society in the future. The prevailing and intuitively rejected indifference towards the suffering of others drives us with increasing maturity into processes of self-discovery, which are composed of an intersection of mindfulness and sociality.

What moves people to enter the cosmos of mindful living? What prerequisites and sensitization steps are necessary to take this step? First and foremost, mindfulness forces us to enter deeply into self-reflection. In this process, human beings are always in a state of tension between what they want to be and how they are, or to put it in the words of Ödön von Horváth: "I am actually a completely different person, I just so rarely get around to it" (Horváth, 1978, p. 67). An unstriving person will criticize the imperfections and limitations of others even though he himself lacks the inclination, good will, and ability to admit his own imperfections and limitations.

Often, between the ages of mid-thirties and fifties, we are very busy organizing our career and providing everything necessary for the family and our neighbors. As far as our spiritual-emotional development is concerned, we are lax, the priorities are set differently. Here existential questions of meaning develop: Should that be all now? Should I go on like this without being able to separate the years that come and go? What should the rest of my life look like? Should it go on according to the same pattern as before? Here we develop ambitions of self-realization with the goal of mindful self-direction. As biographical determinations of a professional and partnership nature now become more prominent, they can—depending on personality and life situation—be perceived as an incentive for change. Any aspects of the self that were suppressed in the build-up phase of young adulthood become increasingly manifest and represent a challenge for many. In any case, not least the fact that we are seeking a life perspective based on sustainability challenges us to explore possibilities for reorientation in various areas of life.

Many people in adulthood find themselves in a seemingly paradoxical situation: On the one hand, they have many options, only they no longer know what is truly meaningful—they have lost their inner compass. On the other hand, these same people feel trapped in so many constraints and responsibilities that they either slowly burn out, suffer in silence, fearfully persist in old roles, or break out abruptly. Often events, especially in the area of relationships, come completely unexpectedly and call everything that has gone before into question. This is also associated with painful experiences of loss of control, uncertainties in reorientation and feelings of guilt. Whether this results in a life crisis and how well one survives it depends primarily on the available personal resources and resilience factors, such as personality, education, partnership, social embedding or health. Regardless of how crisis-ridden this phase of upheaval is experienced, what all those affected have in common is the search for meaning in life or the redefinition of the same. It is a primarily inwardly directed process to bring unquenched dormant needs to light.

This new perspective takes place parallel to the aforementioned confrontation with the original life plans or is determined by it. For the work context, this means that employees seek meaningfulness and appreciation in the work content and in professional interaction across all hierarchies. It is not the social status of the supervisor that determines his acceptance by the employees, but his social and mindfulness-oriented leadership competencies.

1.3 Mindfulness as a New Basic Mental Constant for a Successful Life

Mindfulness is a phenomenon of collective genetics, because all cultures and religions have developed techniques with which mindfulness can be cultivated, practiced and stabilized. Mindfulness is the starting point for the conscious management of one's own awareness in all aspects of life. Western research on mindfulness is relatively young. Since the turn of the last millennium, however, the literature on the subject has grown by leaps and bounds. In 2005, there were about 100 publications on the topic and its clinical applications. Ten years later, there are already over 1500, and there is even a scientific journal called Mindfulness (Kabat-Zinn, 2013, p. 23).

However, the roots of the concept are very old and go back to the contemplative traditions of the East. This also means that mindfulness cannot be separated from contemplation, although there are many secular approaches that are based on mindfulness. In Buddhism in particular, specific methods of mindfulness practice have been systematically practiced and cultivated as the foundation of meditation. Mindfulness is considered a key parameter on the way to overcoming suffering and death.

Mindfulness is not learned through a cognitive process, but only through meditative and contemplative exercises. These can be practiced in the MBSR and mindfulness courses offered practically everywhere in Western societies. Mindfulness is a basic mental attitude, an attitude that contributes significantly to strengthening mental abilities.

The key parameters of a mindful attitude are:

- the greatest possible awareness and attention, clarity and insightfulness;
- the promotion of a spiritual collection and tranquility;
- The concentration on what is now. Consciously experiencing the present;
- respect for others as a central ethical maxim. It calls for empathetic and moderate dealings with others and guides conscientious action;

- the harmonious interaction of body, mind and soul;
- the vision of wholeness and all-round connectedness.

Other important characteristics of personal attitude include the following:

- I do not perceive judgmentally. I put aside my evaluations, let go of my prejudices, am not biased and do not judge.
- I practice moderation.
- I speak at the proper time, practicing wise restraint and abstemious silence.
- I practice composure. Thus, I do not lose the overview in critical situations.

1.4 Building Mindfulness Cultures in Companies

The growing importance of a new mindfulness trend is now being embraced by business. This change of mindset is best demonstrated by companies systematically incorporating mindfulness into their context and culture. Major corporation Google has introduced a program, Search Inside Yourself, based on a mindfulness-based approach to fostering emotional intelligence (Siyli, 2020). The basis of the program is seven meditative principles, which aim to practice and maintain a conscious, focused, and empathic approach to life. Meanwhile, the program is also used and adapted by many other companies. The overall goal is to improve the well-being of each individual and thus also to increase satisfaction and motivation, which is automatically accompanied by lower turnover, fewer absences and improved productivity. In general, one can speak of a win-win situation here, because the quality of life can be harmonized with business management goals. But what can be improved in concrete terms?

- A mindful corporate culture emphasizes enhanced team resilience. Team resilience refers to a team's ability to successfully manage critical situations together. Even under pressure, such a team creates more expeditious solution-oriented approaches.
- Team resilience is characterized by a pronounced willingness to learn. This learning culture is created through open communication, the willingness to also talk about mistakes and weaknesses and to tackle them together.
- The focus is on positive relationships within the team based on a great need for empathy.
- Resilient teams are capable of being pragmatic and flexible. They are able to improvise and use available resources to overcome problems.

The same applies to the organization or company as a whole. Resilient organizations are better able to deal with sudden changes or permanent change than hierarchical and authoritarian ones. Employees, teams and leaders have a strong "unité de doctrine." Team and shared entrepreneurial spirit is not just part of an unread mission statement, but the organization is seen as an organic whole in which each person involved is held in high regard and esteem. This value system provides the basis for mastering difficult corporate phases.

1.5 Mindful Leadership

What does this mean for management? How can you pick up employees mentally, motivate them and involve them as productively as possible? The task of future managers is to enable employees to achieve their goals on the basis of their own competencies and to be able to carry out their activities successfully on their own. A person who believes that he or she can make a difference is highly motivated, self-confident and therefore productive. And this is true even when there is a threat of excessive demands. For management, this means taking technological change seriously as a threat and at the same time mobilizing all available resources with confidence. In order to remain authentic and confident in this tension, mindfulness is indispensable. "Mindful leadership" stands for a leadership practice that focuses on empathy, generosity, and empowerment to promote well-being, self-efficacy, and resilience even under high stress. The generic term for these factors is described as "compassionate leadership". This formulates a claim that is directed at employees as well as managers. Finally, it is about "compassion" and "self-compassion": appreciation and caring for those entrusted to my care. But it is also about caring for oneself. Today, all leadership training must be geared to these factors in order to be able to manage personnel and processes in a timely and system-compatible manner. Competent actions and sustainable interventions result from a mindful attitude. In other words, the focus is not on special leadership techniques, but on resource-oriented attitudes toward competent self-determined individuals. Mindful leadership fosters a collective recognition that people are interconnected. It fosters a supportive, sometimes charitable relationship between leader and staff. Qualities that begin with self-leadership are also important in leadership. Self-leadership requires a critical approach to one's own personality. Self-awareness at every moment and self-reflection are key elements in this. Composure as a basic constant of personal charisma creates security in those whom one is to lead. Trust and consideration create the basis for mindful leadership, which is also always servant leadership. A mindful leader loves his or her employees and exemplifies that work can really be fun if you are given the trust and freedom to work creatively and largely independently in an expert system. Status-, hierarchy- and formalization-oriented managers no longer have a place in digital societies. Instead, mindful leadership is located in a value system defined by the attributes of wisdom, justice, moral courage and moderation. These values are explained in detail in the article by Volker Schulte and Paul Imhof "Ethical cornerstones of people-oriented leadership".

Mindful leadership focuses on clarity, creativity, motivation, and compassion in serving and leading others. Respect, support, and aspects of positive psychology such as fostering positive self-esteem and self-image are the foundation for leading people.

Based on these fundamental considerations, this book now addresses further core aspects of mindful leadership, which illustrate the ubiquity of the approach and which is divided into two parts.

1.6 Topic Overview

The first part deals with the basics of mindful leadership. Here, the historical and philosophical roots are described and, above all, the Asian perspective of mindful leadership is examined. The second part deals with the future perspectives of mindful leadership and with possible solutions on how the approach can be transferred from a theoretical concept to reality.

Volker Schulte and Susanne Hübenthal begin the discourse with the "mechanisms of action of mindfulness as a prerequisite for mindful leadership". In this chapter, they describe the background, methodology and structure of mindfulness programs. In doing so, they take a look at the widespread MBSR program and then also refer to the forms and approaches of East Asian Zen as well as the Ignatian spiritual exercises with their Western Christian connotations. Precisely because the mindfulness approach is still relatively new and there are definitely reservations about this new wave of "soft skills" in traditionally run organizations, the authors also look at the latest results of evidence-based research, current effectiveness studies and the relevance behind its application.

Arie Verkuil, a theologian and lecturer on mindful leadership traces the religious roots of the concept of mindfulness and focuses his analysis and reflections on ethical leadership. He peels away the major traits of mindfulness in different religions and concludes, among other things, that certain core statements are strikingly similar. Thus, one can speak of a global ethic if mindfulness philosophies can be derived directly from the world's major religions.

Volker Schulte and Paul Imhof further narrow the discourse on mindfulness ethics and ask how leadership can be ethically underpinned today. They design a simple and manageable value system, based on the virtue theory, to make the ethical pillars of humane leadership applicable.

Mindfulness has its traditional roots in Asian philosophies. Therefore, the editors have attached great importance to integrating the Asian perspective of mindfulness—especially with the imperative of its current applicability—into the discourse.

The international team of researchers led by Anuradha Sathiyaseelan, Balasundaram Sathiyseelan of Christ University Bengaluru and Michael Zirkler of Zurich University of Applied Sciences present their recently completed findings on the "Jugaad" approach. Jugaad is a common word in the various languages of the Indian subcontinent. It stands for an Indian idiosyncrasy of innovation and creativity that achieves the best possible results even among resources that are often sparse. Jugaad is increasingly being used as a management technique. Companies in South Asia are adopting Jugaad as a practice to reduce research and development costs and maximize resources for a company and its stakeholders through unconventional approaches.

Thomas Zimmer, a sinologist who has taught in Shanghai for more than 25 years, presents another example of Asian mindfulness tradition. In his reflections on the "ideal emperor from a Chinese perspective," he describes the Confucian mindfulness tradition, critically comparing today's power structures in the Middle Kingdom with it with a sharp eye.

In the second, application-oriented part of our discourse, Christoph Steinebach, Álvaro I. Langer and Vanessa Nowak ask about the possible concepts and offers of resilience, mindfulness and leadership in the corporate and organizational context. They answer how positive personal development can be promoted and describe offers for its implementation in the working world. In addition, they introduce the core concepts of positive psychology, which should be part of the toolbox of every mindful leader in the future.

In her chapter, Klaske Veth from the Hanze University of Applied Sciences in Groningen examines the work and the environment in which employees are expected to develop. In doing so, she analyzes the stresses to which a workforce is exposed today and asks how health-promoting management can be implemented and lived via mindful leadership. She introduces the concept of attention economy and shows how calmness, clarity, concentration, happiness and commitment can be found and established in a company.

Martijn de Kiewit is head of the ethics and compliance department of a large international company and works as an international consultant in governance, risk and compliance. In his contribution, the author deals with the practical ethical references in the corporate context. Among other things, he describes the problem of "organizational silence". With his vast practical experience, he points out the dilemmas that managers face. In day-to-day management, there are basic conflicts that need to be resolved. Here the author provides practical assistance.

Kristina Bodrožić-Brnić and Thomas Thiessen address the topic of digital transformation and ask how to apply change management, leadership, innovation and communication as keys to the successful digitalization of companies in the context of mindful leadership. In addition, they use the workshop series "*SparX Digitaler Mittelstand*" to show an application example of how Mindful Leadership can be used concretely as a management tool in the digital transformation.

In their article, Marc Aeschbacher and Valeria Legena reflect on a topic that is slowly finding its way into corporate and individual health management—mental training. The authors are convinced that mental training as a mindfulness approach is worthy of greater attention. First, they describe the reasons why mental training techniques have not yet been an integral part of corporate *health management programs*, and then address the question of how mental training can be used in everyday professional life.

In their chapter, Michael Zirkler, Nikolaus Knoepffler, Reyk Albrecht argue that in an era of power shift from hierarchy to a more egalitarion approach, new tasks and roles for leadership are required. Here lies pivotal role for cooperative leadership. The theory of cooperation is being discussed from an ethical point of view, followed by major implications on the principles and practices of leadership. Ultimately suggestions for the implementation of a corresponding leadership ethics are given.

Jan Willem de Graaf devotes his exciting contribution to the question of mindfulness and technology. The editors have shortened the original text written in English with the title "Mindfulness and Technology" and revised it in the form of an essay. The contribution is therefore at the end of the book. The author spans a broad philosophical and anthropological arc around the topic of mindfulness in a technological context and discusses how the development of automated patterns of behavior and thinking in conjunction with (technological) experience affects humans. Finally, mindfulness is described as a technique for distancing oneself from both the immediacy of already entrenched behavioral and cognitive schemas (brain, psychology) and the "dictating" technological context (technology).

In a final short statement, the editors venture an outlook on the demands on tomorrow's leadership. In doing so, they describe the challenges to future social capital and the dominance of digitized human networks.

References

Kabat-Zinn, J. (2013). *Gesund durch Meditation: Das große Buch der Selbstheilung mit MBSR*. O.W. Barth eBook.

Nell-Breuning, O. (1984). *Worauf es mir ankommt*. Herder.

Schulte, V., Steinebach, C., Verkuil, A. & Hübenthal, S. (2020). *Studie zur Umstellung auf Homeoffice in der Schweiz während der Covid19 Krise*. Accessed May 12, 2020, from https://www.fhnw.ch/de/die-fhnw/hochschulen/hsw/media-newsroom/news/die-mehrheit-fuehlt-sich-wohl-im-homeoffice/media/studie-erhebung-umstellung-auf-homeoffice-17042020.pdf

Siyli. (2020). *Search inside yourself Leadership Institute*. Accessed October 21, 2020, from https://siyli.org/

von Horváth, Ö. (1978). *Gesammelte Werke* (Vol. 3). Suhrkamp.

Part I
Fundamentals of Mindful Leadership: Philosophy, History and Cultivation

Chapter 2
Mechanisms of Action of Mindfulness as a Prerequisite for Mindful Leadership

Volker Schulte and Susanne Hübenthal

2.1 On the Analysis of the Empirical Situation on the Topic of Mindfulness

If one wants to deal in depth with concepts of mindful leadership, the interested person cannot avoid looking at the prehistory and the prerequisite of mindful leadership. Within it is the philosophy, indeed an entire approach to life, that provides a theoretical underpinning for mindful leadership practice. Various philosophical and religious traditions offer theoretical-hermeneutical as well as practical-applicational opportunities to approach the ethical and salutogenetic dimensions of mindfulness. In all religions and cultures there are long traditions of growing spiritually through meditative and contemplative practice, expanding one's consciousness and at the same time immersing oneself in another world. In the process, man's material ego is bound back to find a bridge to the eternal. The strong ego-centeredness is the evil that leads to suffering in all spiritual traditions.

In this chapter, we analyze the background, methodology, and structure of mindfulness programs. In addition, we look at evidence-based research, current effectiveness studies, and the relevance behind the application.

In recent years, interest in mindfulness and mindfulness-based interventions and therapies has increased in many areas of our social life. There are more and more publications on this topic. Some empirical studies and meta-analyses have already investigated the effect of mindfulness and have also been able to prove it (American Mindfulness Research Association, 2019; Lutz et al., 2004).

V. Schulte (✉)
School of Business, University of Applied Sciences Northwestern Switzerland, Windisch, Switzerland
e-mail: volker.schulte@fhnw.ch

S. Hübenthal
Clinic of Neurosurgery, Lindenhof Hospital, Bern, Switzerland

V. Schulte et al. (eds.), *Mindful Leadership in Practice*,
https://doi.org/10.1007/978-3-030-97311-7_2

The focus of any mindfulness practice is not the rational, cognitive grasp of the subject matter, but the experience through continuous meditative practice. The psychologist and neuroscientist Ulrich Ott describes five dimensions for this: The purely physical, *material level* (1) refers to the correct body position and the associated stable posture. The so-called *vital level* (2) makes breathing conscious and influences the biological regulatory processes. When breathing in, the heartbeat speeds up and when breathing out, it slows down. The *emotional level* (3) focuses on bodily sensations and the associated feelings, which are accepted and not evaluated. The *mental level* (4) focuses on the distanced and neutral perception of the restless mind and wants to bring it to rest. Finally, on the level of *non-duality* (5) the actual change of perspective takes place. The ego standing in the center is dissolved by the transcendence of subject and object. The ego we are familiar with in the form we have known it until now as the center of our experience and action temporarily ceases to exist (Ott, 2011).

2.2 MBSR as a Secularized Approach to Contemplation

As early as the late 1970s, a cognitive approach was developed at the Stress Reduction Clinic of Massachusetts, USA, which has since become one of the best-known mindfulness programs and is implemented worldwide. MBSR stands for *Mindfulness-Based Stress Reduction* and is usually translated as *stress management through mindfulness* (Kabat-Zinn, 2013). It is the first stress reduction program to teach formal mindfulness meditation in a standardized clinical setting and free from religious traditions. The mindfulness training-based program improves stress management and also has a positive impact on well-being. Several meta-analyses have demonstrated the positive impact of MBSR on health factors such as well-being, mental health, and physical health, although not every study is strictly evidence-based (Baer et al., 2006).

2.2.1 Theoretical Background of the MBSR Program

The original concept of the theoretical foundations comes from Buddhism. More specifically, MBSR is largely based on the fundamental goals, principles and procedures of traditional insight meditation (Vipassana meditation). Initially, the MBSR course program was used to help patients with chronic pain that could not be further treated. As significant success was noted, Kabat-Zinn's team then successively extended the MBSR approach to other groups of people who were not ill but who exhibited indicators of stress. Remarkable success was seen there as well. MBSR enables participants to cope more effectively with stressful situations and prevents psychological distress. This success is evidence-based. In this sense, MBSR is a non-esoteric, denominationally neutral or secular method of contemplation.

By supporting the Eastern tradition with scientific evidence, Kabat-Zinn has been instrumental in the popularity of mindfulness in the Western world. The MBSR program is about sharpening the skills of focusing and awareness, which in turn is then designed to block out distractions. Moments, thoughts, feelings and body sensations are thus made conscious and the human habit of always digressing can be noticed and interrupted in this way.

Mindfulness exercises help to uncover so-called rumination, musings, and then to consciously not pursue them further, but to return to conscious presence. Rumination is a form of ruminating in which the thoughts circle around one or more (problematic) facts or conceits without generating a solution. This rumination diverts attention from the moment and can be unsettling. The ruminations are usually freighted with fears and problems and can include the future as well as the past. Mindfulness exercises bring people into the here and now. Meditations open the deep sense of the self. We consciously perceive everything around us and focus on what is, which expands our scope of action (MBSR Association Switzerland, 2020).

Hölzel et al. (2011b) analyzed the emotional-physiological events of a mindfulness exercise. During meditation, a stimulus or stressor causes an emotional reaction. The meditating person can now consciously perceive this feeling and its physiological effects.

2.2.2 Structure and Composition of the MBSR Program

MBSR courses are patented and are structured according to a fixed scheme. First, questions and goals are discussed in a preparatory talk. This is where the actual sensitization takes place, because a lot is demanded of the participant. The future course participant must actively participate and, through daily, regular practice, experience a sense of the meaning of meditation and, above all, its effects. The course days are spread over 8 weeks. Up to 3 h must be scheduled per course day. Another full day of silence, usually a Saturday, rounds out the program (Meibert et al., 2006, pp. 166–187).

In the weekly meetings, various mindfulness exercises are introduced and practiced, for example the body scan, low-threshold yoga training, and sitting and walking meditations, guided by the MBSR teacher (Meibert et al., 2006, p. 166). This practice is only effective if the participants continue to practice between the course days. The participants are closely accompanied and can exchange their experiences. In addition to these formal exercises, mindfulness should also be practiced informally, i.e. on a small scale. Course participants are encouraged to adopt a mindful attitude in everyday life, in every action and activity, and to observe themselves (Meibert et al., 2006, p. 166). Sensations, feelings and other physical and psychological reactions should be consciously perceived.

"Over time and with regular practice, it is then possible to experience phases of deep inner calm and power of concentration" (Meibert et al., 2006, p. 173). Experiences are then gradually perceived differently with daily practice and, more importantly, interpreted differently. "Over time, we can develop new ways of seeing our automatic reactions and realize that both pleasant and unpleasant experiences are synonymous and part of life. This realization in depth can lead us to greater equanimity, clarity, and creative possibilities for action. " (Meibert et al., 2006, p. 174). Mental and physical resources have already been shown to be strengthened with an MBSR course. Participants have improved resilience, which helps them continue with daily exercise practice.

Beginners in particular must learn to continue training in a disciplined manner. In doing so, they must also be careful not to fall into old patterns. "Being mindful means nothing other than paying attention to everything and seeing things as they are. It is not about changing anything" (Kabat-Zinn, 2013, p. 67).

2.2.3 Seven-Factor Approach

According to Kabat-Zinn (2013), the following seven independent factors are important in describing the inner attitude, with one factor leading to the next, which then form the basis for mindfulness practice:

1. ***Non-judgment:*** Non-judgment means not having to evaluate and judge everything and anything equally. One should rather take the role of the observer (Kabat-Zinn, 2013, pp. 69–70).
2. ***Patience:*** Patience can be practiced. Everything takes time and eventually matures (Kabat-Zinn, 2013, p. 70). Patience creates freedom and space because one is more open to what is now.
3. ***Keeping the beginner's mind:*** With the "beginner's mind," we admire things that we had known before but had no longer consciously perceived. This spirit allows us to tap into new experiences and helps us to become aware of and excited about things again (Kabat-Zinn, 2013, p. 71).
4. ***Trust:*** This is primarily about building self-confidence. Only when I trust myself do others trust me and can I trust others (Kabat-Zinn, 2013, p. 72).
5. ***Non-forcing:*** Everything is allowed to have its time. "Active doing nothing," the creation of so-called "Empty Action Spaces" (the term used by the authors of this article) gives us the peace and relaxation of not necessarily wanting to bring about anything or to engage in rapid action (Kabat-Zinn, 2013, p. 73).
6. ***Acceptance:*** Similar to trust, acceptance first means self-acceptance. In addition, it should be practiced to show acceptance towards others and to accept different views and attitudes (Kabat-Zinn, 2013, p. 75).
7. ***Letting go:*** Letting go means accepting what is. It also means not fighting against what is unchangeable (Kabat-Zinn, 2013, p. 76).

Other mindfulness attributes are those that can be subsumed under the umbrella term of empathy, such as consideration, generosity, conciliation, benevolence, serenity, compassion, and fellow joy.

Above all, the widespread egocentrism gives way to a reserved self. A meditator no longer puts himself permanently in the center. This self-centeredness is not a phenomenon of our modern age. Montesquieu was already annoyed with his contemporaries when he said: "I observe people everywhere who talk incessantly about themselves. Their conversations are like a mirror in which their obtrusive figure constantly appears. They talk of the most trifling things that have happened to them, and think that the interest they take in them makes them more important in our eyes" (Montesquieu, quoted in Wickert, 1995, p. 698, translated by the authors).

2.3 Zen as a Traditional Asian Mindfulness Practice

An additional approach to the mindfulness dimension can be achieved through Zen. To describe the meaning and purpose of Zen is like squaring the circle. Zen can hardly be conveyed by concepts. If one dares to penetrate the subject hermeneutically at all, it is traditionally done by means of metaphor and narrative. Concerning the practice of hermeneutic penetration of Zen and its limits, the Zen master and mindfulness researcher Michael von Brück points out that sensory impressions and concepts that seek to describe them are produced by consciousness itself. The problem now in Zen and in the various Buddhist teachings is that the human being takes this conceptualization for the real and thus sees a distorted mirror of what is. Perception in that case is dualistic, namely separate, based on judgments and narrowed views. Rather, they are projections of reality (von Brück, 2006, 2016).

2.3.1 What Is Zen?

Zen is, from a scientific point of view, first of all a part of the history of Asian Buddhist religion. For our analysis, however, this is secondary, which is why we give only a side note to the history of religion part. For us, the syncretization of Buddhism and Confucianism as well as Taoism is more important because of the ethical implications. Especially the latter with its ideal of action in non-action (chin.: wu-wei) as well as its teaching that being can be traced back to non-being is relevant for the understanding of Zen. The same is true for Confucianism, which set both moral and ethical standards and landmarks. The over-forming and interpenetration of all three approaches led to a Taoist-influenced Buddhism, shifting the focus of belief in reincarnation to this world with a freedom of consciousness, as is clearly evident in Zen. Zen today and in our context is first and foremost an exercise practice that can only be considered spiritual to a limited extent, since no god is worshipped. On the other hand, an experience of transcendence through Zen meditation is not excluded. Zen claims to be able to solve the mystery of life and death in the time-free moment of an experience through immediate insight into reality. This experience is called awakening or enlightenment (Jap.: kensho). Awakening completely changes one's perception of the world. Zen does not teach asceticism but teaches how man can live sensually and meaningfully in the world. Zen brings us very close to the practice of MBSR, which in turn derives directly from the traditions of Zen. Self-discipline and mindful interaction with oneself and one's surroundings are the prerequisites for Zen practice. Meditation is only one exercise among many. Rather, it is about every behavior and activity of the human being becoming a concrete exercise of mindfulness (von Brück, 2016).

2.3.2 *Process*

The practice of Zen takes place in several steps:

1. By concentrating on an indispensably correct sitting posture and focusing on the breath, psychosomatic energies are released and focused.
2. This builds a mindfulness that does not focus on specific sensory perceptions or things, but builds a perception of the spatial environment, the surroundings.
3. With steps 1 and 2 completed, meditation achieves an alertness that creates insight by conveying things as they are, not as we interpret them.

With this practice, all dualities and contradictions that characterize rational consciousness are dissolved in a mostly unexpected and sudden breakthrough (kensho). The diversity of things and circumstances appears as a coherent whole. All this is perceived with an abundant clarity and as deepest happiness. Zen teaches that this opens up the essence of reality beyond living and dying in this very moment.

The "I" identity merges into a supra-individual "self" which then presents itself disinterestedly in a mindful life.

2.3.2.1 Thinking as Non-thinking

When it comes to thought, we become aware of the difficulty of describing fundamental elements of Zen through words. Hermeneutics and conceptuality are shadows of what Zen wants to teach us (not *tell us*). In Zen, it is important to get rid of the thoughts that are pressing on us. This is not to achieve a state of trance in meditation, nor is it to achieve an emptiness of thought, a vacuum of thought. Rather, it is a matter of letting thoughts move on, which present us with a reality that is not one. The principle of Descartes' sentence "Cogito, ergo sum" (Descartes, 1996, p. 55), which cannot be doubted any further, is wrong and misleading according to the ideas of Zen, because it is only about conceptual images, which are clustered by sense impressions and then interpreted by us. They represent partial areas of something perceived, that is, concepts that are interpreted by us as the real, genuine thing. Buddhist schools, including Zen, teach us that this is precisely where the mistake is made, because our sense impressions are perceived as reality, with judgments and determinations that create a dualism, a separation of the "I" from the environment.

The Zen exercises are now intended to cause the consciousness to become free, by interrupting the taking in, processing and interpreting of the sense impressions that are constantly pelting us. Instead, the consciousness focuses on itself, on a mindful awareness of its surroundings, without wanting to judge and interpret everything from the "I". When a train of thought is held, other thoughts attach themselves and already a (chain of) thoughts is produced as in a coagulation. The non-attachment of thoughts is the basis for the recognition of what really is.

2.3.3 The Exercise as Preparation for a Possible Transcendence Experience

The exercise itself consists of hours of sitting motionless with the spine erect (zazen), interspersed with short breaks, during which the breath is completely calmed. Mind you, this is not inactivity, but bodywork expressed in correct posture. Only in motionless sitting can the divine develop in man, whereby correct sitting is to grasp and harmonize man in his relation to the world.

In Zen, you need a harmony of posture, tension and breathing. Proper sitting brings these three states into balance. The idea is to feel the power of life in the center of the body by slightly protruding the lower abdomen and maintaining a slight tension. This creates a flow of energy that allows the practitioner to be present and collected. Further, the center of gravity shifts to the pelvis, and at the same time tensions in the head, neck and shoulder area ease. On the one hand, one feels supported by the floor, and on the other hand, a feeling of being lifted arises, because the spine stretches upwards as if by itself in this state. This posture is very closely coordinated with proper breathing. "The rhythm of the breath then becomes a constant repetition of a circular movement: during exhalation there is a letting go (surrendering), a letting down (surrendering), and at the end of exhalation a letting in (surrendering) with the supporting ground. When breathing in, a "letting-become-new (finding oneself anew)" arises with ascending movement, whereby the feeling of becoming one with the whole sets in (Baier, 2013, p. 347, translated by the authors).

At the same time, the consciousness observes the ups and downs of feelings without evaluating them or dealing with them. Gradually all thought processes come to rest and only a sharpened attention remains. We practice active concentration while letting go of thoughts and judgments and experience a feeling of all-oneness, timelessness, immediacy, love, bliss and peace. The totality of Zen practice is described in terms of three pillars: Insight ("I do it because it creates insight for me"), Cultivation ("I practice to improve myself in Zen practice"), and Action ("I behave and act mindfully").

Zen is being present in the moment: "A master was asked what Zen was. He answered: 'When I eat, I eat; when I sit, I sit; when I walk, I walk. ' To which the questioners replied in amazement: 'But we do that every day too! The master replied:

'No, when you eat, you already stand up; when you sit, you already walk'" (quoted in von Brück, 2016, p. 16, translated by the authors).

Buddhism is based on the experience of the transience of all phenomena. Impermanence means that all moments of existence are in constant flux, they come into being and immediately pass away again. In this process, the cause of an appearance is changed by the effect it produces. Reality is the interaction of appearances and their causes. Everything is in permanent change. Body and consciousness are a continuum in Zen.

2.4 Ignatian Spiritual Exercises as a Purgatorial Spiritual Mindfulness Practice

While in the MBSR approach and in Zen meditation techniques have been described that aim at behavioral changes and emotional cognition processes through emptying of thoughts and their non-attachment, the Spiritual Exercises of Ignatius is a meditation practice that consistently integrates thought processes in the form of self-reflection and worship of God for gaining cognition and changing behavior. This is a fundamentally different approach. The emergence of the Ignatian Spiritual Exercises is directly related to the transformation or enlightenment process of its inventor, Ignatius of Loyola. The latter was in a life crisis when he made the change to contemplation. We know today that life crises can lead to spiritual growth. Traumatic events in a person's life can unexpectedly bring about positive things. This change is called post-traumatic maturation (Brauchle, 2012, pp. 146–152). The term circumscribes the subjective experience of positive psychological change in individuals following an event that has resulted in a shaking of basic assumptions about life and the world. Posttraumatic maturation in this context involves a changed view of the past traumatic experience as well as a new appraisal of a qualitatively better new life compared to the previous one. This positive change is not experienced as restrictive regressive, but as an expansive further development, as—psychologically speaking—gradual processing and re-attribution. The deep rupture in life finally leads, after a prolonged painful healing and maturing process, to a changed assessment of the world and its values and is thus accompanied by a new value attitude towards the self and life in general. In this way, a new perspective can emerge with which one's own environment can once again be interpreted as benevolent and meaningful. This creates inner strength and self-confidence, which is accompanied by newly developed competencies and coping strategies. This process is characterized by five essential mechanisms of action, as identified by Maercker and Langner (2001) in their studies of personal growth after traumatic events:

- find inner strength and new self-confidence through suffering;
- Develop an intensified appreciation of life and a changed philosophy of life;
- discover new ways of living;

- the experience of an intensified connection with other people and the growth of knowledge of human nature; as well as
- a spiritual development.

2.4.1 *"Spiritual Exercises": Basic Axioms of the Ignatian Way of Prayer*

As emphasized at the beginning, the Ignatian Spiritual Exercises differ in goal and methodology from the other approaches to contemplation and meditation discussed here. Their goal is for the retreatant to order and shape his life according to God's will. This also means giving space to inner growth under the guidance of God. It is about an inner liberation, not about submission. The religious exercises of the Ignatian (individual) Spiritual Exercises consist primarily of personal times of prayer, as described in the Spiritual Exercises Book.

Ignatian retreats, which are individual or group retreats, usually start from a four-week cycle. There are also shorter retreats, e.g. introductory retreats with an eight-day duration or, depending on the institution, also individually adapted retreats. Alex Lefrank has coined the image of a house with its various floors for the didactic structure of the four-week retreat and has integrated the sensitization phase into this metaphor. For before someone gets the idea of opening up his path to God, the need to want to do so must first awaken in him (Lefrank, 2009, pp. 24–32).

2.5 Transtheoretical Model of Behavior Change in the Meditation Process

As described earlier, daily meditation practice is the only key to experienced mindfulness. It is essential to make the step from interest to regular practice. In modern behavioral research, this process is described in an evidence-based way with the Transtheoretical Model. The Transtheoretical Model is originally a concept from the field of Public Health and is mainly applied in prevention and cessation programs. It is used to describe, explain, predict, and influence intentional behavior change. The model, developed by James O. Prochaska of the University of Rhode Island and his colleagues, is based on the assumption that change processes pass through several qualitatively different and successively sequential stages. For this reason, the Transtheoretical Model is also referred to as the "stages of change" model.

Depending on the application, the model postulates five to six stages of behavior change ("stages of change"):

1. In the intentionlessness stage ("precontemplation"), individuals have no intention to change a problematic behavior.

2. In the intention formation stage ("contemplation"), individuals have the intention to change the problematic behavior at some point.
3. In the preparation stage, individuals make concrete plans to change their problematic behavior in the near future and take the first steps toward changing their behavior.
4. In the "action" stage, people change their behavior.
5. In the maintenance stage, individuals have abandoned the problematic behavior for some time.
6. In the termination stage, the old behavior has been permanently abandoned, and the new behavior has been internalized and is maintained (Prochaska & Velicer, 1997).

2.6 Mechanisms of Action of Mindfulness

Mindfulness promotes systematic and networked thinking. Networked thinking is the key competence of the future. Pointing out content interrelationships is extended by looking at effect interrelationships. Networked thinking describes the ability to recognize and analyze the interplay of factors. In this way, we overcome linear reductionist thinking. Mindfulness in daily life produces slowness, accuracy and the ability to dwell on one thing in a concentrated way. This, in turn, promotes intensity of perceptions, including pleasure, without it turning into greed. We also know that mindfulness reduces anxiety and makes us "ready for reality." This is an important process because freedom from anxiety is a process of spiritual and social maturation (von Brück, 2005, p. 147). With mindfulness exercises we achieve to concentrate the scattered inner energy and make it usable. We learn to become inwardly calm and enter a state of deep relaxation and harmony, perceiving ourselves as a whole as well as a part of the whole. Mindfulness exercises are at the same time nourishment for body and mind. At the same time we succeed better in recognizing and accepting our life circumstances as they are. As a side effect, we become more aware of our body and mind, which strengthens our health resources and better equips us to deal with stressors by tapping into energies from within ourselves.

Mindfulness teaches us to shift from the permanent state of action to the state of being. This also leads to a discovery of slowness, self-acceptance, and tolerance. In other words, "if Doing mode is a trap, then Being mode is freedom" (Williams & Penman, 2012, p. 35).

2.7 Current State of Research on Mindfulness

Over the past two decades, there has been a steady increase in research activity around mindfulness (American Mindfulness Research Association, 2019). Mindfulness seems to be a current trending scientific topic. With the possibility of imaging techniques, neuroscience specifically has published many studies examining changes in the brains of meditators or individuals who have completed a mindfulness course (American Mindfulness Research Association, 2019).

A very well-known study on mindfulness using imaging techniques is that of Lutz et al. (2004). Using electroencephalography, the researchers studied eight Buddhist monks who had been meditating daily for years and compared them to ten individuals with little meditation experience. The latter received 1 of meditation instruction daily for 1 week and had no prior mindfulness experience. The monks showed a significant increase and synchronization of gamma waves compared to the new meditators. This difference was evident not only between the two groups, but also between long-term meditators with less experience (approximately 10,000 h) and those with more experience (approximately 50,000 h). These data suggest that meditation trains temporal integrative processes and can cause short-term and long-term neural changes.

Another study comes from Hölzel et al. (2011a). In their pre-post study, the scientists examined the brains of 16 participants in an MBSR course using magnetic resonance imaging. After the course, the experimental group showed an increase in gray matter density in the hippocampus, which supports learning and memory processes, and in regions responsible for self-awareness and compassion. Furthermore, the scientists found a decrease in gray matter density in the amygdala, which is associated with lower stress levels. In summary, it can be assumed that people who meditate have a better memory in the context of learning activities, better self-perception, higher compassion and a lower perception of stress.

Another experiment by Nielsen and Kaszniak (2006) showed that people who meditate are better able to perceive their own sensations. The test persons were shown subliminal images. This means that the images were not consciously perceived, but nevertheless evoked a certain reaction. The images were classified into three categories, pleasant, neutral and unpleasant. The group of meditators reacted more strongly to the stimuli and also rated them more correctly than the group of non-meditators. The latter showed less arousal and differed in assessments of the same stimuli. The research team assumes that meditation improves emotion regulation, which means that the reaction to perceived emotions does not change or changes only slightly.

Some studies with imaging techniques could repeatedly show that mindfulness meditation has positive effects on physical and mental health as well as on cognitive performance (Tang et al., 2015). Interestingly, these could even be mapped to the corresponding brain regions. Tang et al. (2015) wanted to clarify which underlying neural mechanisms are responsible for this. The researchers refer to meditation as mental training for self-regulation. The researchers postulate that mindfulness meditation involves at least three components that work closely together to form a process of improved self-regulation. These are improved attentional control, improved emotion regulation, and altered self-awareness. These findings are still in their infancy and require a great deal more study to truly know the neural mechanisms involved.

Brigit Hufenus (2010) investigated the effectiveness of mindfulness, self-efficacy expectations, and stress management in a quantitative study with 89 participants. The participants completed a questionnaire before and after an eight-week MBSR course to assess mindfulness, self-efficacy, and stress perception.

As a result, the researcher found higher self-efficacy expectations from regular meditation, which then in turn led to a decrease in negative strategies for dealing with stress.

The topic of the impact of mindfulness in the workplace has also increased significantly in recent years. This is due to the fact that perceived stress in the workplace has increased (Grebner et al., 2011). As stress has become an increasing problem for employees and thus employers, the benefits of stress-reducing mindfulness interventions in the workplace should now be investigated. It is important to keep in mind here that the construct of mindfulness in general, however, is difficult to discuss.

To investigate mindfulness, this can either be trained in intervention programs (similar to MBSR) and then measured, or dispositional, i.e., innate, mindfulness can be surveyed using questionnaires (Good et al., 2016). A study by Shonin et al. (2014) examined middle management individuals who engaged in formal mindfulness practices for 8 weeks in a newly designed program. At the final measurement, they showed significantly better results in terms of performance and work-related well-being than their colleagues in the control group.

In a quantitative study, Zivnuska et al. (2016) examined whether and how mindfulness at work can contribute to work-related resources, well-being, and positive workplace attitudes. Among work-related resources, they included work-life balance and work engagement. Well-being is measured by stress and job satisfaction, and job attitudes are measured by intentions to quit and engagement. Results show that employees who practice mindfulness at work gain improved work-life balance as well as increased work engagement. This creates resources that improve well-being (increased job satisfaction and reduced stress), which ultimately benefits the organization by decreasing intentions to quit and increasing engagement.

Reb et al. (2019) examined the effects of mindful leaders on their employees. The researchers found that as the leader's mindfulness increased, the employees' performance and perceived respect increased. In addition, stress levels decreased. The improved quality of relationships indirectly transferred the leader's mindfulness to the employees.

2.7.1 Mindfulness and Well-Being, Performance Enhancement

Research on mindfulness interventions and effects has increased steadily in recent times. Their effects have been measured beyond doubt, although some meta-studies show inconclusive results. Do these data also have the necessary societal support? In this regard, it should be noted that the issue of mindfulness goes hand in hand with the strong dissemination and acceptance of positive psychology.

Positive psychology has seen a major resurgence in the past 15 years. Whereas general psychology has tended to be deficit-oriented over the past 70 years, i.e., focusing on psychological suffering, positive psychology focuses on resource orientation and optimization and on the formation of strengths and personal growth (Steinebach & Brendtro, 2012, p. 19).

People who are plagued with self-doubt and low self-esteem interpret negative experiences and incidents as a natural consequence of their constant failure and bad luck. People blame themselves for negative experiences. This pattern often leads to depression. In contrast, people with a positively oriented thought pattern tend to be significantly less depressed. Positively oriented people do not dwell on the problem, but expend the energy to look for solutions and improvements. People with a negative attitude tend to emphasize failures even more. They expect failure and are not surprised when it occurs (self-fulfilling prophecies). Since mental disorders always have psychosomatic effects, such people also have a weaker immune system. People who think they can make little difference accordingly have a low self-efficacy expectation (SWE). From this it can be concluded that to a considerable extent we have it in our own hands to cultivate and develop our resilience. It is not the external "threats" that are the main problem for these people, but the way they classify and process events. Patterns with negative connotations thus acquire normative power (Seligman, 2008).

Optimistic people will do everything they can to find solutions to problems that arise. For them, these are abnormal conditions. Consequently, they do everything to classify them as temporary occurrences and to restore the usual life balance. Albert Bandura explored this issue in more detail. He came to the conclusion that the degree of self-confidence correlates with one's own resources and consequently determines the speed of recovery and the handling of crises (Bandura, 1979).

2.7.2 Resilience and Stress Resistance as a Resource of Mindfulness

Mindful people exhibit higher resilience and stress resistance. Resilience is not only the ability to withstand stressors and unfavorable developmental conditions, but also the ability to return to a balanced, positive state of functioning after stress (Brandtstädter, 2015, p. 47). Psychologist Suzanne Kobasa explored three basic characteristics in stress-resistant people: control, commitment, and challenge. People with high self-efficacy beliefs have the confidence to make a difference in their environment (Kobasa, 1979). Resilience does not occur by chance. Major factors that influence resilience are personal factors, environmental factors, and process factors. Personal factors include cognitive abilities (e.g., intelligence, interpretive and meaning-making models, religiosity) as well as emotional strengths such as emotion regulation, composure in the face of uncertainty, the ability to actively shape relationships, or the dynamic attitude of being able to solve problems. Environmental factors include family support, identity, and social security. Process factors include the ability to recognize different perspectives, accept realities, and focus one's energies on what needs to be mastered next.

The progressive individualization of forms of work toward digitalized workplaces in home offices, exacerbated by the Covid 19 crisis, is leading to greater work pressure and social isolation. Systematic practice of mindful attitudes can have a stress-reducing influence on this. According to the Dorsch psychological dictionary (Häcker & Stapf, 2004), stress—means "pressure, tension"—and is used in colloquial language as "a subjectively unpleasant situation by which a person is negatively influenced" (translated by the authors). If this negative influence persists and suitable coping strategies are lacking, this can lead to psychological and physical health complaints and even chronic illnesses. In the context of the working life of our society, the word stress is unavoidable and a trigger for many illnesses, especially psychosomatic ones. The increase in psychosomatic illnesses due to high workloads has risen sharply in recent years.

The 2010 Stress Study (Grebner et al., 2011) addressed the potential increase in perceived stress. It found that the proportion of people who perceive stress frequently or very frequently has increased from 26.6% to 34.4% since the last survey in 2000. The following were named as the most significant factors: unclear work instructions, deadline pressure or fast pace, working during free time, working more than 10 h a day on at least 1–2 days a week. The boundary between work and leisure time has become increasingly blurred. It can be assumed that this figure will have increased many times over from 2010 to 2020 due to "constant accessibility" and technical means of communication. The positive results of studies by Grebner et al. (2011), Shonin et al. (2014), Zivnuska et al. (2016), and Reb et al. (2019) clearly indicate that practicing mindfulness exercises results in a significant reduction in stress perception and an increase in subjective well-being at work.

This was recognized earlier in Asia. During an exchange program as part of a study trip of the business administration studies in Asia, the author Susanne Hübenthal visited some companies in Vietnam and Thailand. In most of the companies visited, employees began and ended their shift with a ten-min meditation exercise. This was aimed at strengthening employees' concentration and performance, as well as maintaining and promoting their mental health. Given the increasing number of people with burnout and depression in Western society, these mediation exercises in the form of mindfulness could also be introduced at European companies as a preventive measure.

2.7.3 Improvement of Learning and Memory Processes and Concentration

Many studies could prove an improvement of learning and memory processes. These results play a major role especially for children in school aspects and in their education. In our society, children who are naturally a bit more restless are often diagnosed too quickly with attention deficit hyperactivity disorder (ADHD).

This disorder is characterized by marked deficits in attention and concentration, lack of impulse and behavioural control, restlessness, volatility, and hyperactivity. Associated problems include dissocial behaviour disorders (e.g., aggressiveness, violence), learning disabilities, and autism spectrum disorders (decreased socio-cognitive abilities).

This "supposed" disorder is usually treated with the drug Ritalin (active ingredient: methylphenidate). There are few reliable sources regarding the frequency of ADHD diagnoses in the population, but it is assumed that about 5% of the population are diagnosed with ADHD. Rather, based on the sale of methylphenidate, a large increase in ADHD diagnoses is suspected. "Sales of methylphenidate, the active ingredient in Ritalin, increased in Switzerland from 38 kg in 1999 to 256 kg in 2009" (Schilling, 2010). This drug can have a very good effect in the short term, but in the long term it tends to cause dependence syndromes. The pharmacological effect of Ritalin is similar to that of cocaine, only with a different half-life. Especially in children, more caution should be exercised in prescribing it. Again, Asian culture is on a healthier path in the future. They are taking a preventive approach to this problem. The Pathway School in Saigon (Vietnam), for example, is a normal school with a living philosophy of mindfulness. The children learn mindfulness in the form of frequent mediation exercises throughout the day, in addition to the normal school curriculum.

Thus, mindfulness not only trains learning and performance skills as well as concentration, but also values such as patience, altruism, and morality (Pathway School, 2020). This successful preventive approach could conceivably be applied to our Western schools as well. The effects of mindfulness exercises could be proven several times and should definitely be considered as a side-effect-free preventive alternative to drug therapy. Mindfulness can also be a better therapy alternative for affected adults with the ADHD diagnosis.

2.7.4 Emotion Regulation, Self-Awareness and High Compassion

Mindfulness increases the ability to better perceive one's own emotions and then to regulate them. The most common of all affective disorders in our society is depression. According to a report by the Swiss Health Observatory (Obsan) from 2013, around 7% of the Swiss population suffer from unipolar depression for the first time or repeatedly, and 1–2% each from dysthymia or bipolar affective disorder. This tendency is increasing. The risk of developing an affective disorder at least once within the entire lifespan is around 20% (Obsan, 2013). These figures are alarming. People with bipolar affective disorder are particularly affected by severe impairment of emotion regulation. This means that they move from a depressive phase into a manic phase without being able to control or direct these extreme emotional processes.

The diseases are primarily treated with psychotropic drugs (antidepressants). These drugs usually have strong, sometimes irreversible side effects, and their effectiveness has not been clearly proven to date. This means that sufferers experience severe side effects in addition to the strong emotional fluctuations, which further limits the quality of their lives. Another therapeutic intervention for the treatment of affective disorders is psychotherapy. It remains to be mentioned here that although this has significantly fewer side effects, it is very time-consuming and financially expensive. In addition, this type of therapy requires a great deal of energy, which people affected with depression do not have.

The way of mindfulness could be used as a preventive measure against the affective disorders. If people who have a rather sensitive and anxious personality do daily meditation exercises, there is a chance that they will learn to regulate their emotions better and thus prevent a chronic affective disorder.

2.7.5 *Physical and Mental Well-Being*

It is well known that body and mind influence each other very strongly. If one has a physical problem, then this not infrequently causes the psyche—if one has a mental problem, this often manifests itself in psychosomatic phenomena such as back pain, headaches, etc. In other words, body and mind can hardly be considered separately from each other.

In sports psychology, mindfulness has therefore also been discovered as a mental training. Research has investigated the positive effects on psychologically important aspects, such as the ability to concentrate, emotion regulation and the flow state (Jekauc & Kittler, 2015). The authors believe that these aspects are instrumental in athletic success.

Conversely, this means that in order to be successful in elite sports, athletes must not only train their physical fitness, but also their mental state. Research regarding mindfulness in elite sports is still in its infancy, but with the findings to date, mindfulness is also an extremely positive and promising tool for success in the context of performance and health well-being.

2.7.6 Self-Efficacy

The experience of self-efficacy is one of the most significant active principles of successful intervention in the field of problem solving. People with a high self-efficacy expectation anticipate sufficient coping skills, which results in these people facing problems in all areas of life actively and optimistically can be concluded that a high self-efficacy expectancy acts as a kind of steering wheel in the context of a successful life. In research, an increase in self-efficacy through mindfulness can only be weakly demonstrated so far.

In conclusion, we can generally state that the practice of mindful behavior leads to a mindful basic attitude. This does good to the person who turns to the exercises, both physically and psychologically.

References

American Mindfulness Research Association. (2019). *Journal articles on mindfulness continue to grow in 2018*. Accessed October 21, 202, from https://goamra.org/journal-articles-on-mindfulness-continue-to-grow-in-2018/

Baer, R. A., Smith, G. T., Hopkins, J., Krietemeyer, J., & Toney, L. (2006). Using self-report assessment methods to explore facts of mindfulness. *Assessment, 13*, 27–45.

Baier, K. (2013). Philosophien der Übung unter japanischem Einfluss. Karlfried Graf Dürckheim und Otto Friedrich Bollnow. In M. Schmücker & F. Heubel (Eds.), *Dimensionen der Selbstkultivierung. Beiträge des Forums für Asiatische Philosophie* (pp. 337–369). Verlag Karl Alber.

Bandura, A. (1979). *Sozial-kognitive Lerntheorie*. Klett-Cotta.

Brandtstädter, J. (2015). *Positive Entwicklung. Zur Psychologie gelingender Lebensführung*. Springer.

Brauchle, G. (2012). Posttraumatische Reifung. In C. Steinebach, D. Jungo, & R. Zihlmann (Eds.), *Positive Psychologie in der Praxis*. Beltz.

Descartes, R. (1996). *Philosophische Schriften in einem Band*. Felix Meiner.

Good, D. J., Lyddy, C. J., Glomb, T. M., Bono, J. E., Brown, K. W., Duffy, M. K., Baer, R. A., Brewer, J. A., & Lazar, S. W. (2016). Contemplating mindfulness at work: An integrative review. *Journal of Management, 42*(1), 114–142.

Grebner, S., Berlowitz, I., Alvarado, V., & Cassina, M. (2011). *Stressstudie 2010. Stress bei Schweizer Erwerbstätigen. Zusammenhänge zwischen Arbeitsbedingungen, Personenmerkmalen, Befinden und Gesundheit*. SECO, Direktion für Arbeit.

Häcker, H., & Stapf, K. H. (2004). *Dorsch Psychologisches Wörterbuch*. Hans Huber.

Hölzel, B. K., Carmody, J., Vangel, M., Congleton, C., Yerramsetti, S. M., Gard, T., & Lazar, S. W. (2011a). Mindfulness practice leads to increases in regional brain gray matter density. *Psychiatry Research: Neuroimaging, 191*(1), 36–43.

Hölzel, B. K., Lazar, S. W., Gard, T., Schuman-Olivier, Z., Vago, D. R., & Ott, U. (2011b). How does mindfulness meditation work? Proposing mechanisms of action from a conceptual and neural perspective. *Perspectives on Psychological Science, 6*(6), 537–559.

Hufenus, B. (2010). *MBSR und Selbstwirksamkeitserwartung*. Zurich. Bachelorarbeit. Accessed May 12, 2020, from https://digitalcollection.zhaw.ch/bitstream/11475/829/1/ba0080.pdf

Jekauc, D., & Kittler, C. (2015). Achtsamkeit im Leistungssport. *Leistungssport, 45*(6), 19–23.

Kabat-Zinn, J. (2013). *Gesund durch Meditation: Das große Buch der Selbstheilung mit MBSR*. OW Barth eBook.

Kobasa, S. C. (1979). Stressful life events, personality, and health – Inquiry into hardiness. *Journal of Personality and Social Psychology, 37*, 1–11.
Lefrank, A. (2009). *Umwandlung in Christus: Die Dynamik des Exerzitienprozesses* (pp. 24–32). Echter.
Lutz, A., Greischar, L. L., Rawlings, N. B., Ricard, M., & Davidson, R. J. (2004). Long-term meditators self-induce high-amplitude gamma synchrony during mental practice. *PNAS, 101*(46), 16369–16373. https://doi.org/10.1073/pnas.0407401101
Maercker, A., & Langner, R. (2001). Persönliche Reifung (personal growth) durch Belastungen und Traumata: Validierung zweier deutschsprachiger Fragebogenversionen. *Diagnostica, 47*(3), 153–162.
MBSR-Verband Schweiz. (2020). Accessed February 09, 2021, from https://www.mindfulness.swiss/
Meibert, P., Michalak, J., & Heidenreich, T. (2006). Achtsamkeitsbasierte Stressreduktion – Mindfulness-based stress reduction (MBSR) nach Kabat-Zinn. In T. Heidenreich & J. Michalak (Eds.), *Achtsamkeit und Akzeptanz in der Psychotherapie* (2nd ed., pp. 141–191). DGTV.
Nielsen, L., & Kaszniak, A. W. (2006). Awareness of subtle emotional feelings: A comparison of long-term meditators and nonmeditators. *Emotion, 6*(3), 392–405.
Obsan. (2013). *Depressionen in der Schweizer Bevölkerung*. Daten zur Epidemiologie, Behandlung und sozial-beruflichen Integration.
Ott, U. (2011). *Meditation für Skeptiker: ein Neurowissenschaftler erklärt den Weg zum Selbst*. OW Barth eBook.
Pathway School System. (2020). Accessed October 21, 2020, from https://pathway.edu.vn
Prochaska, J. O., & Velicer, W. F. (1997). The transtheoretical model of health behavior change. *American Journal of Health Promotion, 12*(1), 38–48.
Reb, J., Chaturvedi, S., Narayanan, J., & Kudesia, R. S. (2019). Leader mindfulness and employee performance: A sequential mediation model of LMX quality, interpersonal justice, and employee stress. *Journal of Business Ethics, 160*(3), 745–763.
Schilling. (2010). *Fehldiagnose Zappelphilipp. Beobachter, Ausgabe 19. 2010*. Ringier Axel Springer Schweiz AG.
Seligman, M. E. P. (2008). Positive health. *Applied Psychology, 57*, 3–8.
Shonin, D. E., Van Gordon, W., Dunn, T., Singh, N., & Griffiths, M. (2014). Meditation awareness training for work-related wellbeing and job performance: A randomized controlled trial. *International Journal of Mental Health and Addiction, 12*, 806–823.
Steinebach, C., & Brendtro, L. (2012). Positive Psychologie in der Praxis. In C. Steinebach, D. Jungo, & R. Zihlmann (Eds.), *Positive Psychologie in der Praxis* (pp. 18–26). Beltz.
Tang, Y.-Y., Hölzel, B., & Posner, M. (2015). The neuroscience of mindfulness meditation. *Nature Reviews Neuroscience, 16*(4), 213–225.
von Brück, M. (2005). Geistestraining durch Achtsamkeit – ein Weg der Spiritualität. In V. Kast (Ed.), *Inspirationen für ein gutes Leben* (pp. 137–147). Freiburg.
von Brück, M. (2006). Bild und Bildlosigkeit in buddhistischer Meditation – Tibetischer Buddhismus und Zen. In C. Maar & H. Burda (Eds.), *Iconic worlds. Neue Bilderwelten und Wissensräume* (pp. 209–231). DuMont.
von Brück, M. (2016). *Einführung in den Buddhismus*. Verlag der Weltreligionen.
Wickert, U. (1995). *Das Buch der Tugenden*. Hoffman und Campe.
Williams, M., & Penman, D. (2012). *Mindfulness, a practical guide to finding peace in a frantic world*. Piatkus.
Zivnuska, S., Kacmar, K. M., Ferguson, M., & Carlson, D. S. (2016). Mindfulness at work: Resource accumulation, well-being, and attitudes. *Career Development International, 21*(2), 106–124. https://doi.org/10.1108/CDI-06-2015-0086

Chapter 3
Religious Roots of the Concept of Mindfulness as a Reference Point for Ethical Leadership

Arie Verkuil

3.1 Introduction

The following very general article examines the question of how the concept of mindfulness and ethically oriented leadership can be mutually dependent and interpenetrating. The concept of mindfulness is first presented in the religious context of the Hindu, Buddhist and Judeo-Christian traditions.

In a second step, Mindfulness is presented as a resilience factor within the ideologically neutral context. In a third step, the fundamentals of ethically oriented leadership in the economic context are unfolded. Finally, Mindfulness and ethically oriented leadership are linked.

3.2 Mindfulness in the Context of Religious Traditions

The concept of mindfulness plays a central role in the context of religious traditions. This can be exemplified by the Hindu, Buddhist and Judeo-Christian traditions (Auffahrt, 1999).

The roots of the long and varied *Hindu traditions* go back to the original form of religious experience, animism. Animism experiences nature as animate. Everything that is, be it animals, plants, lakes, rivers, stones and mountains or other natural phenomena, appears animated to the observer, which is why he worships them as divine beings. This view is reflected, for example, in the Rigveda. Later the Upanishads represent the view that behind this appearance with Brahma and Atman two

---

A. Verkuil (✉)
School of Business, University of Applied Sciences Northwestern Switzerland, Windisch, Switzerland
e-mail: arie.verkuil@fhnw.ch

V. Schulte et al. (eds.), *Mindful Leadership in Practice*,
https://doi.org/10.1007/978-3-030-97311-7_3

basic principles stand, which hold this world together in the inside. Brahma, as the creative principle, is the source from which all life has emerged. Connected and inseparable from this creative elemental force is Atman, the individual and indestructible essence of the spirit. It is the divine core of man. The tragedy of human existence lies in the fact that man is not aware of his true divine nature. He does not know that he possesses with Atman an immortal soul and neither ever was nor ever will be separated from the divine source Brahma. The reason for the ignorance about the nature of Brahma lies in the nature of this creative primordial force itself. The multiplicity of appearances of the material world veils his nature as the one and only source of all that exists and puts a veil of ignorance, the veil of Maya, on man. For here in the world of appearances everything seems to exist separate and unconnected from each other. Individuality dominates. The all-dominating force in this individualistic world is egoism. But egoism is the source of all human suffering by making the world of appearances at the same time a world of projections. Projections lead people to the false assumption that they can achieve and have everything they want through the realization of their passions. Greed, for example, leads people to accumulate goods and cling to material things under the illusion that the one who has enough of everything or even an abundance must be happy. This is also the source of envy, which leads to wanting to acquire things that are owned by others. Thus, greed and envy become the cause of people stealing from each other and trying to appropriate other people's possessions in endless wars, leading to endless unnecessary suffering. Already this example illustrates how man clings to this world of appearances with all his strength through the projections of his egoistic desires associated with his passions, which is why he remains bound to it through reincarnation in an eternal cycle of birth and death. Redemption from this eternal cycle brings only the liberation from the illusion of maya and the realization of the unity of Atman and Brahman.

The Bhagawadgita shows how this liberation could take place. In an allegory, it depicts life as an actual battlefield. On this battlefield, human egoistic forces clash with those of the divine order. Only when man overcomes his egoistic forces and becomes aware of his divine nature will he leave this battlefield victorious and be liberated from the eternal cycle of birth and death. The Bhagawadgita describes different ways (yogas) how man can successfully fight this battle. In the sixth canto it names the yoga of meditation. Through the right posture and the right way of life, thoughts and desires should gradually come to rest. Only then and only in this way can Brahman-Nirvana be reached through the constant, mindful life in the self and thus true, boundless happiness be attained.

Buddhism is in its core a philosophy rather than a religion. Rationally, soberly and without compelling recourse to a theistic world view, it analyzes the existential constitution, the Conditio humana, of man. His observation of this Conditio humana leads him to the realization that suffering is the actual existential basic experience of man. From the beginning of his existence, man experiences suffering as the consequences of birth, work, separation, old age, illness and death.

What man does not seem to realize is that he himself is the cause of his suffering. His desire, his thirst for life, his attachment to things, his greed, his hatred and above all his blindness lead to suffering. Delusion can be equated here with ignorance and non-understanding. In this context, we can also speak of the self-fulfilling prophecy, as the Austrian constructivist Paul Watzlawick aptly describes it in his example of the hammer (Pritz, 2008). This is a prediction that brings about its own fulfillment. A certain attitude towards an issue has a decisive influence on the behavior of a person and thus becomes an essential cause for it to occur in the future.

Buddhism offers the practice of meditation as a way out of this delusion. Meditation is supposed to lead to a mindful attitude of mind, which in turn shows itself in the ethical behavior of the famous eightfold path (yogas) to nirvana: right knowledge and mind, right speech, right action and life, right effort, mindfulness and collection.

Mindfulness is the royal road to salvation from all suffering. Whoever lives mindfully does not feel fear, but compassion with his suffering environment.

Mindfulness and compassion also play a central role in the *Judeo-Christian tradition* with its theistic worldview. For this line of tradition, "delusion" means separation from God as the creative source of all life.

The reason for the separation from this creative primal ground is sin, which causes human suffering from an attitude of egocentrism (self-centeredness). In this context, the seven so-called deadly sins are of particular importance: Pride (pride, vanity, arrogance), Avarice (greed, covetousness), Lust (debauchery, hedonism, covetousness, unchastity), Wrath (irascibility, anger, vindictiveness), Gluttony (gluttony, intemperance, intemperance, selfishness), Envy (jealousy, envy), Sloth (cowardice, ignorance, weariness, sluggishness of heart). The ideal way of salvation from the suffering caused by sin, in this tradition, is to follow the double commandment of love. The double commandment of love commands on the one hand to love God with all one's heart, with all one's soul, with all one's mind and with all one's strength, and at the same time to love one's fellow man as oneself. If in the Jewish tradition the keeping of the commandments for the renewal and strengthening of the connection with God stands in the center, in the Christian tradition the life and death of Jesus Christ becomes the reference point for the exemplary embodiment of the basic attitude of the double commandment of love. Faith in the dual nature of his profound compassionate humanity, on the one hand, and in the creative divinity of his person, on the other, becomes here at the same time the ultimate possibility of salvation from the suffering and delusion caused by sin, and thus from separation from God.

Similar to the Buddhist practice of meditation, the Judeo-Christian practice of prayer and contemplation serves to practice mindfulness and strengthen compassion through the visualization of the double commandment of love. In this way, the suffering caused by sin is to be overcome.

Both the example of the Hindu, Buddhist, and Judeo-Christian traditions show how deeply the attitude of mindfulness and compassion is connected to the human existential experience of suffering, regardless of the particular cultural and temporal context, and offers a way to deal with it constructively and productively. All three traditions convey: Practicing an attitude of mindfulness and compassion is able to alleviate the impact of suffering and even opens up a hopeful perspective of final redemption from all suffering through entrance into nirvana, or the kingdom of God.

3.3 Mindfulness in the Context of Modern Resilience Research

Even in the age of postmodernity, human beings are not spared the experience of suffering as a human condition. Reflection on the cause and effect of this experience must also be carried out here, even if the religious context as a self-evident context of interpretation and the religious tradition of meditation and prayer for the strengthening of an attitude of mindfulness and compassion can no longer be assumed.

Current resilience research offers a neutral approach to interpreting the experience of suffering in a constructive way. It, too, observes that people are exposed to the experience of suffering, and at the same time notes that those affected react to it quite differently. Some people retain the courage to face life despite the most adverse circumstances and respond to crises with confidence. This trait is called "resilience."

There are factors that promote the constructive and productive handling of painful experiences. Three of these so-called resilience factors are: Emotion Control, Impulse Control, and Causal Analysis (Mourlane, 2019). Experience shows that reacting impulsively to distressful experiences does not usually mitigate their impact, but rather amplifies them. Not reacting through impulse control buys time and is a basic prerequisite for self-awareness and thus for emotion control. Only the perception of one's own emotions enables the analysis of one's own shares in a painful experience. This analysis of one's own parts is in turn the basic prerequisite for the causal analysis of cause and effect of an episode experienced as distressful. In particular, it becomes possible to better recognize and analyze one's own shares in the causation of experienced suffering. This analysis is the basic condition for reducing or even avoiding unnecessary future suffering experiences. Those who create time for self-awareness through impulse control and increase their ability for self-reflection and emotion control with the help of causal analysis develop more empathy for themselves and others. It is possible and useful to draw parallels here with the practice of meditation and prayer, for the practice of meditation and prayer means, at its core, nothing more than making time for self-reflection in order to be able to make the journey from ignorance and non-understanding to recognition of one's own part in the causes of avoidable suffering. Mindfulness and compassion through the religious traditions of meditation and prayer promote resilience as does practicing the resilience factors of impulse control, causal analysis, and emotion control.

3.4 Leadership in an Economic Context

Leadership in an economic context is primarily oriented to the guiding question of economic activity. This guiding question is: "How can scarcity be overcome?" Behind this question is the existential experience of scarcity. Scarcity of goods and services can lead to sorrowful experiences. The response of economic rationality to these experiences is that scarcity can be mitigated by exchanging abundant goods and services for scarce or absent ones. The impetus for economic activity is not only the experience of scarcity, but also self-interest through the increase of one's own goods. The dominant conception of man in economics is the "homo economicus," a being who seeks to optimize his utility through the exchange of goods and services. This being calculates soberly and rationally. It carefully weighs up the relationship between costs and benefits before engaging in an exchange. However, this superficially sober and rational behavior of "homo economicus" can also lead to an exaggerated focus on self-interest as a result of passions such as greed and envy, which can have an unfavorable effect on bartering in the medium to long term, since it must be in the balanced mutual interest.

The same is true in the context of a leadership relationship. The aspect of exchange also plays a central role in the relationship between the leader and the person being led. It is a relationship based on reciprocity. Reciprocity is a basic human principle and means mutuality. Simplified, this principle is: "Tit for tat". In this context, leadership means that the leader influences the person being led to act in the way he or she wants in order to achieve the results he or she sees as desired. However, this desired behavior on the part of the person being led comes at a price. Without some form of reciprocation by the leader, the desired behavior will not occur.

As determinants for the design of the reciprocity relationship between leader and led person, three essential factors play the decisive role: the leader with his or her characteristics and skills, the led person with his or her motivation to perform as required, and the context in which this occurs.

Just as old as it is controversial is the question of whether the characteristics or the skills of the leader are decisive for exerting influence. Behind this is the even more fundamental question of whether leadership requires very specific skills and can therefore be learned, or whether certain characteristics are decisive that correspond to a person's natural disposition, his or her charisma. At second glance, however, the many different answers are of no practical relevance, since practice shows that, on the one hand, certain characteristics such as emotion control, impulse control and causal analysis are helpful and useful, but on the other hand, it is precisely these characteristics that can be learned and further developed through experience.

Another controversial issue is whether guided persons perform certain actions because they want to or because they are allowed to. In this context, a distinction is made between extrinsic and intrinsic motivation. Extrinsic motivation factors are positive or negative external incentives with which leaders work to enforce their will. If leaders display the desired behavior of their own accord, this is referred to as intrinsic motivation.

The tasks to be performed and the circumstances in which they are performed form the context of leadership. Tasks are distinguished between one-off and repetitive tasks.

The type of tasks is decisive for the leadership role. Types of tasks can be distinguished as follows. See below the differentiation between innovative and repetitive tasks (Fig. 3.1).

Innovative Tasks	⟷	Repetitive Tasks
Elusive	Content of the Task	Clear
Open at the beginning	Course of the Task	Set
Unpredictable	Result	Sure
Never	Repetition	Often
High	Risk	Low
Low	Structurability	High
High	Flexibility	Low
Low	Efficiency	High

Company task types, own presentation

Fig. 3.1 Innovative and repetitive tasks, after Hugentobler, W., Schaufelbühl, K. & Blatter, M. (2020). Integrale Betriebswirtschaftslehre, 7th, revised edition, Zurich: Orell Füssli, p. 97 (own representation)

For the leadership role, the distinction between management and leadership goes back to Zaleznik (1977). This distinction was popularized by John P. Kotter (1990) and systematized by Neuberger (2002).

Management is geared towards efficiency and focuses on repetitive tasks and regulated processes.

Leadership focuses on effectiveness, takes care of innovative tasks, and means leadership by means of a vision or sense of purpose that provides direction and motivation.

Since in lived practice there is always a mix of innovative and repetitive tasks, the two leadership roles, the management role and the leadership role, are always related to each other.

In this context, we also talk about ambidexterity of leadership (Fig. 3.2).

By their very nature, circumstances can be more or less favorable for leadership. The more favorable the circumstances, the more likely it is that the intrinsic motivation of the person being led will come into play. There is less need for influence, but more need for freedom and personal decision-making. If the circumstances are less favorable and the intrinsic motivation is lower, the leadership effort increases and can even go as far as leadership by coercion.

Not surprisingly, there is a lot of potential for conflict in leadership, especially when it comes to the use of coercion. The reciprocity relationship is then based on the exchange of obedience for avoidance of punishment. The leadership relationship is based on fear of negative sanctions of undesirable behavior on the part of the person being led. There is a risk of misunderstanding and misbehavior on both sides due to different perceptions of the circumstances, which may result in unnecessary injury and suffering on both sides.

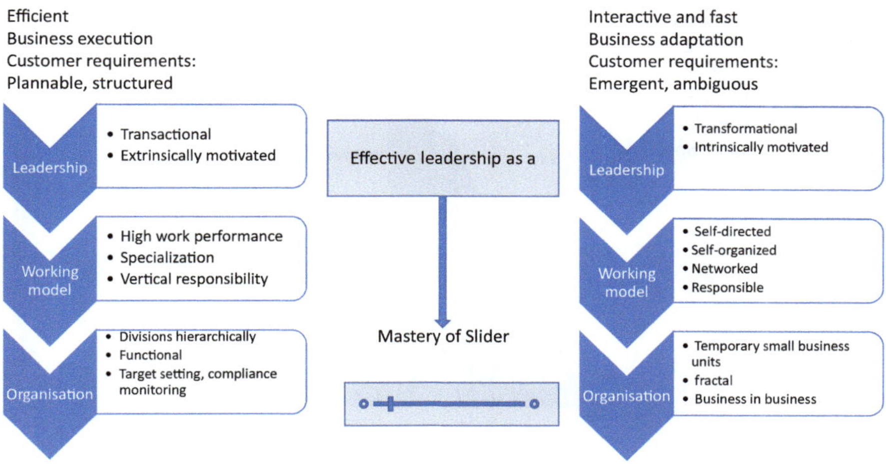

Fig. 3.2 Ambidexterity of leadership at Bosch, after Petry, T. et al. (2019). Digital Leadership, Erfolgreiches Führen in Zeiten der Digital Economy, Freiburg: Haufe Fachbuch, p. 59 (own presentation)

3.5 Ethics and Leadership in the Economic Context of Leadership

If economics asks how scarcity can be overcome, ethics asks about the conditions for a successful life. A distinction must be made between morality and ethics in the narrower sense. Morality knows the conditions of a successful life from cultural, unquestioned habit. One knows what one has to do and what one has to refrain from doing, because one has been told in society, in the family, in the company by all means, even without giving further reasons, which behavior is accepted and which is not (Pieper, 2017, p. 26). In return for conforming behavior, one becomes an accepted member of a group and receives its recognition and protection.

This is where ethics comes in (Pieper, 2017, p. 35). It questions unquestioned moral action by asking for the reasons for justification. From an ethical perspective, moral action may well contradict the conditions of successful life. The argument of becoming an accepted member of a group through conforming behavior is not sufficient from an ethical point of view because this conforming behavior can run counter to the principle of the conditions of a successful life for individual members of a group, for the group as a whole, or for other groups. This may include, for example, the denial of certain rights to women.

Unwanted effects of conformity pressure through morally conditioned views and habits can, for example, be countered by the ethical principle of Immanuel Kant's categorical imperative: "Act in such a way that you use humanity, both in your person and in the person of everyone else, at all times both as an end and never merely as a means." (Kant, 1968).

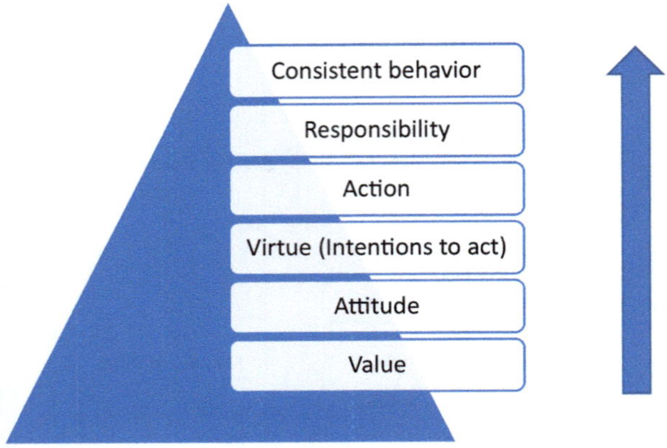

Fig. 3.3 Wertepyramide in Anlehnung an Rokeach, M. (1968). A theory of organization and change within Value-Attitude-Systems. Journal of Social Issues, 1, 13–33

The application of this form of the categorical imperative, which is essentially the same principle as the double commandment of love in Judeo-Christian ethics, can then take on the function of a means of control and correction and counter the unquestioned negative effects of moral action.

Ethics in leadership asks about the foundations of a leadership that, in addition to asserting its own will, also focuses on the conditions of successful life (together). With the question of value orientation, ethics scrutinizes the motivation of the leader to assert his or her will vis-à-vis the people being led. It is interested in whether and which value system underlies the behavior of a leader. Following Rokeach's (1968) value pyramid, this value system can be represented in the context of ethics as follows (Fig. 3.3).

"Values" describe the goal of ethical action. Values are understood to be the conscious or unconscious standards of orientation and guiding principles by which individuals and groups are guided in their choice of action. Values provide answers to the guiding ethical questions of the good life and just coexistence. Such values can be, for example:

1. Reverence for life,
2. Respect for human dignity,
3. Respecting diversity,
4. Keeping Peace,
5. Ensure justice.

Values as standards of orientation only become guiding principles for action when a certain attitude toward them is adopted. Those who adopt a positive "attitude" toward a value strive to realize it out of inner conviction and thus actively contribute to the conditions for a successful life. Reciprocity considerations play no role here. It is about the realization of a value in itself and for the sake of the value itself, out of conviction and inner drive of the acting person and for the time being independent of the concrete context of action. Nevertheless, values only prove to be an attitude, only then to be sustainable, when they prove to be action-determining in relation to passions such as greed and envy.

"Virtues" are intentions of action for the realization of a "value". The cardinal virtues of antiquity were identified by the philosopher Plato in wisdom (prudence), courage (fortitude, determination), prudence (temperance) and justice. Through the application of these virtues, values that guide action are to be put into practice and thus realized.

Putting values into action means acting. A single action for the realization of a value has thereby still by far not the same meaning as often repeated action for the realization of the same value. Through repeated action, values are subjected to the test of whether they are and become actually action-guiding.

Using appropriate virtues to realize values that guide one's actions is one thing; giving an account of the consequences of one's own behavior is another. Only those who give an account of the consequences of their own behavior and draw conclusions from it as to whether this behavior has contributed to a successful life act (ethically) responsibly.

It therefore requires constant critical questioning and consistency checks by the person acting.

The impetus for this critical reflection are dilemmas that challenge value-oriented action in the context of the economy just as fundamentally as the question of suffering as a basic existential experience of the human condition.

Yes, there is even a deep connection between both, the value-oriented action and the existential basic experience of suffering as a human condition. This is especially true when mindfulness is made the reference point of ethically oriented leadership.

The tension field of leadership as an actual basic dilemma is a good reason to do this.

3.6 Mindfulness as a Reference Point for Ethically Oriented Leadership

Leadership in a business context is fundamentally caught between human responsibility and leadership responsibility (Fig. 3.4).

The tension between human responsibility and responsibility for success is based on a fundamental conflict of objectives between an ethical value orientation from the point of view of the conditions for a successful life and the realization of economic added value. This conflict of goals repeatedly confronts executives with decision-making dilemmas in their management role as well as in their leadership role and leads to interpersonal conflicts between executives and those they lead. The decision dilemmas are based on the choice of which goals should be given priority. For example, should jobs be cut to increase short-term profits, or should short-term profit orientation be foregone in favor of mutual loyalty between employer and employees, thus favoring the medium- to longer-term development of the company? These

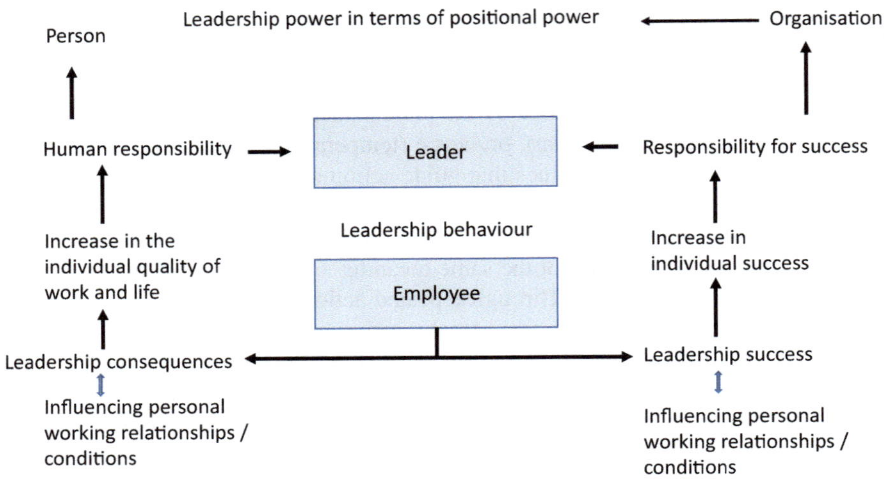

Fig. 3.4 Employee leadership, a problem-oriented frame of reference, after Kuhn, T. & Weibler, J. (2003). Führungsethik, in: Die Unternehmung, 57th Jg., Heft 5, 2003, pp. 375–392 (own presentation)

decision dilemmas caused by conflicting goals challenge leaders to question their values and to take a clear stance on these values.

One way of dealing productively with dilemmas in the area of tension between human responsibility and responsibility for success is to distinguish the respective logics behind the two responsibilities.

Behind the responsibility for success is the purpose-rational logic of economics. The purpose-rational logic of economics is a logic based on an end-means relationship. This logic decides according to the principle of using those means with which the greatest benefit can be achieved in order to achieve certain ends. This also means that those behaviors are most effective in which the highest possible return is achieved with the least possible effort. From an ethical point of view, the economic end-means rationality is initially value-free, since it does not ask about the conditions for a successful life, but about how scarcity of resources can be overcome as optimally as possible.

In contrast, the value-oriented logic of ethics is not a purpose-driven logic, but a principle-driven logic. Ethical logic asks what values should guide human behavior in order to realize the conditions for a successful life.

Economic and ethical logic need not be mutually exclusive. On the contrary, they can complement each other.

On the one hand, ethical logic can act as a corrective by evaluating economic actions that are in themselves value-free and rational in their purpose, by classifying economic actions from the point of view of their contribution to a successful life and thus giving them a deeper meaning.

On the other hand, the end-means thinking of economics can support the realization of ethical values by asking by which means a certain value can be optimally realized as a higher meaningful end of human action.

Ethical and economic rationality, however, requires careful situational weighing and assessment. This weighing requires attentiveness, care and empathy, and requires time until a balanced solution can be found. If a balanced solution cannot be found, then ethics as a guiding star must be given priority over economic logic. Fulfilling the conditions of a successful life, for example, must take precedence over purely economically oriented profit maximization.

Time is a scarce resource. This is why the search for a balance between efficiency-oriented responsibility for success and value-oriented efforts to simultaneously optimize the conditions for a successful life generates stress. In living beings, stress refers on the one hand to mental and physical reactions caused by specific external stimuli (stressors) that enable us to cope with particular demands, and on the other hand to the physical and mental strain they cause. In this sense, stress is also an experience of suffering.

One way of learning to cope well with stress can be the well-studied and widely used method of Mindfulness-Based Stress Reduction (MBSR) developed by Jon Kabat-Zinn in the USA in the late 1970s (Kabat-Zinn, 2013). With the help of this method, self-awareness is increased by purposefully directing attention, with the effect that (leadership) decisions are made less impulsively and more on the basis of empathy and causal analysis. In this sense, the MBSR method strengthens resilience.

Despite these challenges, the basic condition for consistent, value-oriented behavior over the long term is careful and mindful consideration of the possibilities for realizing values that guide action in all conceivable different situations.

Only those who adopt a positive attitude toward values can act responsibly, because their behavior reflects the answer to the question: "How do you realize your values?" or "What does it mean to you to do good and thus contribute to a successful life?"

Acting in accordance with personal values and holding oneself accountable for this increases one's own ethical competence and thus the integrity of the leader. Anyone who acts reliably and in a manner recognizable to others in accordance with personal values is authentic. Authenticity means acting on the basis of the same fundamental values regardless of the different situations and roles in which one finds oneself. Only this reliable, recognizable and consistent action on the basis of the same values gives the person acting an identity and personality that is also outwardly unmistakable. In this sense, authenticity increases the credibility of the leader. Credibility of the leader is the basis for the core value of ethically oriented leadership: gaining the trust of the people being led. The basis of trust is reliability. People rely on other people whose behavior is not based on arbitrariness but on a clearly recognizable attitude that creates identity and shapes personalities. However, trust can only be gained by reducing the pressure of suffering and avoiding unnecessary suffering altogether, both in oneself and in others.

Taking responsibility and being accountable for whether and how one has taken responsibility, drawing conclusions on how to avoid wrong decisions and unproductive behavior in the future, that means mindfulness and compassion in the context of ethically oriented leadership.

Here the circle closes. For spiritually inclined and religiously rooted leaders, being embedded in the Hindu, Buddhist or Judeo-Christian traditions that have been exemplified here can be a source of inspiration and motivation. Regular meditation and/or prayer can strengthen their mindfulness in conflict-prone leadership situations and their empathy and compassion toward their employees.

Leaders without access to religious traditions may strengthen their mindfulness and compassion through neural methods such as Jon Kabat-Zinn's Mindfulness-Based Stress Reduction.

Whether via rootedness in a religious tradition or by practicing a neutral method, improved mindfulness and increased compassion contribute to the reduction of unnecessary suffering. Together with the implementation of the action-guiding values defined by ethics using the cardinal virtues, they are important factors in promoting a successful and productive life and thus increasing (ethically oriented) leadership success.

References

Auffahrt, C. (Ed.). (1999). *Metzler encyclopedia of religion* (Vol. II, p. 50). Metzler.

Kabat-Zinn, J. (2013). *Healthy through meditation: The big book of self-healing with MBSR.* OW Barth eBook.

Kant, I. (1968). *Grundlegung zur Metaphysik der Sitten. Akademie-Ausgabe Kant Werke IV.* Walter de Gruyter.

Kotter, J. P. (1990). *What leaders really do* (pp. 103–111). Harvard Business Review.

Mourlane, D. (2019). *Resilience: The undiscovered capacity of the truly successful* (10th ed.). BusinessVillage.

Neuberger, O. (2002). *Leading and being led: Approaches, results, and critique of leadership research* (6th ed.). Lucius & Lucius.

Petry, T., et al. (2019). *Digital Leadership, Erfolgreiches Führen in Zeiten der Digital Economy.* Haufe Fachbuch.

Pieper, A. (2017). *Introduction to ethics* (7th ed.). A. Francke Verlag.

Pritz, A. (2008). Paul Watzlawick: A guide to unhappiness. In *One hundred masterpieces of psychotherapy* (pp. 195–196). Springer.

Rokeach, M. (1968). A theory of organization and change within value-attitude systems. *Journal of Social Issues, 24*(1), 13–33.

Zaleznik, A. (1977). *Managers and leaders: Are they different?* (pp. 67–80). Harvard Business Review.

Chapter 4
Ethical Cornerstones of People-Oriented Leadership

Volker Schulte and Paul Imhof

4.1 Introduction

In this chapter, we would like to consider the philosophical and ethical framework on which mindful leadership can be built. Mindful leadership is fed by a well-founded and embodied leadership ethic, which can be experienced not only in the attitude but also in day-to-day actions. Mindful leadership is derived from value management, in which certain basic ethical constants are available as a basis for mindful action.

The development of a basic ethical attitude and mindset in human interaction is a profoundly complex process. It cannot be adopted and applied "off the peg," as it were. Rather, ethics is based on a system of values that is shaped by culture, society and individual socialization. In the professional and organizational context, this means developing a credible leadership ethic in which both the value base of the leader and his concrete actions follow a coherent normative logic. In the following, we would like to define and explain some parameters without which mindful leadership is not possible. Mindful leadership can only be based on the maxims of the ethics of responsibility, in that the leader is always aware of the consequences of his actions and has to answer for them (Weber & Winckelmann, 1964).

V. Schulte (✉)
School of Business, University of Applied Sciences Northwestern Switzerland, Windisch, Switzerland
e-mail: volker.schulte@fhnw.ch

P. Imhof
Academy St. Paul, Bonn, Germany

V. Schulte et al. (eds.), *Mindful Leadership in Practice*,
https://doi.org/10.1007/978-3-030-97311-7_4

4.2 Human Service as a Practical Attitude of Virtuous Action

All actions in mindful leadership must be focused on people. The concept of "human service" shimmers with "serving", which is nowadays described in English as "servant leadership". The servant-leadership approach involves an uncompromising orientation of leadership to the interests of those being led. A servant leader lives agape, charity. He likes his employees and wants to help them. The mission of the servant leader is therefore more that of a facilitator who can identify the needs of his employees and help to satisfy them. This is not just about providing support through expertise and advice, but also and especially about creating meaningful, enjoyable work environments. The key therefore lies in the consistent turning of the leader towards the led. Mindful leadership places effectiveness at the center of its work and understands leadership as a direction- and motivation-creating mission and the conveyance of meaning. Everyday leadership is characterized by ambiguity and ambivalence. Mindful leaders can deal calmly with the reality of contradictions in everyday professional life as well as with the ambivalence of actions. They know that there are no simple truths, but they are aware of the existence of multiple levels of being and worlds that can contradict each other. Within this ambivalence, it is important to provide guidance to those being subordinated. Leadership in mindfulness means shaping and coordinating the interplay of interests and tasks of different participants.

One principle of mindful leadership is the invitation to the leader's teachability. Teaching is understood as a gift, not as a reproach, or even more provocatively: The superior person is grateful for advice that helps improve one's own performance. Being able to be told something results from the leader's desire for genuine insight. This requires a humble attitude. Unteachability and know-it-all attitude, today also referred to as resistance to advice, are forms of resistance to reality (Pieper, 2004, p. 31). Therefore, mindful leadership does not mean lecturing or slipping into moralism. The basic prerequisite is to accept people as they are and not as one would like them to be.

The organizational and leadership culture impacts the entire workforce. Leaders at all management levels have the task of breaking down strategies, goals and measures to the individual departments and functional areas and translating and communicating them in their respective context. The leader thus has an important function: he or she must filter the organization's specifications, communicate them in a way that is appropriate to the function and management level, and ensure that the team and the individual employee implement the company's goals. The manager is thus confronted with various conflicting levels. Not every piece of information issued from above is relevant to the team or the individual employee. Not everyone needs to know everything, nor should they. The task of the leader in the unit for which he or she is responsible is to select the information and pass it on in a processed form to those people who need it for operational business. Every activity in an organization is based on the elements of normative management, but they are processed and implemented in a level-appropriate manner. In this process, the mindful leader must also take on a protective role by withholding certain information or adapting it in such a way that there is no unnecessary worry, anxiety or loss of motivation. On the other hand, the leader is responsible for ensuring that the economic guidelines of the organization are communicated and realized based on the functions and competencies of the team (Schulte & Fleckenstein, 2019).

Another conflictual tension can arise when the leader does not agree with the organization's commands and decisions and yet has to communicate them convincingly to his or her own team. In modern organizations, specific codes of conduct are defined with rules and guidelines for external and internal communication and control the desired behavior of employees via leadership principles. The basis for the codes of conduct are the values to which the organization subscribes. This results in a typical overall picture, an image of the organization, to which all employees must align themselves (Schulte & Fleckenstein, 2019).

4.3 Sense of Coherence

This addresses another attribute of mindful leadership, which can be described as a sense of coherence in everyday leadership. The origin of this lies in the "Sense of Coherence " developed by the medical sociologist Aaron Antonovsky (Antonovsky, 1997). For Antonovsky, three aspects are needed for a successful life: First, the ability to understand how my life and that of my environment work. We need a sense of comprehensibility. We also need to be convinced that we can determine our own lives and are capable of developing and shaping them independently. We need the feeling of manageability or comprehensibility. Third, life as such must make sense to us so that we can set achievable goals and feel good about ourselves. We need a belief in the meaning of life.

In summary, the sense of coherence is built on a confidence and basic optimism for life. If we cannot develop this feeling, consisting of the elements of comprehensibility, manageability, meaningfulness, we lack the prerequisites for a happy life.

Traditionally, we deal with a static and negatively defined concept of health. According to this, health is the absence of disease. Therefore, overcoming illness has always been seen as the decisive factor of a satisfactory state of health. According to this reading, health is defined only from the perspective of pathogenesis. The medical sociologist Aaron Antonovsky now turns the perspective around 180 degrees and asks about the conditions of health and its promotion: How do people manage to stay healthy even under difficult conditions? What resources do such people build on, and why do some manage to cope with dire situations better and more easily than others? From this, Antonovsky developed the concept of salutogenesis. He was guided by the question of the conditions under which the maintenance and strengthening of health is possible: "Why are people on the positive side of the health-disease continuum, or why are they moving toward the positive pole, regardless of their current position?" (Antonovsky, 1997, p. 7). The

Fig. 4.1 Three factors of the sense of coherence according to Antonovsky (own representation)

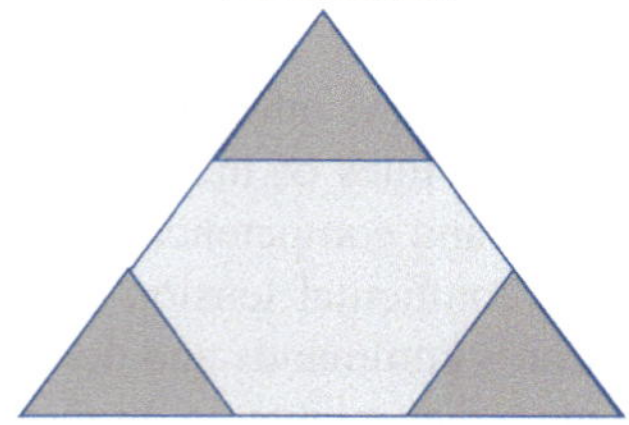

salutogenetic approach therefore asks about resources, which do not focus on suffering itself, but on overcoming it and on everything that is good for us, i.e. on aspects of well-being. What needs to be determined are the patterns and criteria according to which a happy and fulfilled life with all the necessary balances can be achieved.

We are dealing with a broadening of perspective in the salutogenetic approach, because elements of healing are also central and the focus is on coping strategies that seek to optimize our position on the health-illness continuum. Mindful leadership builds on the construct of salutogenesis, because ultimately it is the well-being of employees that is at the heart of mindful leadership.

In his model, Antonovsky also develops resistance resources that are important for salutogenesis and prevent states of tension from becoming a threat. He distinguishes three determinants of salutogenetic resources:

1. Adaptability: By adaptation, the author means immunization in physiological, psychological, cultural and social terms. Stressors (causes of stress) can be countered primarily with social relationships and a clear identity.
2. Deep relationships with others: Here the author emphasizes the importance of so-called primary reference groups, namely close friends, family, and people close to us.
3. Institutionalized ties to communities: Here, identitarian ties to society and religion are meant. Participation in such communities creates a "we" experience that offers protection and a sense of belonging.

From these three determinants, Antonovsky develops three characteristics or skills that are essential for a successful life (Fig. 4.1).

4.4 Support Self-Esteem in the Individual and Team

A mindful leader also always builds on a close bond with the team as well as with the individual employee. The team as a further determining pole develops a collective microclimate in a company. It is up to the leader to form a community of values by means of common rules of the game and rules of conduct, which in the end is more than just the sum of individual employees. Therefore, initiatives for further development are always needed to deepen and renew this process.

The employee has a right to a motivating and supportive environment; it is not a gift of grace from the boss. This makes employee leadership a complex organizational and psychological task. The mindful leader must master the art of getting the employee to perform common tasks and achieve common goals. Where necessary, other colleagues are activated who are happy to support because of the existing community of values. This art is based on a sensitive influence on the individual employee as well as on the team as a whole on the part of the mindful leader. At the same time, the leader must always be aware that he or she is in a hierarchical relationship with the employees. This means that the leader must always seek the necessary balance of closeness and distance from the team. A team member will always seek the greatest possible job-specific proximity to the superior person. If the leader also participates too closely in private, non-job-specific topics of conversation and only sees himself as an integral part of the team in this way, he runs the risk of losing authority. Intimacy makes you vulnerable. Any verbal and thematic intimacy undermines the supervisor's authority function. Therefore, a relationship of trust should always maintain the necessary distance from intimacy; this is primarily the responsibility of the superior. It is counterproductive to participate in every gossip and every relationship problem (Schulte & Fleckenstein, 2019).

Conversely, if too much distance is maintained on the part of the supervisor, there is a risk of a loss of trust on the part of the employee. A superior can never be an equal part of the team, but must be able to live with his privileged role, which can also make him lonely. As a general rule, when a team meets without the boss, the boss is always discussed, usually in a constructively critical way. It doesn't matter whether the boss is doing a good job or not, he or she will always be the focus of criticism. If the boss is present, criticism of the boss is usually dispensed with. Regardless of this criticism, the boss generally has a role model function to fulfill. If a boss is not accepted by the team, a dynamic will develop in which the boss will have to take his or her hat off, or individuals on the team will (Schulte & Fleckenstein, 2019).

4.5 Pleasure and Sensuality Through Work

Sensuality refers to a sense of well-being through the use of the senses, which, in addition to tasting, smelling, hearing and seeing, also implies the passions. In relation to the world of work, this means entering into tasks and projects with pleasure. This, too, is part of the goals and tasks of mindful leadership: to create an atmosphere of cheerfulness and serenity through joy and pleasure in creation. The authors explicitly distinguish this from the term intrinsic motivation. On the one hand, the term has already been so worn down in colloquial language that it is only perceived as a catchword. For another, motivation focuses strongly on the serious spectrum of intellectuality, in that things are mastered intellectually rationally rather than emotionally in a feeling-oriented way. This is not to say that we should only do our work emotionally. However, some corporate cultures would benefit from a life connection to joy, because it releases more creative forces.

4.6 Cardinal Virtues

In recent scientific discussion, virtue is associated with the concept of a person's character. According to this, virtues are character traits. So the question arises, which character, consisting of which virtues, a person should form in his socialization. They should be those qualities that are essential for human well-being (Rippe & Schaber, 1998, p. 11). This implies that another prerequisite is intended. Virtues are not innate, "the virtues, on the other hand, we acquire by practicing them beforehand, as is true of other skills. For what we are to become capable of doing by learning, we learn precisely by doing it" (Aristoteles, 1972, p. 81). Aristotle and also Kant see virtue as a skill that can be learned through practice (Kant, 1990, p. 261).

This already shows that we are dealing with a philosophical discussion that has been going on for more than two millennia. The cardinal virtues are predestined for application in mindful leadership for several reasons. First, the set of values to be heeded is very straightforward. We are talking about only four virtues. From them, many other characteristics of good leadership can be derived. Critical self-leadership, empathy, compassion, warmth, generosity, and many more come entirely from the repertoire of positive psychology.

Humility as a mindful attitude can also be subsumed here and deserves a special mention. Humility is characterized by the fact that the person withdraws as a subject, makes self-reflection, restraint and modesty a basic maxim of his communication and does not appear opinionated. On the contrary, the humble person always questions his actions and articulations. In addition, the referencing of daily actions to the cardinal virtues forms a sharpening of mental and physical sensitivity. They help to lead a resource-oriented life in balance and give a stable support to life. A very highly developed humble attitude of leaders is the gift of self-irony, which, properly applied in speeches, leads to the speaker being taken much more seriously than if he delivers a dry speech with opinionated determinism. Self-irony is the high art of communication and articulation because it makes the person who uses it authentic.

4.6.1 Wisdom

Prudence is the mother of the other cardinal virtues. From the prudence the justice, the bravery as well as the measure develop quasi by itself. Ethically speaking, the decision and resolution made by man to act wisely automatically produces a good action (Pieper, 2004, p. 21). Figuratively speaking, the virtue of prudence "informs" the other cardinal virtues because prudence is the basis for their emergence and expression. Here it is presupposed that in order to realize the good, the agent also knows what reality is actually like. It is not the intention to act wisely that is decisive here, but the wise act in a concrete framework of action. The philosopher Josef Pieper brings another thought into play here. "Perfected ability" is manifested in acting wisely even in the face of sudden situational challenges. Here, the virtue of prudence specifies itself into "dispassion in the unexpected" (Pieper, 2004, p. 31).

4.6.2 Justice

The concept of justice in the political context, especially as a counter-concept to equality, has been degraded to a political fighting term in the 1980s. If we want to approach justice as an ontological concept, it is worth pointing out the counter-concept. Injustice is more tangible than justice. In its positive connotation, the term can be stretched and interpreted broadly. On the other hand, we humans have a sense of when something is unjust or there are inconsistencies. However, justice still takes on a special function in mindful leadership. More strongly than the other virtues, it intends an external effect. It affects the way people live together and the form of relationships. It thus reaches beyond the individual subject. The wise action described above can also and especially work on the concept of justice. In the leadership context, kindness and cordiality would be included as visible attitudes of justice.

4.6.3 Bravery

Especially the third of the cardinal virtues presents itself in an antiquated term. We associate bravery with chivalry, sacrifice and heroism. These are terms that we associate with the Middle Ages or with the poetry of ancient Greece. However, the experience of the perversion of the concept of bravery in the wars of the last century has meant that younger generations no longer have much use for it. On the contrary, the term is misleading today. For the mindfulness context, we use the words "autonomy" and "moral courage" instead. We know from different settings the importance of peer groups, be it in clubs, in youth groups or in the military. An individual wants to feel that he or she belongs to such a reference group, does not want to be an outsider. Thus, a person is also subject to peer pressure. Actions or statements that are carried out dominantly within the group may be disapproved of by an individual in the group as inappropriate or ethically unclean. On the other hand, it is much more difficult to articulate the disapproval because the consequence is the threat of being cut out or expelled from the group. There is a compulsion to conform. "The confession of conscience is always inhibited by the fear of isolating oneself. The fear of segregating oneself is the occasion for joining the crowd" (Ranke-Heinemann, 1975). In the context of virtue teaching, therefore, it makes sense today to replace bravery with moral courage. Those who show moral courage behave autonomously to the passive or active majority. Civil courage always goes hand in hand with the state of one's own conscience. Therefore, also and especially for a mindful leader moral courage is an important attribute of the protection of the persons subordinated to him. This is not always easy, quite the contrary. Reality consists of preferences of people, determined by sympathy and antipathy, "by the peculiar attraction that all mediocrity exerts on each other because it feels comfortable in the absence of high demands" (Jaspers, 1965, p. 193). The majority, according to Jaspers, felt secure in the masses and thought that they could derive from this the right to be in the right. The upright, on the other hand, were in the minority. The majority now lacks a clear compass because certain faith values and virtues have fallen away.

4.6.4 Moderation

When we find our temperance, we always find ourselves. To today's ears, moderation has something anachronistic, almost grotesque. In today's hedonism, the concept of moderation connotes moderation with a negative connotation. It resonates with something mediocre, average. Moderation, on the other hand, means a virtue that leads us to remain mentally and physically healthy. Experience shows that any "lack of moderation" leads to physical and mental imbalances. Therefore, moderation always means finding a mental center. We can find this in many areas. Aristotle, as the founder of the doctrine of virtue and the doctrine of mesotes, illustrates this with the opposite poles of excess and deficiency. To determine moderation, Aristotle seeks the middle ground between two extremes. Self-control (moderation) is the ideal between lechery and dullness. Generosity and munificence stand as a corrective between wastefulness and stinginess, and bravery positions itself between foolhardiness and cowardice.

In terms of mindful leadership, the measure would be equivalent to prudent action. Neither rash reaction nor procrastination lead to the goal, but prudent decision-making and consistent reaction appropriate to the situation. In the following figure, the aspects of leadership and virtue are once again summarised (Fig. 4.2).

4.7 Secondary Virtues

The so-called secondary virtues have fallen into disrepute at the latest since the social upheaval of the 1960s. Yet most of them can also be derived from the cardinal virtues. Values such as loyalty and fidelity, obedience and discipline, diligence and a sense of duty, punctuality and reliability, tidiness and cleanliness, and politeness are

Fig. 4.2 Mindful leadership with consideration of the virtue components (own representation)

values that should be cultivated more strongly again. Particularly in the work context, a mindful leader must be able to refer to these values himself and also demand them from his employees.

4.8 Vices

The teaching of virtue over the past two millennia has also dealt with its evil—or, to put it more cautiously, with its negatively connoted sister, vice. A vice always indicates that a person has a deficit that distances him from the virtues described above. Virtues or vices always lead to human distortions on the one hand of the person who is addicted to them, but are also always reflected negatively in society, because society is also affected by the unvirtuous actions of the actors. In the doctrine of virtue, vices—as negative character traits—always lead to morally reprehensible actions and intentions. Traits such as greed, imperiousness, quarrelsomeness, indolence as opposed to empathy, pride or arrogance, envy, avarice and anger are still today negatively connoted attributes that are socially ostracized.

Related to the work context, we find softer leadership or organizational variants of negative leadership adaptation that can stand in the way of mindful leadership and limit it altogether. The following examples from the work context may serve this purpose:

1. Thinking in Terms of Status Conceit and Hierarchical Positions

   We still find people in leadership positions today who do not build their authority on trust, mindfulness and support, but on mistrust, control and the dominance of the factual. Such leaders are not people-oriented, but live in a system of reporting. The leadership becomes self-referential and hardly knows the reality of the business. The best that can be expected from such management is as little disruption as possible.
2. Non-acceptance of errors

   Typical of this type of leadership is a lack of tolerance for mistakes and failures. People with such psychological dispositions are fear-driven. Narcissistic characters are also frequently found. Such people appear superficially secure, in cutting determinism, thus concealing their own fears as well as their lack of social skills. They are afraid of losing control, which is why they interfere in operational business of the lower hierarchies and confuse strategy and operation. A climate of fear exists.
3. Kitchen cabinets and coterie

   Typical of such management cultures is the development of unofficial information and decision-making structures. The selection of employees for senior management takes place via rope networks, family ties, party books and male alliances. The result is often a dramatic decline in good governance and due diligence. The secret goal is then often one's own advantage, articulated however it may be. Rules and conditions that should apply to the entire organization are relativized by means of exceptions for the management floor. Dorothea and Kurt Faller aptly describe some of these patterns (Faller & Faller, 2018). Decision-making processes in such organizations and companies run vertically, with decisions often being aimless due to the lack of strategically secured planning in self-referential systems. Systems prone to organizational inbreeding function degeneratively at best. In vertical silos, directives are issued, and the message of execution is then passed from the bottom up. Communication is just as one-dimensional, namely vertical. The acting persons do not look to the left and to the right, but downward and upward.

4.9 Psychogram of an Immature Leader

Probably all of us have seen or had to put up with people in leadership positions who should never have been in such a position. And yet there they are again and again, the immature leadership personalities. An example of such a figure is Vice-Questore Patta in the detective novels of Donna Leon. Apparently, the immaturity has less to do with the age of the person than with the lack of mature social competence. When such people are at work, the social environment is often confronted with the suffering of this incapacity. The psychogram of such immature leaders can be summarized as follows:

1. **narcissism**: First of all, such people are narcissists. Their characteristic is a pronounced egocentrism, a cognitive mindset that assumes that their own subjective view of the world has an objective status. They have great difficulty in perceiving their own feelings and drawing conclusions from them. Such persons are always wondering whether they will succeed and how they will be received by those around them. To this end, they are vain and athletic, not so much in team sports, but in individual performance. Often such people are athletes or endurance athletes such as marathon runners or swimmers. As in the workplace, they are self-promoters and achievers in their private lives. They always embody their status and attach great importance to not having their position touched. They are also good actors. They can imitate the tough "Charles Bronson type" professionally. At the same time, they are quite aware that they are performing in a mask. Their life is a single competitive struggle to win or lose, always wanting to be the winner. They work hard and pour all their energy into the work context. This often leads to tension and frustration in the private sphere.
2. **feigned competence: On the** surface, they make a competent and convincing impression because it is important to them to be perceived as competent and assertive. This type of leader is outwardly attractive and overly masculine, regardless of age. He wants to be perceived as a "great guy" and appear dynamic and productive. Once such a boss is convinced of something, the facts are perceived and communicated as exaggeratedly positive. Therefore, they do not allow any discussion or criticism of their strategy. The problematic sides of a project or plan are gladly blanked out. However, if they think they have done something well, it has to be publicized so that people applaud approvingly. It is important to them to win admiration. They like to talk about their successes, list people they have been able to influence, and talk about projects they have pulled off and awards they have received. They always want to be praised and actually depend on compliments. Their dogma is that if you just try hard enough, you can work your way up. Often such characters come from humble backgrounds and have worked their way up into the intellectual world (Rohr & Ebert, 2010).
3. **winners and claqueurs:** They admire winners and despise losers. They hate failure and don't like it when their winning image is questioned. For them, there is nothing more tragic than unsuccessfulness because it is unbearable to have to deal with failure, failing or losing. The next employees have to fit into this image. Therefore, their entourage often consists of claqueurs who eagerly seek to implement what the boss has communicated. If failures cannot be concealed, such bosses like to blame them on others, on political conditions, new trends or poor performance caused by subordinates. What works is true. The objective truth is not even an issue. Actually, such leaders are good salespeople and sad figures at the same time—especially when these people lose their status due to layoffs or retirements and have to adjust to new realities.

4.10 Spirituality in Leadership Practice

This chapter would be incomplete if we did not also consider a look at the spirituality dimension in mindfulness-based leadership practice. According to Pollack, underlying the various manifestations of spirituality is "the conviction that behind the everyday world there exists a higher or a deeper reality that constitutes the core of reality and has an underlying connection with all things in the world that is largely invisible but can be experienced with the help of special techniques" (Pollack, 2019, p. 29). Applied to a Christian leadership ethic, this means that the leader has a threefold responsibility. First, in the responsibility of love toward God, which is expressed in conscious gratitude over creation; second, in an act of self-leadership—here the human likeness to God is reflected, which intends the unconditional dignity of every human being—as well as third, toward the employee, who is shown a concretely shaped love of neighbor and appreciation in the sense of agape. This is the basic framework for the Christian motivated and well-founded leadership of people. In this spiritual context, mindful leadership should always be oriented toward the transcendent good (Nass & Kreuer, 2019).

4.11 Mindful Leadership and Complexity

In today's VUCA world, leadership always means managing high complexity and uncertainty. VUCA stands for volatility, uncertainty, complexity and ambiguity, which ultimately leads to critically questioning one's own possibilities of intervention. Since today's complexity can no longer be controlled, future leadership concepts will only rely on expert systems. Mindful leadership means perceiving different dimensions of reality in a system or an organization. Leadership now only works from a mix of the greatest possible delegation and trust. It is the only key to success.

References

Antonovsky, A. (1997). Salutogenese: Zur Entmystifizierung der Gesundheit. In *Forum für Verhaltenstherapie und psychosoziale Praxis*. dgvt.

Aristoteles, N. E. (1972). *Nikomachische Ethik*. dtv.

Faller, D., & Faller, K. (2018). *Achtsames Management. Führungskompetenzen in Zeiten hoher Komplexität*. Wolfgang Metzler.

Jaspers, K. (1965). Solidarität. In K. Jaspers (Ed.), *Die geistige Situation der Zeit* (pp. 193–194). De Gruyter.

Kant, I. (1990). Von den Pflichten der Tugendhaften und Lasterhaften. In G. Gebhardt (Ed.), *Eine Vorlesung über Ethik* (pp. 261–269). Fischer.

Nass, E., & Kreuer, E. (2019). Christliche Führungskultur. Ethische Systematik und Anwendungen. In M. Warode, H. Bolsinger, & A. Büssing (Eds.), *Spiritualität in der Managementpraxis*. Herder.

Pieper, J. (2004). *Über die Tugenden*. Kösel.

Pollack, D. (2019). Spirituell, aber nicht religiös? Analyse und Thesen zu einer möglichen Entwicklung. In M. Rötting & C. Hackbarth-Johnson (Eds.), *Spiritualität der Zukunft. Suchbewegungen in einer multireligiösen Welt* (pp. 25–42). EOS.

Ranke-Heinemann, U. (1975). Man muss dem Gewissen folgen. In U. Wickert (Ed.), *Das Buch der Tugenden* (p. 383). Hoffmann und Campe.

Rippe, K. P., & Schaber, P. (1998). *Tugendethik*. Reclam.

Rohr, R., & Ebert, A. (2010). *Das Enneagramm*. Claudius.

Schulte, V., & Fleckenstein, M. (2019). Das Führungsdreieck. Ein innovatives Grundlageninstrument. In V. Schulte & A. Verkuil (Eds.), *Entrepreneurship in der Gesundheitswirtschaft* (pp. 77–84). Hogrefe.

Weber, M., & Winckelmann, J. (1964). *Soziologie, Weltgeschichtliche Analysen, Politik*. Kröner

Chapter 5
Is Mindfulness a Key Characteristic of a Jugaad Leader?

Anuradha Sathiyaseelan, Sathiyaseelan Balasundaram, and Michael Zirkler

5.1 Introduction

> Be happy in the moment, that's enough. Every moment is all we need, no more.—Mother Teresa

Mindfulness is an awareness of one's self. This can be achieved by focusing on the present moment with a non-judgmental attitude (Kabat-Zinn, 2003). This psychological process is stimulated through practice and training. In this process, the individual becomes calm, focused, relaxed, and exhibits well-being. Mindfulness helps individuals find peace in their lives (Sathiyaseelan & Sathiyaseelan, 2014). Mindfulness practice begins with deep breathing exercises that help the individual focus on their breathing and direct their thoughts only to "being" and not to anything else. Next is becoming aware of one's body and focusing attention on relaxing the body. The final step is walking meditation, which helps the individual focus his attention on the present moment (Shapiro et al., 2006). The concept of mindfulness derived from what is called "Sati" in Buddhist traditions (Gunaratana, 1992), which could be equated with "Smrti" in Sanskrit. The translation of this word suggests that fundamental to mindfulness is the attitude of looking at things as they are. Mindfulness, then, means paying attention to stimuli as they occur and keeping away the clutter of thoughts that normally occupies the human brain.

A. Sathiyaseelan (✉)
Department of Psychology, Christ University, Bangalore, India
e-mail: anuradha.sathiyaseelan@christuniversity.in

S. Balasundaram
School of Business and Management, Christ University, Bangalore, India

M. Zirkler
School of Applied Psychology, University of Applied Sciences (ZHAW), Zurich, Switzerland

V. Schulte et al. (eds.), *Mindful Leadership in Practice*,
https://doi.org/10.1007/978-3-030-97311-7_5

Moral precepts in Buddhism are considered as sacred as Buddha himself. In Sanskrit, the moral principle is called “sila”, or “sheel”. It is a consciousness that arises from inner ethical behavior. This is one of the three revered sections of the noble eightfold path proposed in Buddhism. Adhering to and following moral precepts is the essential first step to becoming a mindful person in life. Respecting the “Sila” precepts is a great honor for the individual.

There is ample evidence of a mindful tradition in ancient Hindu texts. They emphasize mediation, quiet contemplation and acceptance of things as they are. The Upanishads—a collection of religious and philosophical writings written in India probably between 800 B.C. and 500 B.C.—describe meditation, often suggesting the use of a chant or mantra. Mindfulness practice in the Hindu tradition emphasizes silent meditation—with or without the use of a chant or mantra—to quiet the mind and live in the present moment.

Mindfulness practice entails a conscious way of living that keeps negativity away from the self (Kabat-Zinn, 2013). Dhamma, or mindfulness practices, help individuals nbecome aware of themselves and any attachment, and help them let go of it (Gunaratana, 1992). Dhamma refers to the teaching of the Buddha—a teaching that relates to the eightfold path proposed by the Buddha.

5.2 Application of Mindfulness

Mindfulness practices have been incorporated into disciplines such as clinical psychology, positive psychology, psychiatry, and other social sciences as well. Research in these disciplines (Greeson, 2009) clearly demonstrates the benefits that mindfulness provides to participants in various studies-particularly as it relates to the thought process (Didonna, 2009) and into cognition (Hussain, 2015). Based on mindfulness, several intervention programs have been developed to manage stress, depression, anxiety, adjustment problems, psychosis, and trauma (Hayes, 2004; Khoury et al., 2015; Jain et al., 2015).

Studies show how mindfulness leads to improvements in a number of areas. It serves:

(a) to improve students’ academic performance (Zenner et al., 2014);
(b) to progress among cancer survivors (Hoffman et al., 2012);
(c) to performance enhancement in older adults;
(d) to support individuals struggling with substance abuse (Luberto et al., 2013; Brewer et al., 2009) and nicotine dependence (Vadivale & Sathiyaseelan, 2019).

In the last two decades, mindfulness has been incorporated into almost all disciplines (Bentz & Shapiro, 1998). With the introduction of mindfulness practice, positive effects have been measured in relation to healthy aging (Fountain-Zaragoza & Prakash, 2017). Positive effects have also been found in anger management (Wright et al., 2009), combating weight problems (Asadollahi et al., 2015), and reducing aggression in prison and jail settings (Bouw et al., 2019).

A review of the literature reveals several studies on mindfulness in businesses and organizations. Results show an increase in organizational performance, productivity, and strategic innovation (Sutcliffe et al., 2016), an increase in employee well-being (Reb et al., 2014), an improvement in leader well-being (Roche et al., 2014), a positive correlation between job security and psychological well-being (Ugwu & Asogwa, 2017), and an increase in leader effectiveness (Wasylkiw et al., 2015). Finally, significant positive effects have also been found in relation to resilience in organizations (Baron, 2016; Brendel et al., 2016; Frizzell et al., 2016; Kachan et al., 2017).

Mindfulness practices are integrated into all areas including the corporate world (Langer, 2014). Therefore, adopting these practices to improve employee and leader management and organizational development strategies becomes essential. A study by Morrison (2014) shows how mindfulness and emotional intelligence support the leadership process for organizational development. To develop an organization with positive change, we need leaders who can manage teams mindfully.

Mindful leadership could be defined as a conscious and value-free focus on what is happening in and around the organization on the path to success. A mindful leader is an individual who is aware of the current rapid development phase of the organization, reflects on his or her experiences, and promotes adaptability and optimal use of resources. Becoming such a leader takes time, because individuals need to reflect on their actions, which requires a different mindset. One such mindset is "Jugaad."

5.3 Jugaad: A Way of Thinking

Jugaad is a state of mind. While the concept has only recently been rediscovered and made useful for management, the practice has been around since time immemorial. As stated earlier, Jugaad is a mindset that exists in every part of the world with different names. Most people in India are unconsciously trained on this approach as it is part of their cultural heritage.

In English, there is no equivalent word for it, the closest and most appropriate word is "hack". Radjou et al. (2012) explain in their book that Jugaad comes from ingenuity, resources and cleverness. According to the Oxford dictionary, it is a method that provides flexibility to innovate things with fewer resources in order to maximize resources. In common parlance, it is most often used in situations where limited resources or alternative methods are used as hacks to solve a problem. The term "hack" in this context should not have the negative connotation of cheating. Here in this context, it means "thinking outside the box." Some authors explain this as an emerging culture (Jana, 2009) in the "VUCA" ("Volatile, Uncertain, Complex and Ambiguous Circumstances") world. Several universities, including Harvard, accept this style as a leadership style, namely "**Jugaad leadership style,**" and training programs are conducted for aspiring managers who want to incorporate this style into their leadership.

As pointed out by Tang (2018), a mindful manager must follow the Jugaad approach because he or she must think creatively, innovatively, and unconventionally-like a child. He describes that from Jugaad's perspective, mindfulness helps individuals to enter a creative state in an unbiased way. This state helps individuals explore different perspectives and encourages them to think further. Tang goes on to explain that mindfulness practices help the leader to be calm and focused, which in turn helps with brainstorming as part of a Jugaad innovation process.

Both mindfulness and jugaad focus on immediate experience. Jugaad is a quick remedy, a quick solution to a problem that requires immediate attention. Mumford (2006) points out that effective leadership depends on a leader's ability to bring constructive solutions to crises. Mindfulness is a skill that prescribes these mental models as solutions. Similarly, jugaad means adapting to the ever-changing environment. Jugaad leadership style has been shown to be effective in VUCA conditions where frugality and poverty are prevalent.

The focus of leadership training is shifting from retrospective analysis or future orientation to a focus on the immediate present moment (Drucker, 1999, 2003), with particular attention to change (Heifetz, 1994). Being a leader in today's volatile, uncertain, complex, and ambiguous business environment is a highly responsible task. It requires constant innovation and creativity to change oneself and help employees adapt to the demands of the business environment. This requires certain qualities in the leader. These characteristics demonstrate the effectiveness of the leader in transforming the organization. In this chapter, the authors sought to demonstrate the links between mindfulness practices and Jugaad leadership style through a study conducted in India among mid- to top-level executives who held senior leadership positions in various organizations in 2019.

5.4 Research Method of the Leadership Study

In this part, the steps followed in conducting the above research are considered (Rudestam & Newton, 2001). The design of the study is qualitative in nature. The paradigm used in this study is the interpretive phenomenological approach. Phenomenology is a philosophical approach to the study of the experience of the individual. It provides a rich source for examining and understanding life experiences, identifying how individuals make sense of their physical and social world and the subjective meaning they assign to events and experiences in their lives. This assignment of meaning is influenced by the individual's cultural and socio-historical context (Frost, 2011).

The study is based on the principle of attaching great importance to individual experiences (Creswell, 2007). The process by which individuals make sense of these personal experiences is interpretive in nature. Through purposive sampling, the authors targeted participants who were mid- to high-level male and female managers with at least 5 years of experience in their respective roles. Managers with emotional or psychological problems or addictions were excluded from the study using the 28-item General Health Questionnaire (GHQ 28). Those managers who were not familiar with the concept of Jugaad were also excluded using a self-developed screening tool. To account for other factors, a sociodemographic data sheet and a semi-structured interview guide were used to collect data. The sociodemographic data sheet helped in understanding the differences between various factors such as gender, age, education, experience, and culture.

The semi-structured interview guide was based on an extensive review of the literature on the research priorities. The interview guide consisted of open-ended questions. The process continued with validation of the interview guide. For this purpose, three individuals outside the research team were selected who were experts in the research field and qualitative research. Comments and suggestions from these experts were consolidated and incorporated accordingly. The guide was then sent to the same experts for revalidation. After validation, the researchers reviewed the interview schedule before using it for data collection.

Potential participants, once identified through screening, were contacted personally and asked to participate in the research. The premise of the study was explained to help them make an informed decision to voluntarily participate in the study. Those participants who were easily accessible and located at a short distance were interviewed in a detailed face-to-face interview, whereas those participants who were unavailable or lived at a remote location were interviewed in a semi-structured interview via email or mail.

Researchers proceeded with the interview only after participants understood the necessary information regarding research objectives, voluntary participation, and confidentiality. Participant signatures were included in the consent forms. Interviews were conducted at a time and place that was convenient for both the participants and the researcher. With the subjects' consent forms, the interviews were audio-recorded and later transcribed. The audio files and transcripts were stored on a password-protected computer to ensure the necessary confidentiality.

Data collected in this way were subjected to data cleaning before the process of data analysis was carried out. Each transcript was read a few times to become familiar with the content and to note any additional probing questions as necessary. These probing questions, referred to as "memos," are additional questions that help to bring about needed clarifications regarding the responses given by the participants. Responses to these questions were then obtained from the participants and analyzed for each participant. The complete individual transcripts were then provided to the respective individual participants by the research team members for review. They were asked to read through a copy of their own consolidated transcript and confirm the authenticity of the transcript. The copy of the transcript reviewed by the members was used for data analysis using thematic analysis.

Thematic analysis aims to identify themes and phenomena that recur throughout the study. Patterns identified during the evaluation were recorded as themes, which reduced the data to a minimalistic yet detailed set. Themes were identified in an inductive manner to provide insights that could answer the research questions of the current study (Percy et al., 2015). These themes were further coded to merge and sequence the similar themes. These themes were further used to explain the contexts in response to the research question.

5.5 Results and Discussion of the Leadership Study

The focus of the qualitative study of middle- to top-level managers conducted in India in 2019 was on their understanding of the term jugaad and how the person who practices jugaad becomes a leader. The question of what characteristics Jugaad leaders possess was also explored.

In this part, we discuss one of the characteristics of a Jugaad leader, mindfulness. Participants explained how a Jugaad person practices mindfulness under VUCA conditions to achieve a better outcome for their organization.

There are ten basic themes that emerged from the data under the organizational theme of mindfulness. The following are the initial themes from the data: Leading by Example, Appreciation and Recognition, Leading with Humility, Openness to Feedback, Awareness of One's Thoughts, Emotions, Language, and Behavior, Being Able to Read People, Situations, and Relevant Issues, Intuition, Receptivity to Change, Willingness to Adapt, Willingness to Change, Commitment to Employees, and Commitment to Situations. These themes were grouped under the following basic themes: Creativity, Focus and Goal Orientation, Accountability, Intuition, Adaptability and Flexibility, Efficiency, Emotional Intelligence, Communication Skills, Leading by Example, and Sustainability.

The basic themes were described with statements from the participants. In analyzing the interview transcripts, studies from the literature were also used for comparison in order to achieve a better understanding of the concept discussed.

5.5.1 Characteristics of a Jugaad Leader

The term "leader" is defined in different ways in the literature (Yukl, 2014). Leaders differ among themselves in their characteristics, as each situation requires a different leadership style. Jugaad leaders are individuals who are flexible, adaptable, and use their intuitive power for rapid results. They have a transformative nature with high emotional intelligence. The Downey et al. (2006) article confirms that a leader who is transformational uses emotional intelligence. Therefore, it could be said that a Jugaad leader is also a transformational leader. To be successful in business, a leader must not lose sight of two facts: available material resources and human resources. A Jugaad leader masters both areas. Faced with meager resources and the challenging situation, she works as a role model for the team and with great respect for human resources. Nelson (2018) points out that scarce resources and poverty motivate and guide people to find quick solutions. A Jugaad leader is a visionary who constantly reviews the situation to achieve better results. She is also a kind of person who is ready for change. This helps her with problem solving skills. This is an important characteristic under VUCA conditions (Patton, 2003). This is only possible if the leader has a deep knowledge of her business and the market. Jugaad is a gut-based mindset. With this mindset, a leader is able to quickly analyze the situation and offer solutions based on their experience where their intuition provides the necessary support. A Jugaad leader has a high level of intuition and adaptability and offers quick solutions to problems, keeping in mind himself, the situation, the team and, above all, his business.

5.5.2 Mindfulness

Mindfulness, as we know it, is the directing of thoughts to the present moment. Given the pressures of society and in the business world, a leader needs to be aware of what is happening to them and their team—they need to know the present situation. This awareness is important to create balance within oneself and in the outside world. In particular, the greater responsibilities of being a leader and the personal and professional challenges in life can hinder this balance. The practice of mindfulness helps the team leader to understand all this and helps him to cope with the problems. It increases his attention to the present moment by helping him control his emotions and feelings in stressful and challenging situations, making him an effective leader (Wasylkiw et al., 2015). Mindfulness helps him become aware of how his actions and reactions affect others. This knowledge motivates him to pay attention and participate in the situations. When the leader is aware of himself and others and actively implies, he promotes values and a positive culture among employees. "These practices must be applied every day," the Dalai Lama recommends in response to a question about leadership. Mindfulness helps the leader reflect and find solutions with greater clarity. It promotes positivity and eliminates unwanted trivial things that clutter the mind. When positive, the leader demonstrates compassion and helps empower employees (Baron, 2016; Brendel et al., 2016; Frizzell et al., 2016; Kachan et al., 2017). Mindfulness helps individuals become organized, goal-oriented, and creative in their ideas. This, in turn, helps the individual to become more self-aware and helps them to put their ego aside. Tang (2018) explains how a mindful leader shows the openness and curiosity of a child when it comes to self-identification-which is consistent with the character of Jugaad. Tang goes on to explain that mindfulness practices help the leader to be calm and focused, which in turn helps in brainstorming a Jugaad innovation process, as innovative Jugaad practices are much needed in the VUCA world where frugality is an advantage. Creativity and innovation quickly bring needed solutions to address poverty-stricken conditions.

5.5.3 *Creativity*

In today's competitive business world, creativity becomes critical to survival. Creativity stimulates employee thinking, opens the door to more possibilities and provides the impetus for original ideas. It is becoming part of the job description in many companies. As a result, they are trying to foster creativity by incorporating new strategies such as mindfulness and meditation into their employee training and development programs, such as Google and Goldman Sachs. Creativity is the ability to move from traditional ideas to new meaningful ideas and approaches. A mindful attitude encourages this creative process. The following personal statements from the interviews conducted show how mindfulness helps the Jugaad leader:

- "A Jugaad leader is a creative person."
- "Being in the present moment helps to be creative in getting ideas and making decisions."
- "Jugaad is innovation, you have to be in the present moment to be innovative and creative . . . that takes a meditative state."

The above statements describe the characteristics of a Jugaad leader and clearly indicate that mindfulness is a key characteristic specifically related to their creativity. Rao (2015) states that a Jugaad leader's creativity helps them to innovate spontaneously even in the VUCA world. As mentioned by Tang (2018), a Jugaad person is a creative person who always tries to be in the present moment to deliver results. In doing so, she adapts to the organization at a time. In their articles, Singh et al. (2012) explain that scarcity creates innovation. When someone is mindful and focused on the present moment, creativity flourishes. The last interview excerpt shows that Jugaad requires a meditative mindset.

5.5.4 *Focused: Goal-Oriented*

Focusing on and understanding what is happening in the moment is a key mindfulness skill. This purposeful cognitive skill helps the leader organize thoughts by helping him or her avoid letting unwanted information from the past dominate thoughts and interfere with the present. It also helps the leader to be systematic and calm when making decisions. The following statements from participants show how a Jugaad leader exercises this cognitive skill:

- "A Jugaad leader focuses on the current situation and the current issue—looking at the point of view he is taking at the moment."
- "I would say that a Jugaad leader has to have strong attention, clear focus, to get results quickly."
- A "Jugaad leader is like a guru. . .she has an undivided attention with composure, which helps her to be on the right track and achieve her goal."

These formulations illustrate that a Jugaad leader is also a mindful person, because Jugaad is a process that takes place when the individual is aware of the need to move quickly and with full focus to a solution even in a difficult situation. Patton (2003) explains that Jugaad leaders possess undivided focus—this trait makes them better able to survive in the ever-changing VUCA world. Mindfulness helps the Jugaad leader to be focused and goal-oriented in their efforts.

Times of uncertainty bring with them the need for focus and purpose. The Jugaad leader becomes effective in VUCA conditions and, as the situation is characterized by uncertainty, automatically begins to perceive the various signals coming from the market, from his followers, and from within himself. He is anchored in the present, aware of change. The focus orientation helps him to avoid unwanted judgments and helps him to recognize different approaches to achieve a positive outcome for the situation. We believe that this dynamic quality that the leader achieves through mindfulness and the focus that goes with it is a key characteristic of a Jugaad leader.

5.5.5 Responsibility

The Jugaad leader takes their responsibility seriously and works towards achieving the organization's goal, which is the reason why they achieve more results in their assigned tasks, especially in VUCA conditions. Accountability is one of the main characteristics of a mindful person. The beauty of mindfulness is that it increases accountability on the one hand, and on the other hand, accountability also improves the individual's mindfulness. From the following participants' statements, it is clear how a Jugaad leader is accountable and by what means they show that they are a mindful person:

- "Jugaad leadership equals accountability—paying attention to the outcome by helping employees achieve it."
- "The team leader takes responsibility for decisions and outcomes . . . in particular, he or she must make decisions that result in fewer errors."
- "The Jugaad leader takes total responsibility for the outcome . . . they strive for it."

From the statements, Jugaad leaders are accountable, which also characterizes mindful people. Mindfulness increases a person's ability to act responsibly; it makes him aware of the present and does not allow him to be influenced by past experiences. The leader's attention is therefore focused on the present state of affairs in order to achieve optimal results. In the VUCA world, this particular quality of the Jugaad leader helps to maximize performance.

5.5.6 Intuition

As human beings, we are constantly in contact with others—we listen to signals from our inner voice, we perceive many things intuitively. Mindfulness helps to strengthen our intuitive power by helping us to be present, to recognize ourselves and to have confidence in ourselves. The Jugaad leader listens carefully to these inner signals. In VUCA conditions, intuition is very important as it helps in making quick decisions.

The following statements from the mentioned study indicate the importance of intuition:

- "Jugaad leader is the one who instinctively understands the situation/people and reacts accordingly."
- "The instinctive nature of these leaders makes them more understandable and trustworthy."
- "This leadership style comes from practices of mindfulness in life, mindfulness also helps the intuition of these leaders in business."

The ability to understand something instinctively, without the need for conscious reasoning, is called intuition. It is the art of listening to our inner voice. A mindful person develops this powerful form of understanding through practice. Intuitive experience is easier for people who engage in meditation and self-reflective practices. If we look at the characteristics of the jugaad leader, we can clearly see intuition.

In the VUCA world, the Jugaad leadership style is highly advantageous. The Jugaad leader acts quickly in chaotic and challenging situations where there is ambiguity. The intuitive nature of the Jugaad leader helps them to be present in the situation and detach from the negative emotions.

5.5.7 Adaptability and Flexibility

Adaptability and flexibility are characteristics of an effective leader. Especially in the VUCA world, leadership adaptability helps the organization thrive and compete in the marketplace. It is a practical framework of a step-by-step change process. If you are not able to achieve something in the status quo, then adapting to the situation helps to change it positively and quickly. Jugaad is an innovative mindset. Adaptability is second nature to a Jugaad leader.

To this end, we quote the following statements:

- "There are several managers who don't want any change in their status quo ... But the Jugaad leader is different, she adapts faster and quicker and keeps up to date with the current state of the business ... this quality helps her succeed."
- "Adapting to an ever-changing world is the necessary quality of a leader. I would say a Jugaad leader has it 100 percent ... she's willing to change ... she's willing

to learn . . . like a baby . . . that comes from being present and paying attention to everything that's going on around you."

- "I've seen a team leader who practices Jugaad constantly adapt to change their thoughts, views, and attitudes . . .they are one of the most sought after team leaders. . .these people can make the organization as effective as they want."
- "The Jugaad leader is willing to change his or her views for the good of the organization . . . it is this receptive nature that makes him or her a visionary."

The above examples help us understand how the Jugaad leader practices adaptability as a strategy for effectiveness. Flexibility is a critical leadership characteristic that enhances the leader's ability under VUCA conditions and contributes to quick and effective solutions:

- "In the changing VUCA world, situational flexibility is very important. For me, the Jugaad leader is very flexible . . . this characteristic helps her to change and adapt to the demands of the situation."
- "A Jugaad team leader is flexible, which makes him innovative and creative."

There are studies that show how mindfulness helps with cognitive flexibility. Flexibility helps each individual to be aware of the present moment, their emotions and thoughts (Hülsheger et al., 2013).

5.5.8 *Efficiency*

A very important characteristic of a leader is efficient work. Efficiency means not wasting time and resources in achieving the goal of the organization.

The following statements underscore the importance of efficiency in Jugaad leadership:

- "You can trust the Jugaad leader because they know how to get the job done without wasting time and resources."
- "In a VUCA world, jugaad equals efficiency."
- "He′s like a guru, working and motivating his employees very efficiently and focusing their attention on the present moment."
- "It avoids unnecessary attention to the irrelevant tasks, focuses on the quick solution, helps the others to focus on the current situation as well."

The Jugaad team leader wisely increases the efficiency of his team and employees. Business schools have conducted Jugaad leadership training for their staff to increase the efficiency of their employees. Harvard and Stanford's Jugaad leadership training programs are the best examples.

5.5.9 Emotional Intelligence

Emotional intelligence helps individuals become aware of their emotions and helps them think and behave. Leadership is not a position, but a choice. Jugaad's leadership style falls under the emotionally intelligent leadership styles. It helps those who apply it to become aware of the situation in order to achieve the greater benefit for the organization. This style is highly valued in the VUCA environment. Emotional intelligence includes the following dimensions: Self-awareness, humility, empathy, emotional regulation, dealing with others, dealing with situations, appreciation, and recognition. These dimensions show how mindfulness influences emotional intelligence and vice versa (Baer et al., 2006; Brown et al., 2007). Mindfulness helps us gain insights into how emotions and thoughts influence our behavior.

The following statements support this thesis:

- "This manager knows his positive and negative sides, and that makes him a leader."
- "He has clarity about how others feel and respects that too—you feel comfortable working with him."
- "Whatever the situation, he is stable and controlled in his emotions and always looking for the solution ... very attentive to the situation ... and does not get distracted."
- "This manager I know as a Jugaad leader has good people skills, he is attentive to his employees ... and you won't feel bad sharing your problems with him because you know you will get an answer and patient listening."
- "When you do something good, you receive instant recognition from it, regardless of hierarchy."

Feldman et al. (2007) show how mindfulness is positively correlated with emotional clarity and fewer distractions. The study by Cahn and Polich (2006) indicates that emotionally intelligent people have stronger emotional regulation, which is co-determined by their mindfulness. The empathy mentioned in the previous examples is supported by the study of Shapiro et al. (1998). In their study, they show the relationship between mindfulness and emotional intelligence. The statements about interpersonal relationships described in the interviews are supported by Brown and Kasser's (2005) study, which states that mindfulness helps to create interpersonal closeness. The ability to understand oneself with one's positive and negative sides helps in making effective decisions. Surrey (2005) points out that mindfulness helps with connectedness with others. With mindfulness, it is possible to show respect and accept others. According to our participants, this is a common trait among Jugaad leaders. They show compassion and empathy, which are the characteristics of mindfulness according to authors Fulton (2005) and Morgan and Morgan (2005). They describe that mindfulness increases intersubjectivity, which makes these individuals more tolerant of others. Tang (2018) confirms in his study that Jugaad needs emotional intelligence to be in the innovative and creative state.

5.5.10 Communication

Managers must be open and honest in their communication. They must communicate what they mean to employees so that the execution of the decision goes smoothly. In addition, good communication makes the leader a sought-after supervisor who is valued by his or her employees. Being a good listener and communicator is a skill that comes from practicing mindfulness. A Jugaad leader is also a good communicator. In communicating, she shows her respect to the team and makes employees feel that their contributions are recognized and accepted. This kind of interpersonal relationship doesn't happen by itself. It takes practice. This practice is mindfulness. The Jugaad team leader communicates mindfully with his or her staff and maintains good two-way communication:

- "He knows how to explain the details, even if it's a quick decision, he makes it easy for us to understand so that the work goes quickly and we can expect results."
- "He shows his respect in his words . . . even when he corrects us . . . it doesn't hurt us . . . that's how he does it."

Effective communication needs mindfulness, because it needs clarity in the present moment. Therefore, it could be said that the Jugaad leader also has this quality. These steps taken by the leader should include articulating the company's vision and mission, which sets the broader goal for the company. Employees will also have a better understanding of what they should be moving towards and how fast they should go to achieve the goal. It will also enable them to plan and work according to the requirements. The above formulations are supported by Satyendra's (2015) study. The leaders should clearly communicate the vision and mission statements to his team with proper direction that helps the team to understand their roles and responsibilities. Further, in his study, the author explains the need for clear and concise communication with team members for organizational development.

5.5.11 Leading by Example

A leader must be a role model for his followers. When a leader is a role model, the entire team becomes functional and productive. Avey et al. (2010) show that great leaders are transparent and have a positive attitude that helps them demand more productivity from employees. Some examples from the interviews:

- "This leader who practices Jugaad is a role model for everyone in the organization . . . you follow her and her actions . . . it is enough that you are on the right path . . ."
- "The team leader brings in a lot of positivity . . . They feel comfortable following his directions to get the quick fix . . . They know they'll get to the goal faster and quicker."

If a leader lives what he proclaims, his followers will automatically practice the same. In the words of Mahatma Gandhi, we can explain this phenomenon: "Be the change you want to see in the world." Even though this quote applies to everyone, it can be used here specifically for the leadership role, as the leader is the one who directs the team towards the goal. This particular trait causes a lot of positivity, as mentioned in the study by Avey et al. (2010). You have to be positive to instigate positivity in others. If we are negative and try to instigate positivity in others, it will show in our actions and behavior. This is where the importance of mindfulness comes to the fore. Especially business in the VUCA world needs this approach, and this is exactly what the Jugaad leader practices.

5.5.12 Sustainability

According to the authors Savitz and Weber (2006), sustainability entails an interdependence of living beings. This interdependence causes minimal damage and preserves the environment. The Jugaad mindset is the perfect sustainable mindset because a Jugaad person focuses on how to minimize resource waste and achieve more results. Sustainability is emerging as one of the key characteristics of an effective leader in an organization. The current VUCA world is looking for a sustainable operation of a business where profit and environment are not compromised. Mindfulness is also focused on sustainability. Living in the present with minimal resources is the motto of mindfulness. Sanders' (2008) study shows how mindful leaders bring the vision of sustainability to an ecocentric approach to business. Fulton (2005) and Morgan and Morgan (2005) indicate that intersubjectivity is a key figure of a leader who practices mindfulness. A Jugaad leader contributes to sustainability through his or her innovative style while considering frugal resources. The practice of Jugaad brings in intersubjectivity with nature and resources.

- "Jugaad comes in a frugal world . . . you have to use the resources you have while keeping an eye on the future."
- "You can't separate sustainability from Jugaad . . . the two are inseparable . . . like Siamese twins . . ."
- "In a poverty-stricken country, Jugaad is the quick fix, taking into account the sustainability of resources."

When a person is aware of the available resources and his future generation, he follows Jugaad and that brings a quick solution. Therefore, it could be said that a Jugaad leader follows mindfulness to maintain sustainability. It is the model for sustainable development. Mahatma Gandhi is from the land of Jugaad and he was the promoter of sustainability.

5.6 Conclusion

A leader is the one who gives direction, guidance and motivation to the team. He gives the necessary power by being a role model. Focusing on his actions helps the mindful leader gain the trust of those he leads. A true leader is a visionary, has clear ideas of where to go and how to ripen the fruits of success. Along with success, the leader demonstrates integrity by being sincere in his or her relationship with employees. She communicates honestly, sincerely, and helps people on her team when they are in need. Honesty and integrity are the basis of any good leadership, as already shown by the example of Mahatma Gandhi, one of the most famous leaders in the world.

References

Asadollahi, T., Khakpour, S., Ahmadi, F., Seyedeh, L., Tahami, Matoo, S., & Bermas, H. (2015). Effectiveness of mindfulness training and dietary regime on weight loss in obese people. *Journal of Medicine and Life, 8*(4), 114–124.

Avey, J. B., Luthans, F., Smith, R. M., & Palmer, N. F. (2010). Impact of positive psychological capital on employee well-being over time. *Journal of Occupational Health Psychology, 15*(1), 17–28.

Baer, R. A., Smith, G. T., Hopkins, J., Krietemeyer, J., & Toney, L. (2006). Using self-report assessment methods to explore facets of mindfulness. *Assessment, 13*(1), 27–45.

Baron, L. (2016). Authentic leadership and mindfulness development through action learning. *Journal of Managerial Psychology, 31*(1), 296–311.

Bentz, V. M., & Shapiro, J. J. (1998). *Mindful inquiry in social research*. Sage.

Bouw, N., Huijbregts, S., Scholte, E., & Swaab, H. (2019). Mindfulness-based stress reduction in prison: Experiences of inmates, instructors, and prison staff. *International Journal of Offender Therapy and Comparative Criminology, 63*(15–16), 2550–2571.

Brendel, W., Hankerson, S., Byun, S., & Cunningham, B. (2016). Cultivating leadership dharma: Measuring the impact of regular mindfulness practice on creativity, resilience, tolerance for ambiguity, anxiety and stress. *Journal of Management Development, 35*(8), 1056–1078.

Brewer, J. A., Sinha, R., Chen, J. A., Michalsen, R. N., Babuscio, T. A., Nich, C., Grier, A., Bergquist, K. L., Reis, D. L., Potenza, M. N., Carroll, K. M., & Rounsaville, B. J. (2009). Mindfulness training and stress reactivity in substance abuse: Results from a randomized, controlled stage I pilot study. *Substance Abuse, 30*(4), 306–317.

Brown, K. W., & Kasser, T. (2005). Are psychological and ecological well-being compatible? The role of values, mindfulness, and lifestyle. *Social Indicators Research, 74*(2), 349–368.

Brown, K. W., Ryan, R. M., & Creswell, J. D. (2007). Mindfulness: Theoretical foundations and evidence for its salutary effects. *Psychological Inquiry, 18*(4), 211–237.

Cahn, B. R., & Polich, J. (2006). Meditation states and traits: EEG, ERP, and neuroimaging studies. *Psychological Bulletin, 132*(2), 180–211.

Creswell, J. W. (2007). *Qualitative inquiry and research design*. Sage.

Didonna, F. (2009). Introduction: Where new and old paths to dealing with suffering meet. In F. Didonna & J. Kabat-Zinn (Eds.), *Clinical handbook of mindfulness*. Springer.

Downey, L. A., Papageorgiou, V., & Stough, C. (2006). Examining the relationship between leadership, emotional intelligence and intuition in senior female managers. *Leadership & Organization Development Journal, 27*(4), 250–264.

Drucker, P. F. (1999). *Management challenges for the 21st century*. Butterworth-Heinemann.

Drucker, P. F. (2003). *The new realities*. Butterworth-Heinemann.

Feldman, G., Hayes, A., Kumar, S., Greeson, J., & Laurenceau, J. P. (2007). Mindfulness and emotion regulation: The development and initial validation of the cognitive and affective mindfulness scale-revised (CAMS-R). *Journal of Psychopathology and Behavioral Assessment, 29*(3), 177–190.

Fountain-Zaragoza, S., & Prakash, R. S. (2017). Mindfulness training for healthy aging: Impact on attention, well-being, and inflammation. *Frontiers in Aging Neuroscience, 9*, 11.

Frizzell, D. A., Hoon, S., & Banner, D. K. (2016). A phenomenological investigation of leader development and mindfulness meditation. *Journal of Social Change, 8*(1), 14–25.

Frost, N. A. (2011). *Qualitative research methods in psychology: Combining core approaches*. Open University Press.

Fulton, P. R. (2005). Mindfulness as clinical training. In C. K. Germer, R. D. Siegel, & P. R. Fulton (Eds.), *Mindfulness and psychotherapy* (pp. 55–72). Guilford Press.

Greeson, J. M. (2009). Mindfulness research update: 2008. *Complementary Health Practices Review, 14*(1), 1–8.

Gunaratana, H. (1992). *Mindfulness in plain English*.

Hayes, A. M. (2004). Clarifying the construct of mindfulness in the context of emotion regulation and the process of change in therapy. *Clinical Psychology: Science and Practice, 11*(3), 255–262.

Heifetz, A. R. (1994). *Leadership without easy answers* (Vol. 465). Harvard University Press.

Hoffman, C. J., Ersser, S. J., Hopkinson, J. B., Nicholls, P. G., Harrington, J. E., & Thomas, P. W. (2012). Effectiveness of mindfulness-based stress reduction in mood, breast- and endocrine-related quality of life, and well-being in stage 0 to III breast cancer: A randomized, controlled trial. *Journal of Clinical Oncology: Official Journal of the American Society of Clinical Oncology, 30*(12), 1335–1342.

Hülsheger, U. R., Alberts, H. J., Feinholdt, A., & Lang, J. W. (2013). Benefits of mindfulness at work: The role of mindfulness in emotion regulation, emotional exhaustion, and job satisfaction. *The Journal of Applied Psychology, 98*(2), 310–325.

Hussain, D. (2015). Meta-cognition in mindfulness: A conceptual analysis. *Psychological Thought, 8*(2), 132–141.

Jain, F. A., Walsh, R. N., Eisendrath, S. J., Christensen, S., & Rael Cahn, B. (2015). Critical analysis of the efficacy of meditation therapies for acute and subacute phase treatment of depressive disorders: A systematic review. *Psychosomatics, 56*(2), 140–152.

Jana, R. (2009). India's next global export: Innovation. *Business Week, 2*.

Kabat-Zinn, J. (2003). Mindfulness-based interventions in context: Past, present, and future. *Clinical Psychology: Science and Practice, 10*(2), 144–156.

Kabat-Zinn, J. (2013). *Full catastrophe living: Using the wisdom of your body and mind to face stress, pain, and illness*. Bantam Books Trade Paperbacks.

Kachan, D., Olano, H., Tannenbaum, S. L., Annane, D. W., Mehta, A., Arheart, K. L., Fleming, L., Yang, X., McClure, L., & Lee, D. J. (2017). Prevalence of mindfulness practices in the US workforce: National Health Interview Survey. *Preventing Chronic Disease, 14*, E01.

Khoury, B., Sharma, M., Rush, S. E., & Fournier, C. (2015). Mindfulness-based stress reduction for healthy individuals: A meta-analysis. *Journal of Psychosomatic Research, 78*(6), 519–528.

Langer, E. (2014). Mindfulness in the age of complexity. *Harvard Business Review, 92*(3), 68–73.

Luberto, C. M., McLeish, A. C., Robertson, S. A., Avallone, K. M., Kraemer, K. M., & Jeffries, E. R. (2013). The role of mindfulness skills in terms of distress tolerance: A pilot test among adult daily smokers. *The American Journal on Addictions, 23*(2), 184–188.

Morgan, W. D., & Morgan, S. T. (2005). Cultivating attention and empathy. In C. K. Germer, R. D. Siegel, & P. R. Fulton (Eds.), *Mindfulness and psychotherapy* (pp. 73–90). Guilford Press.

Morrison, J. L. (2014). The leadership experience. *Journal of Education for Business, 89*(8), 457–458.

Mumford, M. D. (2006). *Pathways to outstanding leadership: A comparative analysis of charismatic, ideological, and pragmatic leaders*. Lawrence Erlbaum Associates Publishers.

Nelson, D. (2018). *Jugaad Yatra*. Aleph.
Patton, J. R. (2003). Intuition in decisions. *Management Decision*, 989–996.
Percy, W. H., Kostere, K., & Kostere, S. (2015). Generic qualitative research in psychology. *The Qualitative Report, 20*(2), 76–85.
Radjou, N., Prabhu, J., & Ahuja, S. (2012). *Jugaad innovation: Think frugal, be flexible, generate breakthrough growth*. Wiley.
Rao, B. C. (2015). Rooting frugality in science and engineering. In *Third international conference on creativity and innovations at (for/from/with) grassroots*. Ahmedabad: Indian Institute of Management.
Reb, J., Naravanan, J., & Chaturvedi, S. (2014). Leading mindfully: Two studies on the influence of supervisor trait mindfulness on employee well-being and performance. *Mindfulness, 5*(1), 36–45.
Roche, M., Haar, J. M., & Luthans, F. (2014). The role of mindfulness and psychological capital on the well-being of leaders. *Journal of Occupational Health Psychology, 19*(4), 476–489.
Rudestam, K. E., & Newton, R. R. (2001). *Surviving your dissertation: A comprehensive guide to content and process* (2nd ed.). Sage.
Sanders, D. J. (2008). *Built to serve: How to drive the bottom line with people-first practices* (pp. 42–43). McGraw Hill.
Sathiyaseelan, A., & Sathiyaseelan, B. (2014). Integrating 'mindful living' for a peaceful life. *Research Journal of Social Science and Management, 4*, 187–192.
Satyendra. (2015). *Importance of leadership for organizational excellence*. Accessed October 21, 2020, from http://ispatguru.com/importance-of-leadership-for-organizational-excellence/
Savitz, A., & Weber, K. (2006). *The triple bottom line: How today's best-run companies are achieving economic, social and environmental success - and how you can too*. Wiley.
Shapiro, S. L., Schwartz, G. E., & Bonner, G. (1998). Effects of mindfulness-based stress reduction on medical and premedical students. *Journal of Behavioral Medicine, 21*(6), 581–599.
Shapiro, S. L., Carlson, L. E., Astin, J. A., & Freedman, B. (2006). Mechanisms of mindfulness. *Journal of Clinical Psychology, 62*(3), 373–386.
Singh, R., Gupta, V., & Mondal, A. (2012). Jugaad - from 'making do' and 'quick fix' to an innovative, sustainable and low-cost survival strategy at the bottom of the pyramid. *International Journal of Rural Management, 8*(1–2), 87–105.
Surrey, J. L. (2005). Relational psychotherapy, relational mindfulness. In C. K. Germer, R. D. Siegel, & P. R. Fulton (Eds.), *Mindfulness and psychotherapy*. Guilford Press.
Sutcliffe, K. M., Vogus, T. J., & Dane, E. (2016). Mindfulness in organizations: A cross-level review. *Annual Review of Organizational Psychology and Organizational Behavior, 3*, 55–81.
Tang, A. (2018). *The leader's guide to mindfulness*. Pearson UK.
Ugwu, F. O., & Asogwa, F. (2017). Examining the moderating role of mindfulness in the relationship between perceived job insecurity and psychological well-being among telecommunication workers in Nigeria. *GOUNI Journal of Management and Social Sciences, 3*(1), 72–88.
Vadivale, A. M., & Sathiyaseelan, A. (2019). Mindfulness based relapse prevention - A meta-analysis. *Cogent. Psychology, 6*(1), 1567090.
Wasylkiw, L., Holton, J., Azar, R., & Cook, W. (2015). The impact of mindfulness on leadership effectiveness in a health care setting: A pilot study. *Journal of Health Organization and Management, 29*(7), 893–911.
Wright, S., Day, A., & Howells, K. (2009). Mindfulness and the treatment of anger problems. *Aggression and Violent Behavior, 14*(5), 396–401.
Yukl, G. (2014). *Leadership in organizations*. Pearson.
Zenner, C., Herrnleben-Kurz, S., & Walach, H. (2014). Mindfulness-based interventions in schools - a systematic review and meta-analysis. *Frontiers in Psychology, 5*, 603.

Chapter 6
The "Ideal Ruler" in China: Confucian Tradition and Contemporary Political Practice

Thomas Zimmer

6.1 Preliminary Remarks

The current trade dispute between the U.S.A. and China has given rise to a rivalry of this quality and intensity between the Western superpower and a major power that can only vaguely be attributed to the former camp of the communist "Eastern Bloc" that has not been encountered for many decades. Disappointment has spread over the fact that the "victory" of the democratic-capitalist West once proclaimed by Fukuyama seems to be called into question again. The Soviet Union no longer exists; the new adversary is China.

More strongly than in the case of the former USSR, culture is made an issue in connection with China, and the depth of the divide is hinted at, for example, when there is talk of competition between systems (Fuest, 2018; Chen, 2019; Wambach, 2019; Osnos, 2020). Occasionally, the collapse of the Chinese system is also announced (Ferguson, 2019). In this context, it is striking how much the role of the political leadership has been brought into focus, even if—at least in the Western media—the way it is reported gives a skewed picture. While one can form a fairly comprehensive picture of U.S. President Trump after countless biographies and revealing reports (Hirigoyen, 2020; Acemoglu, 2019), the picture of his counterpart in Beijing remains rather vague, especially when attempts are made to dismiss Xi Jinping simply as a "nationalist" (Böge, 2018). This approach fails to recognize that in the case of Xi Jinping there is very much a separate "Chinese" context of argumentation in which the Chinese head of state is presented to people in China and around the world-for example, as the founder of the "theory" of the common destiny of humankind (Bandurski, 2019; Xi, 2019). In this context, of course, China's decline is then also made the subject of discussion in the press every now and then (Wang, 2020).

T. Zimmer (✉)
Center for Chinese German Cultural and Social Exchange, Tongji University, Shanghai, China

V. Schulte et al. (eds.), *Mindful Leadership in Practice*,
https://doi.org/10.1007/978-3-030-97311-7_6

In the following, after introductory remarks on the emergence and role of ruler images, an attempt will be made to outline the corresponding traditions in China, in order to then deal with Xi Jinping in more detail. The focus is on the topic of mindfulness and its cultural as well as political contexts.

6.2 "Junzi": The Ideal Figure of a "Noble"

Important foundations for images of rulers and the emergence of an "advice literature" in the form of the princely mirrors were already laid in European antiquity in Homer and in classical theory about the state—for example, in Aristotle (Anton, 2003).

Early on, caution and attentiveness in politics were mentioned as a requirement for the persons who were at the head of the state and who were responsible for steering the fate of the community. With regard to the ruling apparatus of the consuls, the Romans used to say: Caveant consules! This meant that those who exercised power should be particularly vigilant and sensitive, probably in order to anticipate dangers to the common good and to their own rule at an early stage and to be able to react to them appropriately.

Of far greater influence than these largely secular-secular sources was then in the Middle Ages above all the theocratic view determined by the Bible and the Church Fathers, which saw in God both the origin and the normative instance and goal of all rule. While the humanist mirrors from the Renaissance period, such as *Institutio principis christiani* (1516) by Erasmus of Rotterdam, were primarily concerned with bringing together classical and Christian thought, Niccolò Machiavelli's *Il principe* (1513, published in 1532) was more of a counter-image to the Christian-natural law ideal of the ruler and placed the reason of state in the foreground.

In contrast to the West, where a culture of conscience developed, especially under the influence of Christianity, centering on responsibility for one's own actions, to which the ruler is also subject, Chinese culture has been strongly influenced by exemplary idols right up to the present day. The idea of spiritual and moral role models to be emulated emerged early on. While a tradition began to develop in the Occident over time, especially since the beginning of the modern era, which guaranteed the individual with his duties and rights within a state-sanctioned legal and constitutional system the possibility of development and endeavored to harmonize the traditional virtue of rulers with the innovations of the separation of powers and legal administrative doctrine, the appeal character with the call to imitate the behavior of ideal figures remained above all in the Confucian-influenced societies of Asia until the present. The focus here was on the figure of the so-called "junzi," in which the philosophers in turn oriented themselves on the figures of the "original emperors," who are almost impossible to grasp historically (Ames, 1983).

Generally speaking, "junzi" refers to the ideal figure of a "noble" who owed his legitimation less to his descent from a noble family than to an ethically and morally founded role, which in turn encompassed not only the human-social space but also the natural-cosmic space. The ideal ruler "junzi" was thus—to put it simply—to be understood as the link between the human world, nature and the cosmos.

6.3 Ruling Traditions

A look at the development of China's real and intellectual history shows, of course, that the traditions that developed there were fed by a wide variety of influences. Of course, these cannot be presented in detail here, but at least one important aspect, especially for the development of the rulership, must be pointed out. As can be shown in particular by new source discoveries at the beginning of the 1970s, two traditions of rulership developed more or less parallel to each other in China. On the one hand, there is—as already indicated—the Confucian way of governance, which was essentially based on justice practiced by the noble (Feng, 1998). In parallel, a tradition of "government by power" (Chinese: badao), which was in many respects opposed to Confucianism, developed that was close to Shang Yang's legalism but made more moderate demands and elaborated a set of guiding principles, strategies, tactics, and ways of spiritual cultivation for a supreme ruler to achieve successful government (Feng, 1998). The so-called "Four Texts of the Yellow Emperor" (Huangdi sijing), attributed to a mythical ruler of antiquity, set forth principles of an "art of governance" that Chinese rulers of the imperial period followed in secret. The differences between the two traditions can be briefly outlined as follows: Confucianism, which became the mainstream of rulership, was an ethico-political philosophy based on a set of moral categories and followed an ethics-of-mind approach. Emphasis was placed on the motives for political action, according to which a ruler should do what was consistent with the moral imperative, regardless of whether or not it would be practically successful. In contrast, in the parallel tradition that developed, which was committed to the concerns of power politics and was more ethically oriented toward responsibility, more attention was paid to the results of politics. This tradition was therefore much more pragmatically oriented.

According to the concepts of Confucianism, all members of society, both the ruler and the common people, depended on moral cultivation to succeed in the process of forming a better society. The techniques of power politics described in the Four Texts, on the other hand, were intended only for the supreme ruler and the ruling elite. Advice for the common people can hardly be found in the Four Texts. Overall, then, Confucianism represented an "overt tradition," whereas political thought as expressed in the Four Texts was based on a "covert tradition" (Feng, 1998). The central content of the discussions in the Four Texts was practical utility in the relations between the governed and the governed. Put simply, this meant that if the ruler benefited the people, then he expected them to provide a "quid pro quo"-a look at the present reveals the current validity of this thinking in a striking way. A quid pro quo for "good government" can be expressed, for example, in the form of servitude or in the recognition of rule (or at least a renunciation of its questioning). What is present in the case of this view is an overtly pragmatic and benefit-oriented form of the ruler's devotion to his people, which differs substantially from the humanitarianism (ren) found in Confucianism, which is oriented toward moral concepts (Feng, 1998). From this, some fundamental differences can be derived for rulership and society: Put simply, "benefiting the people" in the tradition of power politics meant primarily satisfying the material needs of the governed. Spiritual development, education and upbringing were considered secondary. In contrast, the idea of "educating the people" played a prominent role in the tradition of Confucianism (Feng, 1998). In a positive sense, the interplay of the aforementioned traditions-namely, "government by justice" and government aimed at "maintaining power"-allowed two things to be derived for the common people: first, the right to a livelihood, which, although meager by modern standards, can be considered unsurpassed for long periods of history; and second, the right of people to receive an education (Feng, 1998).

6.4 Mindfulness and "Ideal" Ruler

The aim of the following article is now to explore the possibilities and requirements of "mindfulness" in connection with the idea of the "ideal" ruler in Confucianism. Mindfulness, it seems, is highly associated with an attentiveness to change in the practice of political rule. Mindfulness in this context could be understood, first of all, as the need to make appropriate adjustments, weighing the circumstances and any changes that may have already arisen.

Several questions immediately arise here, such as:

1. How and by what means can mindfulness be ensured or maintained over a period of time?
2. Who and what is the focus of mindfulness and who determines that focus?
3. How does the community of the mindful work, how are the hierarchies organized?
4. Is the standard of mindfulness crucial for empowerment as a ruler?
5. What is the scope for implementing the actions sought as a result of mindfulness?
6. How is mindfulness to be evaluated in the context of the complex of consciousness composed of logical-rational and emotional elements, and what rank does it occupy?

It will not be possible to answer all the above questions here. For a better understanding, I will try to work out something on the topic of mindfulness by drawing on a number of the most important sources from Chinese and occidental intellectual history. The focus is on the figure of the *leader*—with regard to the basic theme of this book *Mindful leadership*—here in the classical equivalent of the "junzi" already mentioned above.

6.5 Characteristics of the "Junzi"

The concept of the so-called "junzi", about which something is said early on in Confucius' conversations, for example, is usually translated as "gentleman", "superior man" or "noble man". Although the term "junzi" originally meant something else, "son of a ruler," the descriptions of the "junzi" in the conversations suggest otherwise. Here, the "junzi" is not so much the member of the nobility, but a "man whose nobility derives from personal commitment and a developed moral power" (de Bary & Bloom, 1999, pp. 41–44, translated by the author). "Junzi" could also be understood as "son of the prince" and in this sense could have been a "dignitary of the state." However, what was more decisive was that he belonged to the aristocracy and held a public office. According to Gu, Yu Yingshi "has convincingly demonstrated that the term 'junzi' has undergone a change in content from a 'status-related' term to a 'morality-related' term." Because of this shift from a social to an ethical category, morality has become "the new standard of the noble" (Gu, 1999, p. 137, translated by the author). Accordingly, "one who aspired to become a junzi faced strict moral requirements that applied no less to attitude and motivation than to behavior" (translated by the author). Like most political thinkers in ancient China, Confucius made no distinction between state and society. Since for Confucius the social order was essentially limited to the two strata of the governed and the governed, his political thought revolved primarily around the question of "how to harmonize the relationship between the governed and the governed, and how to create the conditions under which the political community can flourish." For Confucius, the solution lay in the creation of a "Junzi state [...] that is, a state composed of nobles. Confucius thus wishes all members of a polity to be Junzi, and dreams of the Junzi character dominating people's behavior" (Gu, 1999, p. 133, translated by the author).

According to Confucius, perhaps the three most important behaviors appropriate to a "junzi" were filial devotion (xiao), humanity (ren), and ritual decorum (li). Each of these practices was also relevant to government: To the extent that a ruler modelled governance on the family, he was concerned with exerting influence on the stability of society as a whole through the practice of filial devotion. Humanity was associated with compassion and was based on reciprocity. In turn, ritual, which provided an ideal means of ordering personal life, also represented the ideal mode of government, for rites were the vehicle through which the ruler expressed his own virtue or moral power and also fostered a sense of dignity and responsiveness among the people. Dubs lists these possible translations of "li" as "religious rites, ceremony, deportment, decorum, propriety, formality, courtesy, etiquette, good form, good behavior, good manners" (Dubs, 1927, p. 113, translated by the author). In this context, rites cannot be treated without the role of feelings. Martha Nussbaum (2004) also comments on this set of questions, discussing the issue of the complex nature of shame and its role in relation to law. She warns that shame carries dangers that are antithetical to a liberal society, and that at its most primitive, shame means "hiding from our humanity" (translated by the author). For Confucius, the supreme goal of good government was the establishment of harmony (he), which was expressed in the mutual trust of people, and in the establishment of which the "junzi" played a key role. Accordingly, for Confucius, adherence to the middle presupposed, in the realm of external behavior, a spiritual state, which the Gu quoted here describes as "balance of the soul" (translated by the author). The desire for a permanent preservation of the middle and harmony, the balancing between the extremes, "without losing oneself morally" (translated by the author), admittedly had the consequence that the superior man acted with extraordinary caution in new things (Gu, 1999, p. 142).

With the "inner cultivation", which Confucius dealt with in detail, there was always an outward effect. Confucius by no means advocated a "pure inwardness". Rather, he required the "junzi" to "constantly affect his social environment, his state, and even the world under heaven (tianxia) during self-cultivation." The ideal type of "junzi" for Confucius was thus a man "who possesses unshakable moral integrity and considers it a historical task to put the world in order. The sense of being born to create a great being was formative for the junzi" (Gu, 1999, p. 143, translated by the author). Aware of the difficulty of fulfilling the twin tasks of perfection within and impact without, Confucius was confident, according to Gu, that the "junzi" could fulfill his mission "once he had completed the self-cultivation that consisted of 'self-respect, self-strengthening, and self-examination'" (Gu, 1999, p. 144, translated by the author).

An important role in connection with the noble—as noted above—was the example he had to set. Setting a good example meant, on the one hand, immediate practice and, on the other, the will to make improvements in the long term. The principles of good governance became effective as soon as they were put into practice. Interesting in this regard is the passage about Ji Kang asking Confucius about government and Confucius replying, "[. . .] If you, Sir, will good, the people will be good. The virtue of the noble person is like the wind, and the virtue of the little people is like grass. When the wind blows over the grass, the grass must bend" (translated by the author).

The way of people is this: "If they have a constant livelihood, they will have a constant mind, but if they lack a constant livelihood, they will lack a constant mind. If they lack a constant mind, they will succumb to vice, depravity, and excess" (translated by the author). The issue of "good governance" was perhaps the most important concern in the subsequent development of Confucian philosophy. According to Mencius, the "exemplary ruler must be respectful, frugal, and reverent toward his subjects, and must take from the people only in accordance with the regulations . . ." (translated by the author). This was primarily to ensure the livelihood of the people. Good intentions alone were not enough—what mattered was practice. Mencius said, "If you had the way of Yao and Shun, but no humane government, you would not be able to rule the world. Even if someone has a humane heart and a reputation for humanity, one from whom the people have no benefit will not serve as an example for later generations because he does not practice the way of the previous kings. That is why it is said, 'Goodness alone is not enough for governance; laws alone do not prevail.' " (Mencius, p. 136, translated by the author).

6.6 Rule of the Ritual

Now, to summarize what has been said so far at this point, what does the "ideal ruler" have to pay attention to according to the Chinese spiritual tradition? What was the focus of his attentiveness—and what was not? And how and in what way did the "ideal ruler" meet the requirements of the practical exercise of government? Arguably, one of the most frequently discussed questions in the study of the political dimensions of traditional thought in China is that of the relationship between law and ritual, taking into account the role of the ruler (MacCormack, 1996; Schwartz, 1985; Hansen, 1994).

China was only governed well—according to one thesis—when a way had been found to observe the rites and ceremonies exactly (Tan, 2011, p. 469).

As a society without legal ties, China favored the "rule of ritual." According to Tan, in Confucian political philosophy, having virtuous people in government was more important than having a good legal system. While every aspect of life was to be guided by rites and ceremonies as the "proper forms of all civilized conduct," laws remained at best a necessary evil. At worst, in fact, laws then undermined efforts to produce by "natural" means a commonwealth of virtuous people. Not unreasonably, one must add at this point, critics of Confucianism blamed the Confucians' dismissive attitude toward laws for the longevity of despotism, the difficulty of establishing the rule of law, and the lack of respect for human rights in China (Tan, 2011, p. 470, translated by the author). Traditionally, legalists are seen as advocating the use of law as an instrument of "government of the ruler, by the ruler, and for the ruler" (translated by the author). Following the logic of this authoritarian policy meant that the people were not allowed to use the law for their own protection, especially against the ruling class. Nevertheless, Tan insists, "Even though there is a generally more negative attitude toward law, its development in China is complex and cannot simply be attributed to Confucian philosophy" (translated by the author). We should ask whether the objections to the publication of penal codes and the criticisms of a government's use of punishment in early Confucian texts amounted to a rejection of the law itself.

6.7 Formation of the Modern "Noble"

The figure of the Confucian nobleman now played no role for a long time in the complex process of China's modernization efforts during the past century and a half, especially since Confucianism was repeatedly subjected to massive attacks in China well into the twentieth century. Central among these were the May 4, 1919, rallies (Chow, 1960; Siemons, 2009). Given the role May Fourth plays in China's history and culture, the 2019 centennial celebrations were strikingly simple.

Regardless of this, in the "new China" after 1949, a new "noble" was created that supposedly met the ideological orientation and was supposed to meet the needs of the majority of the population consisting of workers and peasants. The "model worker" was a relic from the tradition of the heyday of socialism, which was also cultivated in the USSR and the countries of the Eastern Bloc. Decades later, in the contemporary China of Chinese-style socialism as understood by Xi Jinping, this tradition is cultivated on a far more modest scale, as evidenced by occasional award ceremonies in public and the signs on state "model units." This mixture of individual and collective forces certainly has something "Chinese" about it, but it stems more from the tradition of class struggle than from Confucianism. Decades of campaigning against the "legacies of feudalism" had broken the bridge to the past after 1949. While the party and state in China today have only a moderate interest in reviving the past and actively promoting authentic traditions, there have been repeated attempts in recent years to meet the broader needs of the population by tolerating private schools in which traditions are given space for revival (Gilgan, 2019).

Higher goal of the aimed development—to find here again the connection to the above explanations—is the formation of "nobles" for the solution of the problems in the present. "The learner would absorb content that cultivates his/her natural disposition, aesthetic sensibility and knowledge. Returning to the Confucian classics could be a measure to repair what has been damaged throughout history under foreign influence. By establishing traditionally oriented study halls and academies, Wang hopes to train a new generation of Confucian-oriented and morally upright people (junzi) as the nucleus for a better society" (Gilgan, 2019, p. 69, translated by the author). The aim of all those involved is to make Chinese society more moral, more civilized, and more "Chinese" again: With the help of reading the relevant classics, modern nobles are to be educated who can ultimately enter Chinese society and positively influence it through their own good example. Ultimately, however, it remains to be said that these initiatives coming "from below" to make ancient traditions as authentic as possible for the present are a challenge to the state authorities in the PRC, which are pushing for the realization of their own, i.e., the "utopia" decreed by the Chinese Communist Party-the "dream" of realizing socialism with Chinese characteristics. The endeavor to create a new elite—turned toward Confucianism—is probably doomed to failure for the time being, when it can certainly be seen as a criticism of the currently existing politicians and especially the political leadership.

6.8 Mindfulness of Political Leadership

So, what is the state of mindfulness of China's political leadership in the present? To begin with, a few general remarks must be made. The question of the attentiveness of a leadership in an autocratic system like China's is subject to different criteria of examination than in a political system with democratic legitimacy. In countries with a democratic constitution and a functioning separation of powers by means of legislative, executive and judicial branches, as well as a modern public sphere in the form of responsible free people and media, mindfulness from the leadership's point of view serves to legitimize power, i.e. to acquire *and* maintain power at the same time. In dictatorships, mindfulness on the part of the leadership is subordinated exclusively to the pursuit of maintaining power.

In order to make the course of the investigation comprehensible, it should first be pointed out that there is a particular difficulty in dealing with the attentiveness of leaders in dictatorships, which has to do with the question of the material used. Biographical reliability and density are fundamentally difficult to guarantee, especially for persons still in office in these systems. This is due to the information control generally practiced in dictatorships, so that one sometimes has to rely on anecdotal material.

Having said this, it seems important to me to briefly point out some systemic peculiarities and the relationships between the people concerned in dictatorships when it comes to "attention". (In general, it should soon become clear that the "systemic question" itself is very much at the center of my considerations). If "mindfulness training" in psychology emphasizes above all therapeutic purposes, it should be clear that the processes described can be applied without further ado in the sense of a forced influence typical of dictatorships.

First of all, I would like to briefly mention some of the most important key points that are mentioned in the relevant literature of psychology on "mindfulness" and that can be used fruitfully in my contribution on China. First, there is the "present moment," namely, making it possible, through the practice of mindfulness, "to dwell for a longer time with the attention in the present and not to wander, following chains of thoughts, into the past or future." In psychodynamic therapy, this refers to a trained "inner observer" with the help of which "a continuous, accurate, inwardly directed study of the present activations of the 'implicit memory' can be brought about."This refers primarily to emotional and physical phenomena "that occur when automatic, mostly unconscious reactions occur due to individual triggers" (Weiss & Harrer, 2010, p. 16, translated by the author).

Transferred to dictatorship, this already outlines the "mindfulness control" on the part of the controller on the one hand and the controlled on the other. Nobody is released from the "now". The goal of the controller is to penetrate as deeply as possible into the "I" of the controlled in order to attain the status of the "inner observer" and to achieve an "identification" of the person with their respective states, as they occur especially under strong emotional stress (Weiss & Harrer, 2010, p. 18).

Also the described positive effects of a therapeutic mindfulness training *for* the person (for example, things such as insight, calmness, inner peace, composure and equanimity, compassion and co-joy are cited) can be brought about if the corresponding training is to serve the control *over the* person (Weiss & Harrer, 2010, p. 15).

Controller and controlled thus require—I quote again from the article on the therapeutic use of mindfulness—a systematic "cultivation of special abilities and specific bodily-mental states, both of the patients and of the psychotherapists through regular practice." The "systematic separation of observer and observed"—as demanded by therapy, is probably also present in the case of dictatorship, but admittedly takes place under different power relations and not "at eye level" or in a state of "equality". A mechanism of action which can lead "to fundamental changes in the structure of consciousness itself and thus also to new stages of the development of consciousness" can be used for "therapeutic-liberating" purposes as well as for those of suppression and influence.

"Why people defend a dictatorship" (translated by the author)—this is the title of a 2011 Spiegel article referring to research by two scientists, Aaron Kay of Duke University and Justin Friesen of the University of Waterloo, and their findings presented in the journal *Current Directions in Psychological Science*. Kay and Friesen had explored the question of what leads people to conform to certain situations: "According to the researchers, people always stand up for the government, their university, their company or even a family member when they are threatened or criticized from the outside. Similarly, people protect those institutions on which they depend or when they seem unable to escape the system. But they also do so when they feel they have no control over certain areas of life, such as the health care or school systems" (translated by the author). Overall, loyalty, dependence on the system, and lack of power and escape are cited as crucial reasons, with relevant examples. One of the most important feelings to satisfy the "longing for the leader" seems to be narcissism associated with egoism. According to Wirth, narcissistically disturbed people strive for power because they want to compensate for their lack of self-esteem, whereas the possibility of exercising power nurtures fantasies of greatness and omnipotence. According to Wirth, power acts like a drug: "Self-doubt evaporates, self-confidence increases. Power fantasies often serve to overcome unbearable feelings of powerlessness. If narcissism, power and aggression enter into a close relationship, destructive and self-destructive discharges occur" (Wirth, 2007, translated by the author).

On the one hand, the problem of power is related to the existential dependence of human beings; another reason for the problem lies in the equally existential need for sovereignty. People remain dependent on recognition by others throughout their lives. In order for a "sense of identity" to develop, a counterpart is now needed who confirms the sense of self through love, trust and recognition—or constitutes it in the first place. Exercise of power and (pathological) narcissism now represent strategies to deny this dependence. For the holder of power it is true that by making others submissive he creates the illusion of being independent. This, of course, takes place at an enormous price, as Wirth notes, because whoever has power "can indeed force and buy love and recognition," but in doing so he admittedly only disguises his fundamental dependence, so that a circulus vitiosus is set in motion: "The more the other is enslaved, the less he is experienced as a human subject," and the more violence the self must use against him in order to obtain the hoped-for recognition. This is because the greater the violence used to force recognition, the less it is worth. The addictive character of power processes derives from this dynamic (Wirth, 2007, translated by the author).

Thus, if there is the desire for power on the ruler's side in the interplay between narcissism and power, this is complemented on the other side by the "needs of the ruled for submission, protection, and blind allegiance," which makes the exercise of power by the ruler possible in the first place (Wirth, 2007, translated by the author).

6.9 Culture of Paternalism

How can the above remarks be used in the context of contemporary China? First of all, all dictatorships are characterized by a culture of paternalism propagated by the leadership, which—depending on how it is perceived—can take on the character of a Confucian-like mindfulness in the roles of those affected. As far as the case of the Chinese leader Xi Jinping, born on June 15, 1953, is concerned, the main question is to what extent he lives up to the image of the "ideal ruler" from China's past. Western overviews of Xi Jinping's biography to date are generally more detached and critical than corresponding sources from China.

In addition to the numerous Chinese sources on the relevant websites with information on Xi Jinping's official biography, it is also worth mentioning an early Chinese source from 2008 and thus several years before he assumed the leading role at the head of the Chinese state, which can be understood very nicely as the already long-term attempt to contribute to the narrative of Xi as an ideal and "people-oriented" ruler whose fate is closely connected with important places and events in China's history in the twentieth century. In the text "How Vice-President Xi Jinping Grew Up," the text discusses the sending of intellectual youth to the countryside decreed by Mao Zedong 40 years earlier (i.e. 1968). Xi came to a small town near the city of Yan'an at that time. It was there that Mao Zedong had established his headquarters at the end of the Long March in the late 1930s. Xi's "community of fate" with Mao and other representatives of the early revolutionary phase is also vividly expressed, for example, when reference is made to Xi's accommodation in one of the residential caves. Central contents from Xi's life—including his successful admission to the Communist Party and his minor successes in local administrative work—at that time and contemporary impressions of his character (a suitcase with books carried along), presented in the form of recollections of contemporary witnesses at the site, are intended to help form the breeding ground on which the image of Xi as a "noble" later developed.

But even from relevant China connoisseurs from the West there are now and then statements and representations that have quite obviously been produced out of a desire to present Xi Jinping as a figure in the tradition of the classical Chinese scholar. The German sinologist Helwig Schmidt-Glintzer, who generally continues to see the power of the noble at work in contemporary China, spoke in the fall of 2019 at the Frankfurt Book Fair on the occasion of the presentation of the German edition of a book with speeches by Xi Jinping, among other things, that the texts reveal "the image of the cultivated noble, the wenshi," who stands "in the tradition of the *junzi,*" by which is meant precisely someone who does not seek retreat, but who has the willingness to "assume responsibility for society." "In the formation of political culture, this interplay of speech and written text and corresponding action has always played a very important role in China" (translated by the author). Schmidt-Glintzer's cultural studies summary of Xi Jinping's work a bit further on. "The type of the nobleman, also that of the one who cultivates himself and assumes responsibility, has a renewed appearance in China through the back door with the renaissance of Confucianism, because it is that incorruptible man of letters, interested above all else first of all in self-cultivation, who inherits the ideal of the Confucian nobleman, with which we are in the middle of the re- Confucianization of today's China" (Schmidt-Glintzer, 2018, p. 42, translated by the author).

Although the space of Xi Jinping's activity at the time of writing was limited to the southern Chinese province of Zhejiang, which Xi knew well from several years in various posts, in 1993 Xi first became a member of the Fujian provincial administration, also in southern China, and chairman of the Fuzhou People's Congress. After five and a half years as deputy party secretary in Fujian (1995–2000), he became governor in Fujian and at the same time a member of the party leadership in Zhejiang province. In 2002, Xi was appointed governor of Zhejiang, and in 2003 he became party secretary of the provincial committee and chairman of the Zhejiang People's Congress.

Schmidt-Glintzer suggests, however, that Xi's "visions" had larger goals in mind: "The thoughts and visions from the banks of the Zhejiang demonstrate the commitment to the development of a region of China. They exemplify the care and concern that all of China's regions need, and they give us a sense of the complexity of the tasks that must always be addressed" (translated by the author). It is revealing to what extent the Western expert has here appropriated the extremely positive ductus of official Chinese historiography and contemporary propaganda, without even the slightest mention of the aspects—also present in Xi Jinping—of rigorous enforcement of power politics. One might argue whether the elimination of disfavored opponents like Bo Xilai a few years after Xi's accession to power was necessary and appropriate. It would be difficult to reconcile the character of a nobleman with the fact that a terminally ill Nobel Peace Prize laureate like Liu Xiaobo is not allowed to be released from prison or even to move abroad.

6.10 State Propaganda of the Image of the "Noble" Man

In the following, we will now briefly attempt to show, on the one hand, what efforts have been made by China's propaganda apparatus to create the image of a "noble" Xi Jinping, who has been acting as state president and party leader since 2012/2013, and, on the other hand, to take a look at the effect of these measures. Overall, of course, this can only be a rough assessment.

Under Xi Jinping, the party has gone on the offensive. In recent years, the Chinese Communist Party has begun to specifically recruit new members. Propaganda and grassroots activities are also being actively promoted, and "service centers for party work" (dangjian fuwu zhongxin) have been established in the districts of the cities. In the era of Big Data and the use of social media, the aspect of their use in several ways is of considerable importance in the topic of "mindfulness." How are these media used, for what purpose do they serve? The app we are talking about here is called "Xuexi qiangguo," which is a play on words that at one point can mean something like "Learn to make the country strong." Another reading is "Learn how to make the country strong with President Xi" (translated by the author). The app has been developed by technology company Alibaba and is given to party members by Chinese propaganda offices. The app is able to measure how many texts the registered users have read daily and how many videos have been watched, commented on and recommended. Points are awarded for the corresponding actions. By means of obligatory quiz questions, for example, the app is designed, as surveyed users stated, to "automatically inscribe itself in the memory and influence thinking" (translated by the author)—the party's recognizable goal is to penetrate precisely these spaces of retreat still retained by individuals. There is also considerable social pressure to use the app; users' scores are regularly published within party groups, and there are comparisons and "competitions" with other party cells. It can be assumed that at least some of the users will be driven into internal emigration. Meanwhile, the app is also being used to vet journalists. According to a report in the news magazine "Der Spiegel," President Xi is now testing the loyalty of journalists with a so-called Xi app Journalists must first study the great leader's world of thought in an online training course and then undergo a loyalty test. Only those who answer 80 out of 100 questions correctly receive a press card afterwards. The rest lose their jobs (Der Spiegel, 2019).

6.11 Conclusion

What conclusions can be drawn from China's intellectual and ruling tradition for the present? Culturally and politically, China in many respects draws on traditions handed down from its long history and exhibits more or less conscious traits of ambivalence. Just as Chinese politics was not monolithically Confucian during the imperial period, it is not exclusively committed to an ideologically based "socialist ideal" in the present. While official propaganda outwardly claims to be committed to the socialist values of "democracy," "justice," "prosperity," "harmony," etc. and thus pretends to live up to the Confucian appearance of the government's "legitimacy," the hidden traces of "badao"-"government by power"-are unmistakably present in the practical implementation of policy and appear as totalitarian-autocratic measures in the form of restrictions on information, surveillance, limited freedom of movement, and much more. Instead of idealizing and tracing the traces of allegedly noble Confucian sentiments in China's past and present, it might be appropriate to see everyday political life in China, whether in the long past history or today, as what it has always been-a power game oriented to the interests of a comparatively small minority, of which violence has always been a basic component. It is due to whitewashing Chinese historiography that concrete events have always been presented in a better light than they actually were. Now that Hong Kong has also become a "real" Chinese city in the wake of the new security laws from the summer of 2020, the example of Taiwan continues to show that it is not due to Chinese culture per se that democracy and freedom have so far been denied to a population of billions. "Modernity" is a laborious process, which also includes freeing oneself from the rather primitive power structures of the past and providing space for differentiated and balanced processes based on laws and the separation of powers.

References

Acemoglu, D. (2019). Trump hat wie Hitler ein gewisses Charisma. Interviewgespräch. *Der SPIEGEL, 50*, 74–76.

Ames, R. (1983). *The art of rulership: A study in ancient Chinese political thought.* University of Hawaii Press.

Anton, H. (2003). *Fürstenspiegel des Hohen und Frühen Mittelalters.* Accessed October 21, 2020, from https://web.archive.org/web/20120218182546/http://www.ahf-muenchen.de/Forschungsberichte/Jahrbuch2003/Anton.pdf

Bandurski, D. (2019). *The future of common destiny.* Accessed October 21, 2020, from https://www.echo-wall.eu/state-mind/future-common-destiny

Böge, F. (2018). China fürchtet einen neuen Kalten Krieg. *FAZ, 31*(08), 2018.

Chen, D. (2019). China muss transparenter und offener werden, im Gespräch mit Helene Bubrowski. *FAZ, 31*(05), 2019.

Chow, T. (1960). *The May fourth movement. Intellectual revolution in modern China.* Harvard University.

de Bary, T., & Bloom, I. (1999). *Sources of Chinese tradition* (Vol. 1, 2nd ed.). Columbia Unversity Press.

Der Spiegel. (2019). Accessed May 12, 2020, from https://www.spiegel.de/politik/die-hoecke-app-kolumne-a-00000000-0002-0001-0000-000166735153

Dubs, H. (1927). *Hsüntze: The Moulder of ancient Confucianism.* Arthur Probstain.

Feng, Y. (1998). The yellow emperor tradition as compared to Confucianism. In W. T. de Bary & T. Weiming (Eds.), *Confucianism and human rights* (pp. 154–168). Columbia University Press.

Ferguson, N. (2019). *Auch die chinesische Mauer bröckelt: Warum der Einparteienstaat des Reichs der Mitte keine Zukunft hat.* Accessed June 11, 2019, from https://www.nzz.ch/feuilleton/niall-ferguson-die-chinesische-mauer-broeckelt-ld.1519733

Fuest, C. (2018). Der dritte Systemwettbewerb. *FAZ, 27*(07), 2018.

Gilgan, S. (2019). *Imaginaries of a better Chinese society enacted in the revival of Confucian education. An ethnography of living and learning in contemporary classics reading education "Dujing jiaoyu", Inaugural-Dissertation zur Erlangung der Doktorwürde der Philosophischen Fakultät der Rheinischen Friedrich-Wilhelms-Universität zu Bonn.*

Gu, X. (1999). *Konfuzius zur Einführung.* Junius.

Hansen, C. (1994). Fa (standards: Laws) and meaning changes in Chinese philosophy. *Philosophy East and West, 44*(1994), 435–488.

Hirigoyen, M. (2020). Ich bin der Nabel der Welt. Die Psychoanalytikerin Marie-France Hirigoyen über Donald Trump und die Frage, wie wir uns gegen die toxische Macht von Narzissten wehren, Interview mit Ute Cohen. *FAZ, 07*(06), 2020.

MacCormack, G. (1996). *The spirit of traditional Chinese law.* University of Georgia Press.

Nussbaum, M. (2004). *Hiding from humanity: Disgust, shame, and the law.* Princeton University Press.

Osnos, E. (2020). *The future of America's contest with China. Washington is in an intensifying standoff with Beijing. Which one will fundamentally shape the twenty-first century?* Accessed

October 21, 2020, from https://www.newyorker.com/magazine/2020/01/13/the-future-of-americas-contest-with-china

Schmidt-Glintzer, H. (2018). *Chinas leere Mitte. Die Identität Chinas und die globale Moderne*. Matthes & Seitz.

Schwartz, B. (1985). *The world of thought in ancient China*. Harvard University Press.

Siemons, M. (2009). *Das datum Aller chinesischen Daten*. Accessed October 21, 2020, from https://www.faz.net/aktuell/feuilleton/die-4-mai-bewegung-das-datum-aller-chinesischen-daten-1799316-p2.html

Tan, S. (2011). The Dao of politics: Li (rituals/rites) and laws as pragmatic tools of government. *Philosophy East and West, 61*(3), 468–491.

Wambach, A. (2019). Im Systemwettbewerb mit China. *FAZ, 06*(08), 2019.

Wang, W. (2020). *Eastern mind-set foretells global future*. Accessed October 21, 2020, from https://www.globaltimes.cn/content/1176673.shtml

Weiss, H., & Harrer, M. E. (2010). Achtsamkeit in der Psychotherapie. Verändern durch 'Nicht-Verändern-Wollen' – ein Paradigmenwechsel? *Psychotherapeutenjournal, 1*(2010), 14–24.

Wirth, H. (2007). *Macht, Narzissmus und die Sehnsucht nach dem Führer*. Accessed October 26, 2019, from http://www.bpb.de/apuz/30600/macht-narzissmus-und-die-sehnsucht-nach-dem-fuehrer?p=all

Xi, J. (2019). *Xi calls for international scientific cooperation for 'shared destiny of mankind'*. Accessed October 21, 2020, from http://www.globaltimes.cn/content/1168384.shtml

Part II
Transfer from Theory to Practice

Chapter 7
Resilience and Mindfulness: Concepts and Interventions for Organizations in Times of Change

Christoph Steinebach, Álvaro I. Langer, and Vanessa Nowak

7.1 Shaping Life in a Changing World

One of the basic truths is probably that we live in a changing world. People change in their behavior and in their experiences. But their social and physical environment is also changing. At the same time, people show changing attitudes and behaviors, which also represent changing social norms and values. Perhaps it is a sign of our times that in all of this there is an increasing emphasis on people's responsibility for themselves and for their environment. Resilience and mindfulness are important in order to be able to adequately face the many challenges and pitfalls. Resilience and mindfulness represent particular competences of individuals as well as of the groups and organizations in which these individuals live and work. This chapter seeks to present resilience and mindfulness as concepts and assets for work contexts in the changing world in which we live.

7.1.1 Social Change

The social change we are facing has been described many times. Globalization, pluralization, acceleration and the strong focus on knowledge in all its forms and

C. Steinebach (✉)
School of Applied Psychology, ZHAW Zürich University of Applied Sciences, Zürich, Switzerland
e-mail: Christoph.Steinebach@zhaw.ch

Á. I. Langer
School of Psychology, University Austral de Chile, Isla Teja, Valdivia, Chile

V. Nowak
Centre of Competence and Development, Valdivia, Chile

V. Schulte et al. (eds.), *Mindful Leadership in Practice*,
https://doi.org/10.1007/978-3-030-97311-7_7

contents are current topics. Worryingly, the consequences are pointed out: demographic change, increasing freedom and the associated problems of a meaningful orientation of one's own life. And last but not least, polarization in attitudes and value-based behavior. The consequences are problems that strongly influence our public life. On the one hand, conflicts between individual groups are increasing, and on the other hand, our natural environment is under massive threat, e.g., through the phenomenon of climate change. All this has a negative impact on people's physical and mental health (World Economic Forum, 2020). Proposals on how to counter these problems and their causes call for sustainability, regionalization, the participation of all in social life and a slow down and deceleration, also in the sense of mindfulness.

The sciences play a particularly important role in developing solutions. In terms of evidence-based practice, appropriate measures are designed based on theory and empirical evidence. Rationale and impact of these measures are reflected upon. This is an opportunity to improve theory and practice. In all of this, it is important to note that the sciences are not merely observing from a safe distance but are themselves the objects of these fundamental changes. In addition, the different sciences each have their own perspective and can therefore examine only one part of the highly complex issues. Therefore, it is necessary to combine findings from different sciences to arrive at good, reliable and sustainable solutions (Smedslund, 1972; Wilson, 1998). Together, it is necessary to investigate what contribution the different sciences can make to a better understanding of resilience and mindfulness and how they can participate in solving the problems at hand in the everyday management of organizations and companies.

7.1.2 Change in the World of Work

The social change already described is reflected in the world of work. In many respects, we can speak of a globalized world of work. Development, manufacture and sale of products take place worldwide in many industries, which is reflected in global value chains (Gereffi & Fernandez-Stark, 2016). And the same is true for many sorts of services. This requires not only communication and cooperation across national borders, but also professional mobility. For many, living and working in foreign countries is a matter of course. The result is a higher degree of plurality and diversity within organizations. Many work processes are being accelerated, not least through digitalization. This is associated with many opportunities, but also risks. Companies, but also their employees, must keep up with this pace. With increasing acceleration, many complain about a life on slippery slopes (Rosa, 2017). Dissatisfaction, depression, and burnout can be the result.

The knowledge that is important for work is growing and can be called up virtually at any time. It is important to absorb new knowledge and process it appropriately in order not to lose touch and thus even one's job. The consequences can be felt in many companies: Demographic change means an aging workforce.

Here, it must be ensured that older employees are also able to keep up with the current changes. Increasing freedom is also a challenge for one's own professional career. It is important to shape one's own career path accompanied by lifelong learning according to one's own needs (Council of the European Union, 2018). This always requires investment in one's own professional training and in the development of one's own team and company. Such demands on the shaping of one's own professional development often lead to orientation crises. Everyone is called upon to provide further training, advice and mutual support. Where individual interests and needs become important, where people from different cultures with very different professional biographies come together, conflicts over resources and power can also arise. Increasing polarization makes it difficult to find good compromises time and again. The problems that arise from this are obvious: We are increasingly experiencing conflicts in companies. We observe that companies are being given more responsibility, for their environment and for the sustainable use of their resources (Sáez-Martínez et al., 2016).

We observe that workload and working conditions are becoming a constant threat to health and well-being. In view of the aforementioned solutions, entrepreneurship today means taking responsibility for sustainability and for anchoring the company responsibly in the region. However, it is also important to ensure the participation of everyone in order to secure all competencies, skills and abilities as resources for the sustainable development of the company. As will be shown below, the concepts of "resilience" and "mindfulness" help managers, employees and the company as a whole to adequately counter the negative consequences of global trends.

7.1.3 Changing Education and Training in Work Contexts

Similar to self-development, learning is increasingly the responsibility of the learners themselves. Vocational education and training are therefore increasingly understood as an individualized process. Regardless of what skills and abilities are to be imparted, learning is particularly successful when it is authentic, i.e., when practicable solutions to realistic problems are sought. Reflecting on the learning process, talking with colleagues deepens learning and consolidates learning success (Gomez et al., 2019). Work-based learning seeks a close connection between knowledge and practice. In this way, the world of work becomes the world of learning. Learning success must then be proven in everyday life, new skills must be acquired, or the knowledge base must be further developed. A broader knowledge base and the multitude of options for action make it necessary to reflect on the ethics of one's own conduct. The interests and concerns of all stakeholders must be considered. Theory is necessary to justify one's actions and assess their consequences. Here, the close connection between theory and practice becomes clear (Merrill, 2012).

Formal offerings for imparting knowledge and building skills and abilities are conceivable. Courses or programs to promote mindfulness or to introduce meditation techniques should also be mentioned here. The purpose of such courses is then not the training of job-specific competence profiles. Rather, it is to develop skills useful in specific occupations or, more generally, to promote subjective well-being, health, or personal development. Increasingly, counseling services offered in connection with professional development tasks, crises, and critical life events are gaining in importance (Schreiber, 2020). This offers the opportunity to reflect on one's own situation and to learn new skills and abilities on a very individual basis. Thus, it is conceivable that in a counseling process not only one's own professional biography and current stress at work become the subject of discussion, but also techniques for promoting mindfulness are taught. In this case, job-related counseling is about promoting job resilience. However, it can also be about clarifying how one's basic needs (Ryan & Deci, 2000) of autonomy, belonging, and competence can be met in one's career and work. The needs orientation also leads to a shift in the relationships between leaders and their teams. Leaders are advised to empower autonomy and to support as advisors or facilitators rather than as hierarchical controllers. New leadership paradigms that focus on concepts such as culture, individual responsibility, mindset, and feedback, whether as adaptive leadership (Heifetz et al., 2009) or agile leadership, come to mind (Zirkler & Werkmann, 2020).

7.2 Promoting Resilience: Models as Maps in Difficult Terrain

Resilience is demonstrated by a successful balance of individual vulnerabilities and strengths as well as environmental risks and support. It is demonstrated in dealing with special challenges, developmental tasks, crises and critical life events. We define resilience "as the positive adaptation and sustainable development of a system to respond to short- or longer-term everyday challenges or severe stress. Based on internal system processes and through dealing with the environment, the system defines new reference values and develops required competencies, and the ability to cope with future stresses improves" (Steinebach, 2015, p. 557). This makes it clear that resilience is a prerequisite and outcome of positive development. However, it also shows that not only a person can be resilient, but also social systems such as groups and organizations, the neighborhood or the local community.

7.2.1 Shaping Self and Environment

From a systemic point of view, the individual is a system, which itself consists of systems on different levels. Biochemical, muscular-neural, emotional, and cognitive processes are each controlled by different system elements with different functions. It is critical that these levels, as semi-autonomous systems, can define new control variables when there is an internal or external need for improvement. Such adaptation is understood as self-optimization (Brandtstädter, 1980, 2001; Steinebach, 1988).

From a systems theory perspective, the individual system is integrated into a nested structure of different environmental systems. The microsystem includes, among other things, interaction with colleagues, one's own team as a whole, and one's supervisor(s). The next system includes contacts with other employees in the company as well as with relevant external actors. The exosystem reflects the characteristics of the legal principles relevant to the company. The macrosystem reflects the norms, values and attitudes of society, for example, on good leadership (Steinebach, 1988).

More resilient organizations, it is said, have employees, teams and managers who are willing to acknowledge and deal with reality. They can perceive critical developments at an early stage and are able to evaluate them appropriately. They can design and examine alternative courses of action. In the company, everyone has a differentiated picture of strategy, goals, and processes (Scharnhorst, 2008; Sommer et al., 2017). This relates to the ideal, such as vision, mission, and guiding principles, or the real, such as specified tasks, roles, and functions. Accordingly, in the Job Demand-Resources Model (Bakker & Demerouti, 2017; Albrecht, 2013), basic needs, sense of duty, but also work pressure, physical and emotional demands, commitment, and roles are important conditions for predicting individual or team performance. This model also shows how much "meaningful work" is linked to individual cognitive, emotional, and physical, but also social and ergonomic working conditions.

7.2.2 Understanding Mindfulness

Mindfulness is a 2500-year-old Buddhist practice traditionally understood as part of the process of "awakening" (Gethin, 1998, 2011). In the teachings, mindfulness is described as a process that involves increasing physical awareness of internal or external stimuli and emotional states (Davis & Thompson, 2015). The most common definition of mindfulness found in the psychology and mental health literature is "the practice of paying attention in a particular way: on purpose, in the present moment, and non-judgmentally" (Kabat-Zinn, 1994, p. 4) or in a more recent work: "Mindfulness can be thought of as moment-to-moment, non-judgmental awareness, cultivated by paying attention in a specific way, that is, in the present moment, and as non-reactively, as non-judgmentally, and as openheartedly as possible. When it is cultivated intentionally, it is sometimes referred to as *deliberate mindfulness*" (highlighting in original, Kabat-Zinn, 2015).

Based on the proposed definitions, at least two aspects of mindfulness can be highlighted: (1) attentive orientation to what is present and (2) openness, curiosity, and acceptance as an expression of a particularly successful example of current emotional regulation. In this regard, mindfulness, understood as a trait (i.e., dispositional mindfulness) or practice (i.e., mindfulness-based interventions), has been used in primarily to address health problems (Howarth et al., 2019), but also preventively as mental health promotion in schools (Langer et al., 2015, 2020) and in the workplace (Vonderlin et al., 2020).

7.3 Mindfulness in Organizations

When we want to use mindfulness training to promote the resilience of employees, but also the resilience of teams or the entire company, then it is not enough to offer introductory mindfulness training to individuals. Rather, from a systems theory perspective, it would be important to strive for a change in social interaction and corporate culture in addition to promoting the skills and abilities of a mindful lifestyle. On the part of employees, it is certainly about experiencing mindfulness as a holistic physical and mental experience. But it is also about fostering a particular social interaction in which mindfulness is part of a shared experience of coherence. To achieve this, measures are necessary both on the part of the individual employees and on the part of the company. This requires responsible leadership. Since the culture of the company is to be influenced, it is necessary that leaders support and exemplify this change in corporate culture. This makes it clear that leadership takes into account the basic needs of all and that the current challenges are tackled together and with mutual support.

Where mindfulness in organizations is addressed, the question of leadership deserves special attention. It is about mindfulness as a personality trait of a leader. Various facets of mindfulness as a character trait resonate here. Mindfulness in leadership also requires that managers make offers to promote mindfulness in the company. And that each manager also cultivates and develops his or her own mindfulness. For example, there may be moments when the manager shows him or herself to be particularly mindful or appreciates the mindfulness of others. Despite all current stresses and distractions, mindfulness rests in the here and now and does not adjust to external events in a judgmental way. Such moments of mindfulness are particularly important for dealing with negative emotions and for unbiased reflection on conditions and developing solutions to current problems (for a general discussion of facets of mindfulness, see Bergomi et al., 2013).

If we place mindfulness as a protective factor in the service of a person's resilience, the team's resilience, and the entire company's resilience, then it must be a concern of managers to promote mindfulness comprehensively. Mindfulness is in itself a protective factor because it reduces negative feelings and experiences of stress. But it also supports the development of other protective factors, such as a differentiated perception of one's own body, a positive perception of other people and the environment.

When promoting mindfulness in the company, social interaction is of particular importance. Colleagues can support each other in their quest for greater mindfulness. Joint offers to enhance mindfulness also foster the need for belonging. The experience of being able to accompany others on their learning journey strengthens one's own competence. Mindfulness is anchored in the here and now of one's own physical and emotional experience and in the current situation. Mindfulness therefore also promotes autonomy. Offers to build mindfulness also address basic needs and create a climate of engagement, connectedness, and trust (see the work of the Mindful Peers Network, Langer et al., 2019; Steinebach et al., 2019a, b):

- Mindfulness is associated with greater social empathy.
- Features of the physical environment are perceived more accurately and re-evaluated.
- Mindfulness increases well-being. With it, individual resilience grows.
- People who are better able to empathize with others are also more likely to be helpful and generous.
- People who act generously feel self-efficacious and have a more positive view of themselves.
- Mindfulness promotes social responsibility for resources.
- A supportive social environment provides positive self-esteem.
- Mindfulness training in companies creates an organizational culture in which basic needs and mutual support are firmly anchored.

7.3.1 Wellbeing in the Workplace

Special attention in organizations is paid to the well-being of their employees. It is a basic personal insight that is backed up by many research findings: mindfulness is closely linked to well-being. From the work of Ryff and Keyes (1995), we know what constitutes well-being: a positive attitude toward oneself, good social relationships, a life of freedom and self-determination, the ability to control one's environment and to make sense of one's life. Under the impression that our own life is meaningful, that we are developing positively and that we are supported by our social environment, we feel good. The possibility to direct one's own life according to one's own goals, norms and values is another important basis for one's own well-being. Openness to new experiences and the possibility to deal with new things are also very important. Involvement in positive social relationships, the possibility to determine one's own life, corresponds to the basic needs as we find them in Ryan and Deci (2000). We can therefore assume that the satisfaction of basic needs not only promotes well-being but is also an important basis for tackling challenges and tasks with perseverance and commitment.

Furthermore, personal well-being is only conceivable if the well-being of others (in this case employees, superiors, customers, and other stakeholders) is taken into account. This is where empathy and generosity are needed. In fact, generosity is seen in research as an underappreciated and neglected virtue (Miller, 2018). Those who act generously do more than just do good for others. Acting generously represents independent choices, something that goes beyond the expected and serves the good of others. "The common underlying assumption seems to be that human generosity is a beneficial act that may be directed towards other human beings, the community or the society as such" (Komter, 2010, p. 443). Although a universally accepted definition may be lacking, the proximity of this concept to altruism, prosocial behavior, and helpfulness is obvious. Prosocial behavior is an umbrella term for actions that attempt to do good to others. Very different factors are responsible for whether prosocial behavior is exhibited. Individual factors come into play here, as well as situational or external factors. On the individual side, temperament, empathy, analysis of the existing situation play a role, as do personal moral concepts and ethical convictions. All of this can be influenced by education and socialization.

In the situation itself, it is decisive whether we ascribe to ourselves the competence to be able to help and whether help is really needed. A dividing line is drawn between altruism and helping, because altruism excludes that the helper himself derives a benefit from the helping action. "While inherent in most definitions of altruism is the tenet that the helper must not benefit from the altruistic act, helping lacks a similar precondition. Helping is any act that one does to assist another, regardless of whether the helper benefits from the act or not" (Collett & Morrissey, 2007, p. 6). The positive effect for the helper may also occur later, for example, when the helper is seen as particularly trustworthy because of the helpfulness attributed to him or her (Przepiorka & Liebe, 2016). The close connection between mindfulness, empathy, and generosity makes it clear that it makes perfect sense to further develop the organizational culture as one of mutual help and support. This, too, promotes mindfulness in the organization.

7.4 Interventions to Promote Mindfulness

When considering interventions to enhance resilience through mindfulness, different levels and processes come into view: On the individual side, it is about fostering health and well-being. This involves the physical, emotional and cognitive levels. Within the company, this involves employees, managers and, depending on the concept and requirements, ideally also customers and other stakeholders. But it also affects work groups and teams, the company, and the corporate environment.

A basic problem of all interventions is probably that there is a gap between the intention and the actual behavior. Good intentions and the firm conviction that it would be good to change one's own behavior and "live healthier" or "go through life more attentively" are no guarantee of appropriate, new and better behavior. How can we design interventions to bridge the gap between intention and behavior?

Heckhausen and Gollwitzer (1987) distinguish in their phase model of action different phases. And depending on the phase of an action, we are more or less open to information. In the initial phase, there are different options for action to choose from. Initially, actors are still open to information. With the formation of the intention, a conclusion is increasingly drawn from initial considerations. The step from motivation to volition follows. In this pre-actional phase, the decision is then more likely to be secured and defended. As the work of Ralf Schwarzer (such as Schwarzer & Hamilton, 2020) shows, risk perception, outcome expectations, and self-efficacy beliefs are important for the formation of intention. The latter are also important when it comes to action planning or when it comes to assessing whether and how possible disruptions in implementation can be blocked. This shows that, depending on the action process, information is absorbed, and that the implementation of the action must be increasingly safeguarded against interference.

New information alone is therefore not sufficient and is only processed appropriately in certain phases of action. In principle, the following is important for us in offers to promote mindfulness:

1. Information is not everything. Information is important at the beginning and during the reflection of experiences. It also requires practice and, for example, "reminders" to stay on the ball and block out interference.
2. Practicing mindfulness does not necessarily require extensive, i.e., intellectual, or academic, knowledge of mindfulness. Although it is common practice to teach mindfulness from the "top down" and to teach theories and concepts of mindfulness, alternative offerings that focus on practice are nevertheless effective (bottom-up processes, Guendelman et al., 2017).
3. Early interventions are more effective, efficient, and sustainable than later curative interventions.
4. Offerings should focus on aspects of behavior and experience that are relatively easy to influence.
5. They should be close to people and extend over a longer period.
6. They should be based on people's needs and not be problem-focused, but help people appreciate and develop their strengths.
7. When it comes to the environment, it's not just social factors. The conditions and effects of the physical environment can and must also be included in the promotion of mindfulness in the company (cf. summary of contributions in Steinebach & Langer, 2019).

7.4.1 Person

When it comes to enhancing resilience on an individual level, stress and stress management are often discussed. It is about preventing burnout or other physical and psychological problems. Various strategies can be pursued to manage stress: On the one hand, it is possible to work directly on the stressors. This involves skills in conversation and conflict management, time management, and promoting positive social integration within the team. Another strategy may be to change attitudes and evaluations. This involves setting appropriate goals and designing processes appropriately. This does not necessarily mean that the person suffering from the given conditions alone must change. In concrete terms, it may also be a matter of realigning teamwork, for example by promoting a culture of mutual support and help. On the individual side, it will be about re-evaluating problematic situations and changing negative thinking patterns. Another strategy may be to gather and activate strengths to better face current stresses and future challenges. Offers to promote relaxation and mindfulness are at the top of the list here. A healthy diet, sufficient sleep, exercise, and hobbies are other ways to reduce stress reactions through healthy living (Schuster, 2018).

What can leaders do? According to the World Economic Forum's Future of Work report, active learning and learning strategies, leadership, innovation, problem solving, emotional intelligence, and creativity and initiative are among the skills that will be most in demand in the workplace in the future (World Economic Forum, 2018). Delegation of tasks and active resolution of workplace conflicts through mediation can also be very helpful. Managers should acquire knowledge and skills about coping strategies. They should take steps to embed such strategies with and among employees. They should increase their own resilience through, for example, exercise, healthy eating, relaxation, and positive social contacts, and they should try to balance current stresses in their free time. In addition, meditation and relaxation help them to keep a "cool head" in crisis situations and remain capable of acting. Here, too, mindfulness exercises show their effect: (1) Non-judgmental attention reduces inappropriate self-attention and facilitates constructive confrontation with difficult emotions. (2) Non-judgmental attention helps to focus on the current process, to set aside goals and expectations in favor of the current experience, and to better experience oneself in the current situation. (3) Dis-identification represents the inner withdrawal from the current stressful experience. This creates the opportunity to observe oneself and reevaluate the situation from observation (Chambers et al., 2009; Davidson, 2010).

Managers increasingly see themselves as service providers, as supporting employees to promote their health and well-being. Such an attitude strengthens cohesion and social ties. Health and well-being become corporate goals for which human, financial and material resources are made available. The diversity of employees, their particular biographies, their self-image and their convictions are respected. Based on this attitude, employees are called upon to help shape conditions and measures to promote health and well-being in the company. In this way, these processes become examples of successful systemic self-organization of the company, in which new answers to pressing questions are developed in a solution-oriented manner.

7.4.2 Team

What are suitable interventions to enhance resilience and mindfulness in teams? Teams are of particular importance because, as units of the organization, they represent special social groups. Teams can differ from one another in many ways: for example, in terms of their structure, size, mission, and culture. Unlike project groups, we would assume that teams have diverse and ever-changing missions. For the individual members, the team is important because the identity of a team can be derived from its composition. In principle, this is true for all groups to which we belong. A positive view of the team also requires a positive identity of its own. Team resilience refers to "the team's contribution to overcoming the challenges faced by the team as a whole. Team resilience ensures successful management of these tasks and opens up reliable perspectives for positive developments of the members as well as the group as a whole. From a systemic ecological perspective, team resilience provides the framework for the resilience of individual team members. At the same time, it is also the basis for sustainable performance of the entire organization" (translated by the authors, Steinebach et al., 2013, p. 185). The resilience of a team is reflected on the one hand in the positive accomplishment of concrete tasks and challenges, but also in the well-being of the individual members and the group as a whole. Important group characteristics include confidence in the group's performance, enthusiasm, optimism, recognized leadership qualities, mutual respect, cohesion and commitment, and everyone's knowledge of the goals at hand. To achieve this, everyone's contribution and commitment is necessary. The evaluation of the dynamics in the group depends crucially on whether the appreciation of one's own group and the devaluation of the foreign group bring an advantage for one's own identity. The need for positive identity also influences how I evaluate my own contribution to group goals. In this dynamic, closeness and distance on the one hand and hierarchy on the other hand prove to be important group characteristics. Overall, it can be assumed that these teams are particularly good at mastering challenges in which cohesion and mutual influence are moderately strong and flexible (Steinebach et al., 2013).

What are suitable interventions? To create transparency about the mission, processes and functions, the team discussion is certainly helpful. To ensure the integration of new team members and to facilitate a change of perspective in the event of conflicts, expectations and fears, the group's own strengths and weaknesses and its previous handling of challenges should also be discussed. Conflicts between team members or individuals and the group, common and different expectations and fears should be discussed openly. Positive experiences in the work process, but also outside the work process, promote group cohesion. This is one of the reasons why outdoor training can be useful. But also, a course and regular meetings for joint mindfulness exercises can promote cohesion and mutual understanding within the group. Peer group supervision and a positive peer culture have been shown to be very effective in building a culture of mutual support within the group. Group discussions based on the Positive Peer Culture approach (PPC, cf. Steinebach et al., 2018) follow a set procedure that allows problems in and with the work to be addressed openly and reflected on in the group. Solutions are developed and, if necessary, support is provided from within the group to implement the solution. This can be done during the session itself, but also between sessions. Such group sessions are thus also a model for open and purposeful dialogue within the team. They promote participation and cohesion in the group and thus also the resilience of the team.

7.4.3 *Organization*

For an organization, it is also crucial to what extent it can adapt to new challenges, whether the organization can continue to develop, and whether central values and norms can be aligned in such a way that the achievement of goals is possible. It therefore makes perfect sense to apply the systemic developmental definition of resilience to organizations as well. Norms and values, as well as the social and physical conditions in which these values are reflected, provide a framework against which the organization's groups or each individual member can orient themselves. Guidelines and rules determine the extent to which there is an obligation to align one's own behavior or the group with the rules of the organization.

If Höher (2018) speaks of dialogic organizational resilience, dialog is the foundation on which seven different pillars of resilience are built:

1. Social capital, such as leadership culture, values and relationships;
2. mindfulness as a characteristic of the organization;
3. culture, identity and meaning;
4. organizational learning;
5. the ability to integrate the unexpected;
6. settings and types of dialogue; and
7. structures that enable dialogue within the organization.

Mindfulness proves to be an important characteristic of the organization. We can assume that mindfulness is reflected in leadership behavior and interaction. We can assume that offering or promoting mindfulness will also have a positive impact on leadership culture, values within the organization, and social relationships. If we promote mindfulness, the organizational culture and thus the identity of the organization will also change. With increasing competence in adequately regulating emotions in stressful situations, the ability to process the unexpected in a goal-oriented manner will also grow. Therefore, it seems obvious to build structures and settings for developing mindfulness and for mindful dialogue in general.

Following Bolman and Deal (2006) and Andersson and co-authors (2019), we can assume that companies can be seen, sometimes more, sometimes less, as a factory, a family, a jungle, or a theater. Companies get into trouble when they focus on only one or two of these perspectives. Versatility and flexibility are needed to meet the challenges of everyday life. Therefore, companies should position themselves in such a way that they can live and shape all four perspectives if necessary. A company that only functions as a factory, an organization that only stages itself, will quickly reach its limits. It can be assumed that mindfulness is most likely to serve the image of the family. However, arguments can be made as to why mindfulness is important in all four perspectives. Regardless, mindfulness first allows for a realistic assessment of how the four perspectives stand in one's own organization and where improvements are needed (Deal & Peterson, 1999).

Mindfulness helps to arrive at a realistic assessment of what (1) makes the company what it is and what it can be in the future. Mindfulness also makes sensitive

(2) to the boundaries between people and institutions, to the similarities and differences in needs, attitudes and necessities. (3) Mindfulness also makes it possible to accept change as necessary and positive while appreciating the stability of overriding values. Mindfulness (4) prevents hasty actionism and promotes reflective action even under great pressure. Paavo Nurmi's (1897–1973) phrase "We don't have time, so we should slow down" (translation by the authors, Wichor, 2015, p. 170) impressively reflects this attitude. (5) Mindfulness of all also promotes a new understanding of leadership that emphasizes the responsibility and competence of all. New leadership models, e.g., with the goal of greater agility, are replacing classic forms of hierarchical control (Zirkler & Werkmann, 2020).

7.5 Mindfulness in Organizations: Connecting the Dots

We have based our reflections on a systemic, developmental understanding of resilience. From this perspective, the individual itself consists of various subsystems of different system levels. These levels are arranged hierarchically and are in close exchange. Together they form a complex structure, which in turn is integrated into various environmental systems. In the world of work, employees represent such individual systems and are themselves part of teams and the organization. Here, too, there are complex interactions that also extend into the relationship between employees and customers or clients. From a systemic perspective, the goal must be to ensure that positive developments are adopted at the various system levels and promoted in the various environmental systems. At the individual level, this can entail preventing burnout and measures aimed at promoting health and well-being. In systemic interactions with customers or clients, the focus is on promoting strengths. Working together and doing something on your own offers the opportunity of satisfying basic needs and thus promotes the intrinsic motivation of all involved. At the team level, the focus is on appropriate forms of dialogue, on a culture of mutual support in which basic needs are taken into account and joint action is shaped. Here, too, the strengths of individual team members as well as the team as a whole will be addressed. The effort to create a culture of mutual support continues at the organizational level. It is driven by a desire to meet the needs of all. At the same time, there is a need to continually assess external challenges and provide the necessary resources. What remains is the expectation that individuals, teams and companies have an impact on the business environment, neighborhood, local community and ultimately society. Mutual responsibility and care for one another can thus ultimately be fostered in society.

Not surprisingly, we demand in the outlook that more research is needed. Research is needed that reflects the complexity of what is happening, using a variety of research methods. We need research that accompanies the process of change. We need research that examines measures to enhance mindfulness in companies, taking into account the diversity of organizations in different cultures and societies.

What needs to be considered in designing interventions in the future? In short, companies need settings where mindfulness can be practiced and lived. When dealing with problems, one must focus on solutions, supported by an attitude of empowerment. When deciding on possible measures, the basic needs of those affected should be taken into account, and those affected should be given the opportunity to help shape the measures with regard to their basic needs. Needs orientation necessarily goes hand in hand with participation. In addressing challenges, the here and now is important. However, it is also important to anticipate upcoming changes in good time and to assess the consequences of measures. Strengths and weaknesses of employees and the organization must be appropriately perceived and evaluated. On this basis, it is possible to expand the options for the company. For all this, transparent communication seems to be the right approach. Everyone has their own strengths and therefore their own know-how. If responsibility is shared among everyone, then leadership means encouraging dialog and supporting the search for joint solutions. However, this dialog is not only directed at everyday problems and their solutions. It is also about finding common meaning, about the common image of the company, its culture, and its goals. All this happens under great entrepreneurial pressure. To be able to deal with this pressure, you need resilience and a mindful view of yourself, your employees, and the organization.

References

Albrecht, S. L. (2013). Work engagement and the positive power of meaningful work. *Advances in Positive Organizational Psychology*, 237–260.

Andersson, T., Cäker, M., Tengblad, S., & Wickelgren, M. (2019). Building traits for organizational resilience through balancing organizational structures. *Scandinavian Journal of Management, 35*(1), 36–45.

Bakker, A. B., & Demerouti, E. (2017). Job demands-resources theory: Taking stock and looking forward. *Journal of Occupational Health Psychology, 22*(3), 273–285.

Bergomi, C., Tschacher, W., & Kupper, Z. (2013). The assessment of mindfulness with self-report measures: Existing scales and open issues. *Mindfulness, 4*, 191–202.

Bolman, L. G., & Deal, T. E. (2006). *The wizard and the warrior*. Jossey-Bass.

Brandtstädter, J. (1980). Gedanken zu einem psychologischen Modell optimaler Entwicklung. *Zeitschrift für Klinische Psychologie und Psychotherapie, 28*(3), 209–222.

Brandtstädter, J. (2001). *Entwicklung, Intentionalität, Handeln*. Kohlhammer.

Chambers, R., Gullone, E., & Allen, N. B. (2009). Mindful emotion regulation: An integrative review. *Clinical Psychology Review, 29*, 560–572.

Collett, J. L. & Morrissey, C. A. (2007). *The social psychology of generosity: The state of current interdisciplinary research*. University of Notre Dame. Accessed October 21, 2020, from https://generosityresearch.nd.edu/assets/17634/social_psychology_of_generosity_final.pdf

Council of the European Union. (2018). Council recommendation of 22 May 2018 on key competences for lifelong learning. *Official Journal of the European Union*, 2018/C 189/01. Accessed from https://eur-lex.europa.eu/legal-content/EN/TXT/PDF/?uri=CELEX:32018H0604(01)&from=EN

Davidson, R. J. (2010). Empirical explorations of mindfulness: Conceptual and methodological conundrums. *Emotion, 10*, 8–11.

Davis, J. H., & Thompson, E. (2015). Developing attention and decreasing affective bias. In K. W. Brown, J. D. Creswell, & R. M. Ryan (Eds.), *Handbook of mindfulness: Theory, research, and practice* (pp. 42–61). Guilford Publications.

Deal, T. E., & Peterson, K. D. (1999). *Shaping school culture*. Jossey-Bass.

Gereffi, G., & Fernandez-Stark, K. (2016). *Global value chain analysis: A primer*. Duke University, The Duke Center on Globalization, Governance & Competitiveness.

Gethin, R. (1998). *The foundations of Buddhism*. Oxford University Press.

Gethin, R. (2011). On some definitions of mindfulness. *Contemporary Buddhism, 12*, 263–279.

Gomez, J., Nüesch, C., & Löhrer, A. (2019). Weiterbildung von Führungskräften: Beispiel einer Wissenschaft-Praxis-Kooperation. *Zeitschrift für Hochschulentwicklung, 14*(4), 75–89.

Guendelman, S., Medeiros, S., & Rampes, H. (2017). Mindfulness and emotion regulation: Insights from neurobiological, psychological, and clinical studies. *Frontiers in Psychology, 8*(220), 1–23.

Heckhausen, H., & Gollwitzer, P. M. (1987). Thought contents and cognitive functioning in motivational versus volitional states of mind. *Motivation and Emotion, 11*(2), 101–120.

Heifetz, R. A., Grashow, A., & Linsky, M. (2009). *The practice of adaptive leadership: Tools and tactics for changing your organization and the world*. Harvard Business Press.

Höher, F. (2018). *Menschliche Resilienz in Unternehmen – Dialog als Ressource. Grundlagen und Methoden*. Budrich.

Howarth, A., Smith, J. G., Perkins-Porras, L., & Ussher, M. (2019). Effects of brief mindfulness-based interventions on health-related outcomes: A systematic review. *Mindfulness, 10*, 1957–1968.

Kabat-Zinn, J. (1994). *Wherever you go, there you are: Mindfulness meditation in everyday life*. Hyperion.

Kabat-Zinn, J. (2015). Mindfulness. *Mindfulness, 6*(6), 1481–1483.

Komter, A. (2010). The evolutionary origins of human generosity. *International Sociology, 25*(3), 443–464.

Langer, Á. I., Ulloa, J. V., Cangas, A. J., Rojas, G., & Krause, M. (2015). Mindfulness-based interventions in secondary education: A qualitative systematic review. *Estudios de Psicología, 36*, 533–570.

Langer, Á. I., Steinebach, C., García-Rubio, C., Andreu, C. I., & Torres-Díaz, L. (2019). Looking for a broad framework for the integration of mindfulness-based interventions in the educational system. In C. Steinebach & Á. I. Langer (Eds.), *Enhancing resilience in youth. Mindfulness-based interventions in positive environments* (pp. 19–35). Springer.

Langer, Á. I., Medeiros, S., Valdés-Sánchez, N., Brito, R., Steinebach, C., Cid-Parra, C., Magni, A., & Krause, M. (2020). A qualitative study of a mindfulness-based intervention in educational contexts in Chile: An approach based on adolescents' voices. *International Journal of Environmental Research and Public Health, 17*, 6927.

Merrill, M. D. (2012). *First principles of instruction. Identifying and designing effective, efficient and engaging instruction*. Pfeiffer.

Miller, C. B. (2018). Generosity. A preliminary account of a surprisingly neglected virtue. *Metaphilosophy, 49*(3), 216–245.

Przepiorka, W., & Liebe, U. (2016). Generosity is a sign of trustworthiness—the punishment of selfishness is not. *Evolution and Human Behavior, 37*, 255–262.

Rosa, H. (2017). *Beschleunigung. Die Veränderung der Zeitstrukturen in der Moderne*. Suhrkamp.

Ryan, R. M., & Deci, E. L. (2000). Self-determination theory and the facilitation of intrinsic motivation, social development, and well-being. *American Psychologist, 55*, 68–78.

Ryff, C. D., & Keyes, C. L. (1995). The structure of psychological well-being revisited. *Journal of Personality and Social Psychology, 69*(4), 719–727.

Sáez-Martínez, F., Díaz-García, C., & González-Moreno, Á. (2016). Factors promoting environmental responsibility in European SMEs: The effect on performance. *Sustainability, 8*, 898.

Scharnhorst, J. (2008). *Resilienz – Neue Arbeitsbedingungen erfordern neue Fähigkeiten*. Accessed from http://www.bdp-verband.org/aktuell/2008/bericht/BDP-Bericht-2008_Gesundheit-am-Arbeitsplatz.pdf

Schreiber, M. (2020). *Wegweiser im Lebenslauf. Berufs-, Studien- und Laufbahnberatung in der Praxis*. Kohlhammer.

Schuster, S. (2018). Förderung Emotionaler Intelligenz durch Achtsamkeitspraxis am Arbeitsplatz. In H. Gölzner & P. Meyer (Eds.), *Emotionale Intelligenz in Organisationen* (pp. 247–258). Springer.

Schwarzer, R., & Hamilton, K. (2020). Changing behaviour using the health action process approach. In *The handbook of behavior change* (pp. 89–103). Cambridge University Press.

Smedslund, J. (1972). *Becoming a psychologist*. Universitetsforlaget.

Sommer, D., Kuhn, D., Milletat, A., Blaschka, A., & Redetzky, C. (2017). *Resilienz am Arbeitsplatz*. Mabuse-Verlag.

Steinebach, C. (1988). Wege zu einem integrativen Modell interdisziplinärer Frühförderung. *Frühförderung interdisziplinär, 7*(3), 417–425.

Steinebach, C. (2015). Resilience. In J. D. Wright (Ed.), *International encyclopedia of the social & behavioral sciences* (Vol. 20, 2nd ed., pp. 555–560). Elsevier.

Steinebach, C., & Langer, Á. I. (Eds.). (2019). *Enhancing resilience in youth. Mindfulness-based interventions in positive environments*. Springer.

Steinebach, C., Gharabaghi, K., & Steinebach, U. (2013). Teams. Positive Umwelten schaffen. In C. Steinebach & K. Gharabahi (Eds.), *Resilienzförderung im Jugendalter. Praxis und Perspektiven* (pp. 183–196). Springer.

Steinebach, C., Schrenk, A., Steinebach, U., & Brendtro, L. K. (2018). *Positive Peer Culture. Ein Manual für starke Gruppengespräche*. Beltz-Juventa.

Steinebach, C., Langer, Á. I., & Tri Thi, M. T. (2019a). Enhancing resilience in youth: Sustainable systemic effects in different environments. In C. Steinebach & Á. I. Langer (Eds.), *Enhancing resilience in youth. Mindfulness-based interventions in positive environments* (pp. 3–17). Springer.

Steinebach, C., Schaer, M., & Knafla, I. (2019b). Generosity, peer-support, and positive development in youth. In C. Steinebach & Á. I. Langer (Eds.), *Enhancing resilience in youth. Mindfulness-based interventions in positive environments* (pp. 57–78). Springer.

Vonderlin, R., Biermann, M., Bohus, M., & Lyssenko, L. (2020). Mindfulness-based programs in the workplace: A meta-analysis of randomized controlled trials. *Mindfulness, 11*, 1579–1598.

Wichor, M. (2015). *Sport – Geschichte. Zitate, Fotos, Anekdoten*. epubli.

Wilson, E. O. (1998). *Consilience. The unity of knowledge*. Knopf.

World Economic Forum. (2018). *The future of jobs report*. WEF. Accessed October 21, 2020, from http://www3.weforum.org/docs/WEF_Future_of_Jobs_2018.pdf

World Economic Forum. (2020). *The global risks report*. WEF. Accessed October 21, 2020, from http://www3.weforum.org/docs/WEF_Global_Risk_Report_2020.pdf

Zirkler, M., & Werkmann, B. (2020). *Psychologie der Agilität. Lernwege für Individuen und Teams*. Springer.

Chapter 8
Taming the Mind

Klaske N. Veth

8.1 Introduction

In this chapter, we examine the work and environment in which employees are expected to thrive and the extent to which managerial mindfulness might impact employee health. Certainly, it is not just leaders and managers who struggle with stress. However, as figureheads, pioneers, inspirers and leaders of organizations, they act as mirrors, touchstones and role models for others. And so it is with the way leaders and managers deal with stress. How can calm, clarity, focus, happiness and engagement be found in the here and now. The chapter begins with an examination of the (stressful) work and work environment and explores what the challenges are that people face today. The next subchapter focuses on a particular aspect of promoting healthy work—the attention economy. We then delve into the topic of health in the workplace and ways to work and lead mindfully. In general, what are the relationships to health in this regard, and what are the benefits of mindful work? And finally, the role of mindfulness is explored by leaders in terms of managing their own work lives and those of their employees.

8.2 Changed Work

Based on the thesis "Happy worker—productive worker", we know from research that work and its environment influence the well-being of workers and consequently their performance (Nielsen et al., 2017). Organizations need to know how to provide

K. N. Veth (✉)
Hanze University of Applied Sciences Groningen, Groningen, The Netherlands
e-mail: k.n.veth@pl.hanze.nl

V. Schulte et al. (eds.), *Mindful Leadership in Practice*,
https://doi.org/10.1007/978-3-030-97311-7_8

for employee well-being. The extent to which employees are happy and productive during their daily work depends not only on their individual characteristics, but also and especially on the work environment they perceive around them (Amabile et al., 2004). Employees, managers, and executives alike work in environments characterized as fast-paced, volatile, and complex. Jon Kabat-Zinn, the founding father of today's mindfulness movement, mentioned this (work) life environment, including pain, illness, and stress, as "the whole disaster." Over the past few decades, we have changed our work and its environment, resulting in an overcrowded work environment where employees' health and consequently their performance deteriorates. This ultimately leads to costs that offset the financial gain.

First, let's take a look at physical characteristics. We know that physical office conditions significantly influence employee attitudes and behaviors (Morrow et al., 2012). The consequences of adverse office situations that affect employee well-being and performance consist of indoor environmental factors and values such as noise levels, visual distractions, air quality, lighting, thermal comfort, plants, colors, furniture, and interior design (Manning, 1991). However, the term workplace or work environment is used to describe a broader concept of the working conditions under which employees work. The work environment refers not only to a place where a job is done. It typically involves other factors that characterize the workplace, such as additional perks and benefits of employment. Therefore, the workplace should be defined as "the environment" where people are connected, interact socially, and come together for the work to be done. This broader definition includes the identification of various elements:

- Work that needs to get done—in the office, at home, in a restaurant, on a plane or in a car, at a seminar or conference.
- Processes (such as transaction processing, innovation, communication, learning, etc.) that define the work to be done.
- Technology as a tool for the work to be performed (such as data access, groupware, mobile ware, etc.).
- Physical environment to support work, such as office design and layout, furniture, equipment, temperature, lighting, etc.
- Interaction of people to share knowledge and information.

Thus, the term "workplace" encompasses "physical and emotional sensations" that include comfort, aesthetic views, and social relationships (Preiser & Schramm, 2002).

In today's offices, workplace design, technology and culture are meant to promote employee health and organizational performance. Minimalist design, rows of employees sitting close to each other in open-plan offices, with possible impromptu collaboration around a ping-pong table, commuting to work made easy by technology—if presence work is necessary at all. Breaking down walls and overcoming time and distance should encourage spontaneous interactions, increase flexibility, and foster a more engaged and productive workforce (Oxford Economics, 2016).

But there are some weak spots on the road to this utopia, from the noise and distractions endemic to the open office to employees' frustration with technology and their inability to disconnect from it after hours or during vacation. To help people get more done during the workday (and make it easier for them to unplug after hours), leaders should understand the challenges their employees face and become aware of their own challenges. This is even more true in the wake of the Covid-19 crisis, as employees need to exercise greater self-discipline to distinguish between work and leisure.

The ultimate goal of these changing work environments and workplace technology is increased productivity, engagement and satisfaction at work, for both leaders and their employees, and as work and life become increasingly intertwined, these changes are likely to impact hours outside the office as well. Today's leaders must recognize the challenges of this new environment and develop a strategy to meet them. Oxford Economics conducted an interesting study on this in collaboration with Plantronics (2016). While managers are working hard to build a culture of openness where employees are encouraged to interact with each other, an open-plan office also has its drawbacks. Noise and distractions pose huge challenges in the workplace, especially in the age of open-space offices and telecommuting. Ambient noise and lack of privacy can make it difficult for employees to focus and get things done. With privacy disappearing, people have less room to shield themselves from the sounds of their colleagues' chatter, sneezes or phone calls. Another problem is work equipment. Only about one-third of employees say they are equipped with the necessary devices to work outside the office without distractions. This is another example of managers not understanding the magnitude of the challenge—far more say their employees are equipped with the necessary tools than employee responses suggest. When technology meets expectations and works flawlessly, employees are happier, more productive and free to focus on bigger problems. Ideally, they reap both the benefits of remote work and a central hub. In addition to all of this, the modern workplace and the factors that shape it—heavy technology use, shrinking personal space, noise exposure and distractions—contribute to a larger problem: Many feel the pressure to be "always on" and experience the strains of constant connectivity and information overload. Despite awareness of information overload and burnout, many people have difficulty putting down their devices for some time. More than one-third of respondents cite habit or compulsion, fear of missing out, or social pressure as the main reasons for frequent use of phones, tablets, and laptops. Many realize that this could have potentially serious consequences: One-fifth of respondents say that technology has a negative impact on their health.

As a result, employees and managers alike face increasing work pressure. Hougaard et al. (2016) focus specifically on the role of managers, noting that the current pressure on managers is forcing them to do more in less time. So it is because of work and its environment, which is changing more than ever, that the demands on leaders are becoming more complex. Work requires being constantly on and overloaded with information. In addition, leaders face these challenges in a work environment full of distractions. These demanding requirements are also referred to as **PAID reality** (Hougaard et al., 2016). This acronym stands for *"under pressure (**P**ressured)," "**A**lways on," "overloaded with information (**I**nformation overload)," and "**D**istracted."* Our work has changed dramatically in recent decades, especially in Western countries and Asia. While we used to have easier access to attentive focus on the task at hand, today we experience distractions everywhere and every day. Nowadays, due to the PAID reality, we are gradually losing our ability to perform at the highest level because we have lost our knowledge of how to manage attention.

If you ask any leader about work and the demands it places on them, the answer will be how many tasks need to be completed each day-often too many to manage. Therefore, when Warren Bennis states that "leadership is the ability to turn a vision into reality" (Bennis, 2008a, b, p. 13), this sounds too simple to be true. Straw et al. (2013) state that leaders have three main responsibilities: Firstly, crafting a **v**ision, secondly, building **a**lignment, and lastly, championing **e**xecution. As it seems, it takes a lot to master these skills. Straw et al. also give some definitions of these responsibilities: To build Vision, one must envision an improved future state that the group will make a reality through its work. To build Alignment, one must get to the point where everyone in the group understands and is committed to the direction. Finally, championing Execution is about ensuring that the conditions are in place for the imagined future to become a reality. This all is encompassed into the VAE model. But amid the challenging environment with employees exposed to the same stressful stimuli, leaders find themselves under pressure. They should proactively combat this problem by protecting their employees from information overload and burnout, but also by protecting themselves.

That's why noise, technology and culture are critical issues in the modern workplace. Getting these things right will boost employee engagement and improve business performance. It pays to make sure employees do their jobs well with a minimum of stress and distraction. The first step to solving this problem is recognizing that it exists. Only 39% of managers say that ambient noise affects their employees' productivity, and only 33% think that noisy colleagues are a problem. Not surprisingly, very few companies have taken meaningful steps to address the problem: Noise has only belatedly been perceived as a factor in office construction, and managers overestimate their employees' ability to solve the problem with the technical tools at their disposal. Leaders who recognize and respond to these challenges are more likely to empower employees to do their jobs effectively, stay engaged with their work, and feel passionate about the organization. The question, however, is how to lead in this volatile, uncertain, complex, and ambiguous (VUCA) world. It seems that the VAE model is no longer sufficient. Let's now look at these changes that have taken place in the last decades.

8.3 Attention Economy

In recent years, Herbert A. Simon's (1996) statement describing the problem of information overload as an economic problem has become very popular. Economic strategists such as Thomas H. Davenport have adopted the term "attention economy" (Davenport & Beck, 2001). But it was back in 1971 that Simon articulated the concept of attention economics in writing, "...in an information-rich world, information abundance implies a scarcity of something else: a scarcity of what information consumes. What information consumes is fairly obvious: it consumes the attention of its recipients. Therefore, an abundance of information creates a scarcity of attention and the need to divide that attention efficiently among the abundance of information sources that might consume it" (Simon, 1971, pp. 40–41).

Too much information can also lead to so-called "social interaction overload" in the long term. Therefore, the attention economy is also relevant for the social sphere. Nowadays, anyone can use social media to reach a wide audience by distributing their own content and commenting on the content of others. Therefore, in today's information-overloaded world, the scarcest resource is not ideas or even talent, but attention.

So one megatrend we see in internet use is that attention is one of the most important currencies of the twenty-first century. With the increasing proliferation of content that can be accessed instantly, attention is proving to be the limiting factor in the consumption of information. A fundamental reason for this effect is that human mental capabilities are limited. Therefore, the ability to absorb information is also limited. Attention serves to filter out the most important information in the human brain from a large pool of information that surrounds people in the digital age. Using attention economics as an approach to information management, organizations thus treat human attention as a scarce commodity. Simply stated by Crawford (2015), "Attention is a resource—humans only have so much of it." In this perspective, Davenport and Beck define the concept of attention as, "Attention is focused mental effort on a particular piece of information. Objects reach our consciousness, we engage with a particular object, and then we decide whether to act" (Davenport & Beck, 2001, p. 20).

In this distracted world, a leader must create a safe place for employees to express frustration and solve problems. So a leader needs the ability to "contain" the problems of their employees. To be more engaged and truly connected to others, silencing inner voices and being fully present in the mind are prerequisites (Hougaard et al., 2016). This first requires discipline to stay focused and not be disturbed by nonsensical challenges or distracted by mental background noise. It also requires the ability to stay focused and in the here and now. Only through mindful presence can a leader be successful. She must not fall into the trap of trying to solve, fix, manipulate or control others' problems.

Leaders who understand how to contain their own distractions find mindful presence to be an appropriate strategy for engaging their employees, creating better connections, and improving organizational performance (see also Hougaard et al., 2016). The results of a survey of 2000 employees conducted by Bain & Company showed that of 33 leadership traits-including "*creating* compelling goals, expressing ideas clearly, and *being* receptive to input"*-the* ability to be mindful *presence, being centered is the most important leadership trait.* Derived from research data, there is also a direct correlation between leader mindfulness and employee well-being and performance. In other words, the more a leader is present to their employees, the better they will perform. The question now remains, what strategies may prove

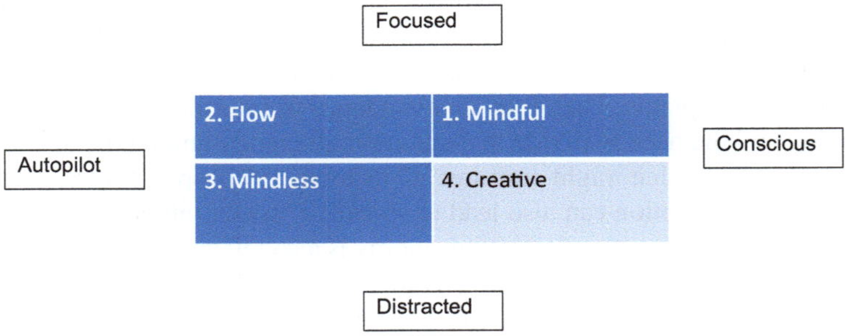

Fig. 8.1 Mindfulness matrix, after Hougaard and Carter (2018a, b) (own illustration)

helpful in the leader's quest to be more present in our daily lives? The mindfulness matrix is very useful in this regard (see Fig. 8.1). Optimal effective leadership can be achieved by being focused and aware (quadrant 1). Mindless/careless is when one is neither focused nor aware (quadrant 3). A leader should always avoid this mindset because it will never lead to engaged or productive team members. Being creative means being aware but easily distracted. Be sure to focus on good ideas and bring them to the quadrant above the state of creativity to ensure they become innovative solutions. Quadrant 2 represents the state of flow. This state can be useful in performing routine tasks without the risk of missing valuable information. Leaders should strive for the state of being mindful -that is, focused and aware. These key elements contribute to being mentally agile and effective.

8.4 Occupational Health

Sure, there's a lot a worker can do themselves to improve health in a work environment. We understand that while this advice is obvious, it can still be seemingly difficult to implement in daily life. Eight hours in a chair in front of a computer, five days a week can take a toll on your body (Hougaard & Carter, 2018a, b). That's why you should take a walk during your lunch break and eat only something light. Staying healthy and in shape through exercise are obvious ways to create healthier habits in the workplace. Not only do these habits burn calories, but they also relieve stress and refresh you. Less obvious, but still of great value, is not eating snacks. The snacks that employees place so nicely on their desks can add several hundred calories to the daily diet. In addition, drinking an adequate amount of water-eight to ten glasses per day-can help keep you hydrated. Since we know that Tension Neck Syndrome (TNS) can occur when the neck and upper shoulders are held in a fixed, uncomfortable position for extended periods of time, make sure to provide headphones, sit-stand tables, bike tables and the like. Eye strain is another problem that can occur when sitting in front of a computer for long hours. It can cause headaches, difficulty focusing, and increased sensitivity to light. The distance to the screen should be about an arm's length from your eyes. If you can't read your screen from an arm's length away, simply increase the font size on your computer. Another healthy tip is to take a long vacation, which will help you recharge your batteries. Vacations help relieve stress and take your mind off work, especially if you have a conflict, such as a problem with your boss, a colleague, or a project. Another way to live a healthy life at work is to avoid long stretches of long workdays. Finally, keep your keyboard, mouse and phone clean, as they can harbor thousands of germs just waiting to make you sick. Many hand movements can be useful on the way to a healthier workday.

Despite the abundance of tips mentioned, one important tip has not yet been mentioned: The most important thing you can do to stay healthy at work is to increase your self-awareness. This includes conscious self-observation in order to know one's own limits.

8.5 Mindful Leadership to Promote a Healthy Workplace

Anyone who has experienced an effective and engaged leader knows how satisfying this is—a leader who knows how to shape his/her place in the workplace, who knows when to change course. How to implement this, however, is somewhat unclear when you are just starting out in this position in the field of work.

The effective and committed manager is aware of the position of the company and the employees. While work is generally considered to be tasks performed for pay as part of an employment relationship or through self-employment, it can take place in very different environments. It can take place in formal or less formal settings, in large or small and medium-sized enterprises (SMEs), in primary (mining, agriculture, fishing), secondary (manufacturing and construction) or tertiary (services) industries (banking, insurance, police). The manifestations of these different environments can lead either predominantly to health impairments in the physical domain or primarily to effects on mental and emotional health. Differences in social positions also have a similar impact. In general, we can conclude that the lower the social position, the greater the vulnerability. So while work is primarily thought to positively affect health and well-being, it can also have significant negative effects on physical, mental, and emotional health. We know that work also significantly impacts individual identity, social status and self-esteem. So, as a leader, it is critical to appropriately classify the work in which you and your employees are engaged. Given the changes that have already taken place in post-industrial societies, and given the predictions about the amount and type of work that is likely to be available in the future, how should a leader view their work-related health promotion?

Knowing both their concrete and social position within the organization and that of their employees, it is now up to the leader to keep themselves engaged and productive in their work life and, as a result, to keep their employees engaged and productive as well. We know little about what successful leadership looks like and the environments in which it occurs. What is it that leaders say and do day in and day out that leads people to perceive an improved healthy workplace?

We know that the results of an organization do not only stem from the overall strategy of the company, but are also fundamentally shaped by the attitude of the employees who carry out the work of the organization on a daily basis. Therefore, cultivating a deep self-understanding is a prerequisite for effective leadership. This evolves around questions such as: *What are your most valuable strengths and most dangerous weaknesses? How do you learn and collaborate with others? What are your deepest values? And in what kind of work environment can you make the greatest contribution?* (See also Drucker, 2004). Effective leaders are aware of this, and they also know that sustainable results are only possible if their attention is first focused on their relationships with their people, based on thorough self-knowledge. Good relationships are a sine qua non for performance.

To do this, a leader must have the right levers at his or her disposal. In this world of speed, uncertainty, complexity and ambiguity, it is mindful leadership that counterbalances this and enables reflection, smarter rather than harder work, less stress, more job satisfaction and more sustainable performance. An important role of the leader is to ensure inner calm, both in themselves and in their employees. All of this contradicts the collective contemporary image of the boss with thick skin and calluses on his or her soul; someone who withstands constant work pressure, the relentless flow of information and incentives, is always on the run and changes frequently. Leaders are expected to be available all the time, everywhere, 24/7. How then can one take care of oneself? When is it time to rest and schedule recovery time for yourself?

Mindful leadership means leading by example, creating a "green zone" (Koole, 2012), and bringing the right mix of taking responsibility, embodying honesty, and being productive. It pays to know your own limits and ask yourself what you need yourself. Hougaard and Carter (2018a) provide interesting interviews with leaders in which they are asked how exactly they implement mindful leadership on a daily basis to, as one of the leaders said, just be there now, "even with a daily schedule of back-to-back meetings." All of these meetings are important, all involve complex information, and most require far-reaching decisions. Under these conditions, it is a challenge to actually be present every moment and hold meeting after meeting. One of her interviewees said, "When I'm with people during the day, I do my best to be focused, I'm present with them. This is partly because I get energy from being with people. But secondly, it's also because it's discouraging for the other people if you're not focused, if you're not present. They lose motivation. If you're not present, you might as well not have the meeting. It can be difficult to do it that way sometimes, but it's always important."

Being mindful throughout the day requires discipline and skill. To stay focused, you must be disciplined and not allow yourself to be distracted. Distractions can come from others or from your own lack of concentration. The cornerstone is presence, only this guarantees high performance. Also, make sure to be visible to your co-workers. To do this, plan your presence. Make sure you set aside a good portion of your time to walk and talk with employees. Memorize their names, stand by them closely during loss, grief and other life events, and show your human side. If you have a sincere interest in your employees, it will be felt and reciprocated in good to exceptional performance. To underscore the importance of this interest, let's say it again: it is a sincere interest that will be felt by others.

Do less and be more. As one of the interviewees, a senior vice president, notes, sometimes even a simple solution can be helpful to the employee facing a challenge. Often, an employee simply wants to be heard. What is also helpful in this regard is to sit back and lend an ear to the situation. That's why it's important to be present and fulfill the role of a container, that is, to create a safe space where people can vent their emotions and frustrations and thus work safely on their development. As a leader, you leave people in charge of themselves, but you make sure they feel safe.

Thus, it may be clear that mindfulness and presence in and of themselves do not solve problems. However, these states lead to higher subjective well-being and better positive functioning (Mandal et al., 2012), such as engagement, happiness, and positive emotional experiences, and they reduce stress. The authors note that these processes are interrelated and that they can even lead to *spirals of gain*. One of the findings is that in order to achieve this state of mind, one should not speed up. Thus, the key to improving leadership performance and well-being in today's fast-paced work environment is to slow down (Hougaard et al., 2016). In addition, mindfulness also involves training the body to be present in the mind. A prerequisite for this—not just a recommendation—is a daily moment of practice. One must sit back, take several deep breaths, and then make contact with the body and breathing. Counting the breaths helps to focus attention on the breaths and keep it there, rather than on the thoughts and emotions that come up. After this pause, for which even 5 min is enough, one is more present mentally and physically. This also leads to more relaxed postures, which ultimately affects the way people think, behave, communicate and relate to others.

Leading in the modern workplace also requires open attitudes at the organizational level. A healthy workplace requires a change in focus on the context in which people work, in addition to mindfulness. An environment that is demanding because it applies pressure 24/7 without allowing time for good relationships to develop will never lead to a healthy workplace. Carter and Hoograad (2018) present this as the following overarching structure for better leadership (Fig. 8.2).

Some companies are ahead of others in developing and benefiting from strategies for the modern workplace (Oxford Economics, 2016). Only 15% of executives agreed that new and emerging technologies have a positive impact on their employees' productivity. However they agreed that digital technology enables employees to do higher-value work for the organization and contribute to growth and success. They also described that their organization balances noise exposure through wellness programs work-life balance time off or other methods. This group of leaders also tends to better understand the impact of distractions and technology on their employees. They address these issues at the executive level resolve critical issues such as device integration and are more likely to provide technology to help employees avoid distractions. Implementing similar strategies to embrace the opportunities and overcome the challenges of the new workplace should be a priority for all companies

Fig. 8.2 Three levels of mindful leadership, according to the model of Hougaard and Carter (2018a, b) (own illustration)

8.6 Conclusion

All in all, leading in a PAID reality, as exciting and rewarding as it is, has its setbacks. Hougaard et al. note that leaders who act unconsciously choose "mindless busyness over mindful business" (Hougaard et al., 2016, p. 55). We also now know the benefits of being mindful for leaders themselves, the people they lead, and their organizations (Hougaard et al., 2016). By putting themselves first as people, they develop the qualities that enable positive emotions, engagement, happiness, and lower stress levels. In this world of volatility, uncertainty, complexity, and ambiguity (VUCA), the leadership model of Vision, Alignment, and Execution (VAE) can no longer meet the demands of the times. In this world fighting for attention 24/7, in this tsunami of challenges coming our way, we can be prepared. We can start with building more mindfulness that is beneficial for yourself, the team members, and the organization as a whole. Sure, it can often feels like 'battling a hurricane'. So, leaders can choose whether they tame the hurricane or tame themselves. We know hurricanes cannot be tamed. Only people can tame their minds.

References

Amabile, T. M., Schatzel, E. A., Moneta, G. B., & Kramer, S. J. (2004). Leader behaviors and the work environment for creativity: Perceived leader support. *The Leadership Quarterly, 15*(1), 5–32.

Bennis, W. G. (2008a). Leadership is the capacity to translate vision into reality. *Journal of Property Management, 73*(5), 13–14.

Bennis, W. (2008b). The art of followership: Great followers create great leaders. *Leadership Excellence, 25*(4), 4.

Crawford, M. B. (2015). *Introduction, attention as a cultural problem. The world beyond your head: On becoming an individual in an age of distraction*. Farrar, Straus and Giroux.

Davenport, T. H., & Beck, J. C. (2001). *The attention economy: Understanding the new currency of business*. Harvard Business Press.

Drucker, P. (2004). *Managing oneself*. Harvard Business Review.

Hougaard, R., & Carter, J. (2018a). *The mind of the leader - how to lead yourself, your people, and your organization for extraordinary results*. Harvard Business School.

Hougaard, R., & Carter, J. (2018b). If you aspire to be a great leader, be present. *Harvard Business Review, 13*, 2017.

Hougaard, R., Carter, J., & Coutts, G. (2016). Mindful leadership: Achieving results by managing the mind. *Executive Forum, 2016*, 49–56.

Koole, W. (2012). *Mindful leadership*. Publisher Business Contact.

Mandal, S. P., Arya, Y. K., & Pandey, R. (2012). Mental health and mindfulness: Mediational role of positive and negative affect. *SIS Journal of Projective Psychology and Mental Health, 19*(2), 150–159.

Manning, P. (1991). Environmental aesthetic design: Identifying and achieving desired environmental effects, particularly "image" and "atmosphere". *Building and Environment, 26*(4), 331–340.

Morrow, P. C., McElroy, J. C., & Scheibe, K. P. (2012). Influencing organizational commitment through office redesign. *Journal of Vocational Behavior, 81*(1), 99–111.

Nielsen, K., Nielsen, M. B., Ogbonnaya, C., Känsälä, M., Saari, E., & Isaksson, K. (2017). Workplace resources to improve both employee well-being and performance: A systematic review and meta-analysis. *Work & Stress, 31*(2), 101–120.

Oxford Economics. (2016, June 13). *When the walls come down - How smart companies are rewriting the rules of the open workplace* (pp. 1–12).

Preiser, W. F., & Schramm, U. (2002). Intelligent office building performance evaluation. *Facilities, 20*(7/8), 279–287.

Simon, H. A. (1971). Designing organizations for an information-rich world. *International Library of Critical Writings in Economics, 70*, 187–202.

Simon, H. A. (1996). *Models of my life*. MIT Press.

Straw, J., Davis, B., Scullard, M., & Kukkonen, S. (2013). *The work of leaders: How vision, alignment, and execution will change the way you lead*. Wiley.

Chapter 9
The Role of Ethics in Leadership: A Practical Model for Mindful Ethical Leadership

Martijn de Kiewit

9.1 Good Leaders and "Good Leadership"

9.1.1 Introduction

A leader can be defined as someone who can get others moving to bring about change. The question is whether "leadership" is synonymous with "getting others to do what the leader wants." If we look at history, we find many examples of leaders who were able to get the masses to do what they wanted them to do as leaders: from Caesar to Stalin and from a mafia boss to all kinds of dictators. These leaders had the talent to impose their will on others. But if we look at history, we also see leaders like Gandhi and Mandela. They not only had the talent to move the masses, but they added something more. The difference between these groups of leaders is that the second group of leaders is viewed more positively because their goals are perceived as good and righteous.

However, it is complicated to define what "good and just" goals are. People often disagree about this and heated discussions break out. Think of the different political views held in society, or organizations like the mafia. It may be hard to imagine, but perhaps the people who work for a mafia boss actually think that they are acting in the name of good and just goals. And the mafia also operates with a clear set of values and norms, such as omertà—they never talk to the police—or the rule that you don't look at friends' wives. Even terrorists are driven by a strong set of beliefs and goals that drive them to actions that are difficult for others to understand. Throughout history, we have seen many examples of groups who followed a leader and truly believed they were doing the right thing—while ignoring reality. For example, think of those who belong to a religious sect and commit atrocities that they are convinced are for the common good.

M. de Kiewit (✉)
Rotterdam School of Management (RSM), Erasmus University, Rotterdam, The Netherlands

V. Schulte et al. (eds.), *Mindful Leadership in Practice*,
https://doi.org/10.1007/978-3-030-97311-7_9

We must therefore ask ourselves what is an actual distinguishing characteristic to distinguish claimed good goals from really good goals. The effect of the goals on other people enables us to make this distinction: Goals that are beneficial only to the leader (or to the ingroup), as opposed to goals that are also beneficial to a larger group of people. We can call these types of goals "constructive goals." To return to our example of the Mafia: Although it operates with a strong set of values and norms, its goal is to gain wealth for its own group by hurting others.

Therefore, the definition of good leadership should include all three of the above characteristics: first, the appropriate ability—*to move* others—second, the positive orientation—to lead others toward the *right goals*—, and third, the broad scope—to set one's own goals that also benefit others. Ethical leadership can therefore be defined as: *moving others to constructively achieve the right goals.*

In this chapter, we look at ethics as part of mindful leadership and how to constructively engage leaders who are looking for the right ethical direction to take a mindful approach.

9.1.2 The Ethical Reality Is Much More Diverse than a Binary Evaluation of Right/Wrong

In the examples, we saw two types of leaders: those who could move the masses and those who could do so as well, but also in the right ethical direction. However, it could be argued that some "bad leaders" also thought they were really moving their followers in the right direction. Usually, all leaders at least claim to their followers that they know the right direction, sometimes with an approach that emphasizes this by claiming divine support for their direction and using extensive propaganda to convince followers to follow the leader.

So the essential question is: What are the "right goals"? On the one hand, this can be an ethical question. Moral philosophy and religion have long been the primary domains when it comes to ethics, as they deal with abstract concepts such as values, norms and rules. The ethics discussion is a never-ending one, as circumstances and society are constantly changing. But the question of "right goals," on the other hand, can be a more specific one, focusing on what an organization's goals should be and how those goals can be achieved. The point, then, is not to prescribe the moral direction a leader should take, but to show how a leader can take into account his or her own values and the different interests of the various groups of people involved in the organization, and to think actively about what the "right goals" should then be.

Knowing and agreeing on what "the right goals" are is not easy because we cannot define in a binary way what is the "right" and what is the "wrong" direction. Reality is a multitude of different interests and values of different people. A mindful ethical leader tries to take into account as many of them as possible in order to find a balance between them.

9.1.3 Dilemmas Force Leaders to Get Their Hands Dirty

In addition to the leader's difficulty in actually knowing and deciding what the right ethical direction is, the leader must also face the problem that what is good and right for one person may be very bad for another. In reality, you often can't please all the people all the time. So, as a leader, if you make a decision for the good of many, it can sometimes have negative consequences for certain people. In extreme cases, it may even be necessary to do something bad for the good of the group. This ethical theory is called consequentialism or teleological approach and differs from deontological ethics, which focuses on moral principles. For practical leaders, it quickly becomes clear that in reality there is always a need for a consequentialist approach. Here, many leaders face dilemmas that they find difficult to resolve.

We can illustrate this with a famous example from Foot called the "trolley dilemma" (Foot, 1967).

Trolley Dilemma
A driverless trolley races along the railroad tracks. In front of it, on the tracks, five people are tied up and unable to move. The trolley is heading straight for them. They are standing some distance away in the marshalling yard, next to a lever. When you pull this lever, the trolley switches to another track. However, you notice that there is a person on the siding. You have two options:

1. Do nothing and allow the trolley to kill the five people on the main track.
2. Pull the lever and divert the car to the side track, where it will kill one person.

Which is the more ethical option? Or, more simply, what is the right thing to do?

The trolley problem has been the subject of many surveys, in which the majority of respondents generally chose to kill the one and save the five (Bleske-Rechek et al., 2010). For example, in a 2007 study, 85% of respondents indicated that this was permissible (Hauser et al., 2007).

What makes the trolley dilemma (and any real dilemma) so difficult is that neither option is perfect. A leader who makes decisions will realize this very quickly. A leader must constantly make decisions and take actions that are not perfect for everyone!

9.1.4 The Need for Action: Courage Is Needed to Be a Good Leader

The Trolley Dilemma showed us that sometimes a leader has to choose the common good. This is already difficult in a thought experiment, but imagine you were faced with such a dilemma in real life: Would you really pull the lever? In real life it is even more complicated because you have to act—and usually you have to act quickly—without having all the information! This requires courage, and many people find it difficult to actively intervene. We can see this in the example of the Trolley Dilemma. In 2017, a group led by Michael Stevens conducted an actual trolley problem experiment in a YouTube channel broadcast, where the subjects were convinced that a train would hit five people if they didn't pull the lever, and one person if they did. When the problem is presented as a thought experiment, people have a hard time deciding, but the majority claim they would act and pull the lever toward the one person to save five. However, in Stevens' experiment, which involved a *real-life* situation, most participants simply froze and did not pull the lever. It turned out that it takes courage and is much more difficult to act in real life than to analyze the issue as a thought experiment.

9.1.5 Summary

We can summarize the lessons from this first part as follows. First, we discussed that there are different views on what good leadership means: is it enough to be able to move people, or must it include morality as a foundation? Then, we concluded that defining what the "right goals" are involves complications because this depends on people's interests and values, which vary depending on the person, society, time, etc. Further, we see that leaders must deal with a reality that is diverse and complex. This means that what is good for one person or group may not be ideal for another (group) in the long run. Leaders must constantly work on these dilemmas, sometimes readjusting their original goals, direction, and values. The fourth insight was that although it is complicated enough to come to a decision about what is the right action, good leaders must also have the courage to actually take the action.

In the next chapters, we will look more closely at what the key characteristics of a good, ethical leader are. Being a leader who is "mindful" of others can help the leader develop ethical leadership skills. The four characteristics of a mindful ethical leader that will be considered here are authenticity (Authenticity), openness (Hearken), reconciliation (Reconciliation), and authority (Authority).

9.2 Authenticity: Clarity About a Leader's Own Values

9.2.1 Introduction

As we have seen, part of leadership is defining the "right goals" for the group. Leaders set the course and communicate that course to those being led. While there may be debate about direction, it seems that a characteristic of successful leaders is that they are able to set the course very clearly and express their values. In other words, they are authentic in their values. This is because the direction is also clear to the leader, because it is truly his or her own.

This can easily be demonstrated with an example. Leaders who try to convey a direction that is not their own, but something they have to pass down through the ranks on the orders of higher management, and which they themselves also do not agree with or understand, are easily recognized by their group as not being "authentic".

9.2.2 A Definition of Authenticity: Clear Boundaries, Ideals and Values

A description of this part of leadership can be found in Kaptein's model (Kaptein, 2003). He describes in his article "The Diamond of Leadership Integrity" that integrity "refers primarily to authenticity" (Kaptein, 2003, p. 101). Authentic, in the literary sense, means original and not a copy, that is, genuine. For leaders, this means that authenticity refers to having a clear sense of direction and knowing what to accomplish. "Authentic leaders have clear boundaries, ideals, and values" (Kaptein, 2003, p. 101). These own clear values and goals give authentic leaders a kind of compass in guiding their own behavior and decision making. An inauthentic leader, then, is one who acts based on stereotypes or expectations of his or her role. Since these expectations change regularly, an inauthentic leader can usually be recognized by the fact that they regularly change the direction in which they are moving ("*but yesterday you told me to do just the opposite!*").

Authenticity also helps against undesirable (unethical) behavior, because clarity about one's own values also gives employees clearer messages about where the moral boundaries lie (Kaptein, 2003, p. 101).

9.2.3 The Clear Communication of One's Own Values Is Part of Authenticity

If the values are clear in the formulation, this helps others to achieve the goals defined by the leader. A good leader therefore has the ability to communicate very clearly what the right values and goals are. Therefore, it is not only necessary for the leader to have authentic values, but it is equally important for the leader to be able to communicate them clearly to others. For this reason, Kaptein's model makes this distinction visible by consisting of two layers. The first layer is about the manager as a person: the manager must be a person of integrity, that is, have the right values and goals. The second layer is about how a manager influences his employees: the manager should encourage the development of his employees' integrity. The way this is done is through communication with employees. After all, if no one knows what the desired values and goals are, others cannot be expected to follow. Communication skills are therefore an essential ingredient for ethical leaders.

Communication as a key factor is often forgotten in discussions of ethical leadership, which tend to focus on controversies about what exactly is the right course of action in an ethical dilemma. As we saw with the example of the trolley dilemma, this can be a long, difficult, and interesting discussion. However, since a dilemma by definition does not allow for a clear right/wrong assessment, it is not sufficient to arrive at a solution to the dilemma by making a decision. This decision must be "sold" to the team so that they understand the reasoning behind the decision. This is especially true since many people will see the other sides of the dilemma and may reignite the discussion by asking or criticizing why that particular direction was chosen rather than the other option(s). Then, the risk to the organization could be that the whole discussion will flare up again and again or that people will not support the leader's decision and will not cooperate to achieve the organizational goals. For these reasons, it is obvious that good communication is a part of ethical leadership.

There are different communication styles that leaders can cultivate, but again, there is a connection with authenticity. People can easily sense whether the communication style is authentic. A command style carried out by a meek person is unlikely to work. Likewise, a previously less optimistic leader who suddenly tries to communicate in a coaching style will be met with distrust.

9.2.4 *The Authenticity Multiplier: Charisma*

Why is one leader's communication so much more effective than another's? Some leaders seem to have something special in the way they communicate-something that is difficult to define. Weber spoke of "a certain quality of an individual personality" (Weber, 1947, p. 359) and was the first to coin the term "charisma" in the context of leadership. He adopted the term from the Roman Catholic Church, which first used the Greek word "charisma" (gift) to describe the Holy Spirit, but later used it to describe the basis of the organizational aspects of the church, which were based on the "gifts of God," "not man-designed rules or procedures" (Conger & Kanungo, 1987, p. 638). Academics have also examined the concept from a behavioral perspective to determine if there are certain individual characteristics that make leaders more attractive to those they lead. "Certain personal attributes of charismatic leaders consistently identified in this literature include" (Conger & Kanungo, 1987, p. 639):

1. Vision or appealing ideological goals;
2. Behavior that instills confidence;
3. The ability to inspire and/or create inspiring activities;
4. Self-confidence;
5. Dominance;
6. a need for influence;

7. rhetorical or articulation skills; and
8. unconventional and/or counter-normative behavior.

In these elements we see a mixture of the leadership skills already identified, as in the first case: vision or appealing ideological goals is very similar to our description of showing clear direction and authenticity. However, other elements are more related to communication with those being led. The "self-confidence", the "dominance" and more directly the "articulateness" are personal qualities that clearly contribute to a good communication with them.

9.2.5 *Summary*

This chapter has discussed that authenticity in the context of leadership means that leaders have clear boundaries, ideals, and values that guide them to the right goals. The ability to communicate all of this clearly helps the leader to be successful. There are leaders who demonstrate a great ability to communicate, often referred to as "charisma." Although charisma is difficult to define, elements such as clarity of purpose, a confident attitude, self-assurance, dominance, and articulateness seem to be personal qualities that help leaders.

9.3 Realignment of Values Through Openness and Attentiveness to Feedback

9.3.1 *Introduction: Authenticity as a Balance Between Flexible and Dogmatic Values*

People think a lot. We think about what is right and what is wrong. However, as we saw in Sect. 9.1, this is not always clear because we regularly find ourselves in dilemma situations. We will not find a one-solution-fits-all approach to our moral questions revealed in our dilemmas. We all spend our whole lives searching for definitions of our own ideals, values and their limits. We are constantly examining this within ourselves. This is an internal process where we sometimes realign our values because we have gained more insight, received more information, or learned something new.

Some people tend to review this more often than others. Some people don't do this at all and are very dogmatic in their beliefs and are unwilling to change because it makes them insecure. Or they are extremely convinced and are not receptive to anything that challenges their beliefs; sometimes they even become hostile to people who hold different opinions. Others are very flexible and perhaps adapt their values too easily to each new situation. Authenticity is at the heart of this. A truly authentic leader would seek the balance of reconciling his or her own beliefs with the input of others and examining that input to see if the values need adjustment. In this part, we focus on this process: how a leader can remain authentic but also be open to input on realigning his or her values.

9.3.2 Organizational Silence as an Obstacle to Change

When I started working after graduating from university, I was quickly a bit surprised and shocked by messages from top management. They kept raving about all the good things and positive aspects within our company. Actually, things were not going well at all, and everyone was complaining about it. It turned out that top management found this out months later. My surprise was that, for some reasons, higher management didn't really have a true idea of what was going on at the lower levels of the organization. What was even funnier was that later, when I was working with clients, I saw the exact same thing: senior management was not hearing or getting the real information about negative aspects of the organization. An important role for us as consultants was to tell them the real story (with bad news). I began to wonder: maybe this was something that was a broader phenomenon and not unique to my company?

In their brilliant 2000 article, "Organizational Silence: A barrier to change and development in a pluralistic world," Morrison and Milliken describe how organizational hierarchy can prevent information from moving up the hierarchy and being used effectively by managers (Morrison & Milliken, 2000). In their model, they describe many different factors that influence "employee withholding of information about potential problems or issues" (Morrison & Milliken, 2000, p. 706). However, all of these factors generally assume two main conditions. First, the fact that managers fear negative feedback, and second, managers' implicit beliefs. These implicit beliefs are that employees have a vested interest, that management knows better, and that dissent is bad. Because of this fear and these implicit beliefs, managers will be less open to feedback from their employees. These conditions, among other elements Morrison and Milliken describe, drive what they call organizational silence.

Organizational silence not only poses a threat to regular operations within an organization (production, sales, etc.), but also prevents leaders from being open to information that could help align their values. Particularly in the case of ethical violations within organizations, we regularly find after the fact that many employees knew about the misconduct but either did not raise their voices or leaders were not receptive to employees' criticism of the behavior.

9.3.3 Why Do Managers Fear Negative Feedback?

People often feel threatened by negative feedback and try to avoid it (Morrison & Milliken, 2000, p. 708). When people are confronted with negative feedback, there are usually four types of reactions. They may accept the feedback as correct and then try to change the situation. However, people are regularly difficult to persuade and, when they receive negative feedback, most likely tend to ignore the message, dismiss it as inaccurate, or attack the credibility of the source (Ilgen et al., 1979).

Managers seem to have an even greater fear of negative feedback because they want to avoid embarrassment, threats, and feelings of vulnerability or incompetence (Argyris & Schön, 1978). Especially when the negative feedback comes from employees, managers fear it (Ilgen et al., 1979). Part of the reason for this increased fear is probably that managers fear that the negative criticism will undermine their authority and position as a leader among employees. After all, if they accept the criticism, aren't they implicitly acknowledging that they were wrong and the employee was right? So why should the employee listen to the leader next time?

9.3.4 Why Do People in Organizations Give Negative Feedback?

It is a misconception to think that negative feedback comes from negative people. As we learned from Milliken and Morrison's concept of organizational silence, managers have implicit beliefs that many of us also share. For example, the implicit belief that employees have self-interest. For example, when employees bring up a problem via negative feedback, "This new machine won't work right!", the implicit belief could be that employees are saying this out of self-interest because they see their jobs being jeopardized by the installation of a machine that could make things more efficient. However, there could be many other reasons for employees to give this feedback. Perhaps because they really feel that the machine is not a good investment or is not working properly. Again, the motivation behind this could be self-interest (employees will have to spend more time and effort to correct the machine's work), but it could also be that employees see that it really is not an improvement, and out of the motivation to be a good and loyal employee, they fear that this could have an impact on the company. It seems to be a paradox that probably the employees who give a lot of negative feedback are actually the employees who are very loyal because they care about the issue and raise their voice.

9.3.5 How Can Organizational Silence Be Prevented?

The simple answer to how to prevent organizational silence would be to say, "Listen to your employees!". We now understand that even negative feedback can be seen as something that loyal employees bring forward as an impetus for improvement.

The second implicit belief Milliken and Morrison mentioned in their explanation of organizational silence was that "managers know better." Managers usually became managers by recruiting from within their own ranks, implying that they were more experienced or knowledgeable than their peers. It could also be that the manager was recruited externally, meaning that a better candidate than current employees was needed to fill the vacancy. This implicitly states that the manager has more skills than the employees to make the right decisions. Finally, the manager was **selected** based on his qualities and proved to be a better fit than the other team members.

But even though this manager should then theoretically have more qualities than the employees, this of course does not mean that the manager is infallible and therefore always right about everything! The combined knowledge and experience of the team could be much more valuable than that of the individual manager.

It may be difficult for some leaders to acknowledge this, but: You are not always right, even if you think you are! And even if you ARE right, you are not always right, because the perception of your employees IS the reality of your employees. In other words: If the majority of your employees see things differently, that could be the reality. Therefore, a key skill of a mindful leader is to take into account feedback from others, especially from his or her employees.

9.3.6 Active Appreciation of Feedback: Listening

Being open to feedback is the first step. The second step is to value the feedback and pay attention to it. This means not just receiving the feedback, but really listening to it and thinking about it. The term "openness (hearkening)" is introduced here to summarize the actions that must be taken to avoid organizational silence. A good leader should be genuinely open and appreciative of feedback about ideas, goals, and the means to get there. The leader should actively encourage feedback and the gathering of this information. Listening means paying attention to what is being said, listening with attention. This does not mean that everything said is true or adhered to, it means that what is said is truly listened to with the goal of evaluating it appropriately without bias or implicit beliefs.

9.3.7 Summary

As our world is constantly changing, we need to constantly review whether we need to realign our values because we have gained more insights, received more information, or learned something new. To prevent leaders from being dogmatic, it is important to be open to feedback from others. In organizations, a major pitfall is the occurrence of what we call "organizational silence": the effect of fear of negative feedback and implicit beliefs that lead to a barrier to information moving up the hierarchy. A key skill for good leaders is the ability to be open and consider feedback from others, especially employees. We use the term "openness (hearkening)" for this. Openly accepting feedback will provide better information for leadership actions in dealing with dilemmas. In the next chapter, we will look at how to deal with the different views, values and interests that exist.

9.4 Reconciliation of Different Directions: Dealing with Dilemmas and Different Interests

9.4.1 Introduction: Good Leaders Try to Solve Dilemmas

In the first part of the chapter, we discussed the ambivalence of good leaders and "good leadership."

The difference between the two lies in the goals they pursue. Even though both types of leaders think they are doing something good, the distinguishing factor is whether they make an effort to take into account the interests of multiple stakeholders and whether they recognize the fact that reality may not be perfect for everyone involved. Dictators of the past saw it as a necessity to pursue their own goals, even at great cost to the other stakeholders. This can easily lead to major incidents and atrocities. The leaders we consider to be truly "good" leaders are those who have understood the dilemmas they have encountered in trying to achieve their goals.

Kaptein describes this element in his "diamond of leadership integrity" model and calls it "congruence." This means that this type of leader sees the organization as a means of creating value for society as a whole and tries to deal with the dilemmas and different interests of the stakeholders in such a way that they achieve a balanced situation via some kind of compromise, reconciliation, or ideally a win-win situation (Kaptein, 2003, p. 103).

Another author who has tried to describe a model for dealing with dilemmas is Trompenaars. In his dilemma-consequence model, he presents a kind of helix that shows how the different values and interests can conflict with each other, but that a better solution should be sought through arguments and compromise (Hampden-Turner & Trompenaars, 2000).

9.4.2 *What Is a Dilemma?*

As we saw in Sect. 9.1, a dilemma is a situation in which two options are obviously in conflict. A dilemma can be defined as a difficult choice between two or more interests or values that requires moral deliberation and consistent action. The example of the trolley dilemma described earlier showed that doing nothing would result in the death of five people. But pulling the lever would result in the killing of one person. Neither option is perfect. One could say that doing nothing would lead to the additional death of four people. You could also say that pulling the lever would make you responsible for the death of that one person.

As a (business) leader, many decisions you have to make involve dilemmas. Actually, we all make dilemma decisions every day. But being a leader means that you have to make more decisions that have an impact on others.

Life cannot simply be squeezed into a binary scheme where there is a right and a wrong answer; it is much more complicated. What is good for one person may be bad for another. Some examples might further explain this point.

Example Dilemmas: Being CEO of a Production Company
You are the CEO of a production company in the Netherlands. As a leader, you really try to do the right thing, but during your tenure you face the following dilemmas.

(a) **Profitability vs. employee interests**
The profitability of the company is declining. This is mainly due to the legal changes in social and tax contributions, which have led to an increase in personnel costs in recent years. You have the option of moving production to another country in Asia, where lower personnel costs and favorable tax assessments await you. On the one hand, you want to support the current loyal workforce, but for the profitability and long-term survival of the company, a move to Asia is better. Shareholders prefer the option of relocating production. They also know that the proposed area for the new site has a very high unemployment rate, so these people would really be helped by the new investment. What would you do? And if you decide to relocate: When exactly will that point be reached, since it's a gradual process?

(b) **Profitability vs. environmental impact**
You have moved your production to another country where the costs are much lower. It turns out that not only the personnel costs are much lower, but also the environmental costs. This is due to the fact that the environmental laws in this country are less strict than in the previous location. This has a very positive effect on your profitability. However, your environmental consultant tells you that even though you comply with

(continued)

local legislation, he still suggests investing more in environmental measures such as filters to avoid environmental damage. However, the investment would have a negative impact on profitability. What would you do?

(c) **Employee interests vs. individual human rights**

Having solved the environmental problem, you hope for less stressful times as CEO, but unfortunately you are confronted with the news that one of your employees has been arrested by the police for violating local legislation that prohibits organizing a workers' union. Your company's code of conduct clearly states that everyone should always comply with local laws and regulations. Your code of conduct also states that your company respects basic human rights (which includes the freedom to bargain collectively). You happen to know the local police chief very well in private and you could call him. What would you do?

(d) **Loyalty to your friend vs. honesty**

After these difficult years of being a CEO, you are retiring and longing for some peace and quiet. Every week you and your wife play tennis with a neighboring couple who have become good friends. As you visit a restaurant, you suddenly bump into your neighbor who is eating there with another (much younger) woman. He confesses to you that he is having an affair, but begs you not to tell his wife about his infidelity. Under duress, you agree not to tell her. Later in the week, you meet his wife at the tennis club while he is away, and she breaks down in tears that she has no idea why their relationship is falling apart. She asks you if you know why her husband has been acting so strange lately. What would you do?

9.4.3 The Different Options for Resolving a Dilemma Through Reconciliation and Feedback

In the examples, the dilemmas clearly have two values that appear to collide. These values can be plotted on a graph to show what the theoretical options are for resolving the dilemma. Take the first example of the "*profitability vs. employee interests*" dilemma. These values can be plotted against each other in the diagram (Fig. 9.1).

In this example, the x-axis would represent the value "profitability" and the y-axis the value "employee interests". Now let's go through the different options. Option A would be an action where you would not contribute to the profitability of the company or the welfare of the employees. In this example, that would be if you as the CEO (and let's also assume for the benefit of the discussion the owner and sole decision maker) thought that the company was obviously no longer profitable and decided to close the company. Everyone would be laid off and the company would cease operations.

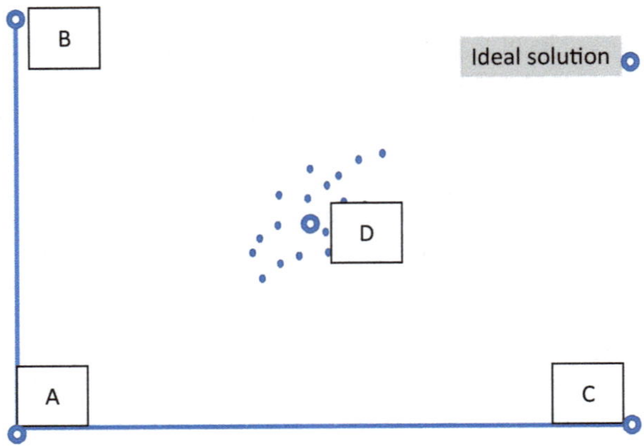

Fig. 9.1 Graphic of reconciliation options

Option B would be the variant where you, as CEO, would opt for "employee interests". In this case, this could be an option where you would stay at the current location and try to keep the jobs of your loyal employees. Your outcome on the "employee interests" axis would be great, but the outcome on the "profitability" axis would be zero. In fact, if the situation worsens, you will start losing money, which could also lead to bankruptcy in the long run. This would be an argument against this option, put forward by proponents of options that are more focused on profitability.

Option C would be the option where you go for full profitability. You try to operate at the new location in the new country with a minimum of relocation costs and no severance payments for the laid-off employees. Thus, no points are scored on the "employee interest" axis. Focusing on minimizing costs can have unexpected consequences in the long run. One example might be that pressure to obtain permits can lead to illegal actions such as falsifying documents or bribing local officials, which can have serious personal and financial consequences later.

Option D would be an option where you try to find some kind of compromise. In other words, you try to reconcile the two values by finding a solution that supports both values. In this example case, you want to move to the new location, but you also have a redundancy plan for your employees, which costs you some profitability. Not a perfect solution, and you achieve 50% on both axes.

Well, what would be the perfect solution to this dilemma? The ideal solution would achieve maximum on both axes. How could you achieve full profitability while ensuring the well-being of your current employees? Please consider for yourself for a moment if you can come up with a new and creative solution to this case that is different from the options presented.

You probably don't know the perfect answer directly, but you would also have some alternatives. You decide to share your dilemma with many different people. You discuss the issue with the works council and unions and ask other CEOs how they have dealt with similar situations. You involve shareholders and outside investors. In other words, you ask other people what they would do. Many share their views with you and provide feedback on your plans. There are many alternative courses of action. These are shown as gray dots in the graphic. The reality is that they are probably all not the perfect solution to your problem, but some of them will offer you new insights, spark creative out-of-the-box thinking, or provide truly innovative ideas. By sharing the dilemma and listening to feedback, you will be able to come up with a better alternative solution than what you initially had in mind. Again, the reality may be that even then you won't get the perfect answer, but very likely there will be an alternative that is better than what you initially considered as extreme options or alternatives.

9.4.4 Summary

Leaders are constantly confronted with dilemmas. Good leaders try to resolve their dilemma in a constructive way by taking into account the different values and interests that clash in the dilemma. When people are first confronted with a dilemma, they tend to look at it from an either-or perspective. For example, it's either profitability *or* employee well-being. This binary view leads to the selection of "extreme" options. The reality is much more balanced. When people take a little more time to think about an issue, they become aware of this complexity and try to resolve the dilemma in a constructive way that reconciles opposing interests. If they take the time and effort to gather information and feedback from others, the chances of finding a more balanced solution to the dilemma increase. Reality is not a perfect world, so finding a perfect solution to a real dilemma will usually be difficult.

9.5 Use Authority as a Leader for the Common Good

9.5.1 Introduction: The Role of Managers in Ethical Incidents

Before we describe the Mindful Ethical Leadership (MEL) model in Sect. 9.6, let's explore a bit of the opposite. Unethical leadership would consist of a leader manipulating those being led into doing something really bad. History shows that many unethical behaviors originate from bad leaders giving orders to their led. Why do people follow these orders from unethical leaders, sometimes even when they see and understand that the actions they are asking them to do are unethical? Why are people so easily manipulated? This is what we explore in this chapter to learn how to use this knowledge as a "force for good" in our model of Mindful Ethical Leadership.

9.5.2 All Organizations Are Hierarchies with Leaders

Human collaboration is usually based on organization. An organization is a tool that facilitates cooperation to achieve specific goals. The term is derived from the Greek word organon, which means a tool or instrument (Morgan, 1997, p. 15). Within an organization, people work together to achieve a common goal. Individuals work together on the basis of mutual consent. A key element of organization is that work is divided within the group so that some sort of specialization occurs. However, this separation also requires coordination tasks. This leads to a structure in which a hierarchy is created: "coordinators" stand above various others to coordinate their collaboration. In a sense, then, the managerial task is separate from the executive task. Therefore, almost all human organizations have a hierarchy.

Biologist de Waal asserts that our ancestors evolved over millions of years into hierarchically structured societies with strong personal interconnectedness (De Waal, 1996, p. 194). While they may disagree on the origin of formal cooperation, both anthropologists and biologists agree that humans cooperate in organizational contexts and that this organizing aspect of society has slowly but steadily evolved into a regulated society. Family, neighborhood, friends, work, government, army, religion, and business are types of organizations.

Therefore, when something fails, people always look for two things: first, the person who made the mistake, and second, the manager who is partly responsible for the mistake. We expect leaders to also monitor the work of employees. You will hear that leaders are "responsible." This applies to the primary process, but also to ethical incidents. For example, if there is a compliance violation in a bank, not only would the rogue trader be brought to justice, but management would also be held accountable to determine if they are taking their responsibilities seriously enough. You can read examples of this in the newspapers every day.

In addition to the issue of responsibility, we also regularly see ethical incidents emanating from people in leadership positions (Machiavellians are not surprised by this). Usually, it involves a person in power ordering others to perform unethical activities. It seems that people are extremely inclined to follow leaders. As we can learn from De Waal, this originates from the fact that we are trained from early childhood to follow authority (think of parents telling the child what to do). This effect has been going on in our evolution for thousands of years.

9.5.3 The Extreme Power of Authority

As De Waal has pointed out, humans have inherited this evolutionarily developed system for our behavior. Our behavior is certainly not based on rationality alone. Because of our cognitive and temporal limitations in reality, it is simply not possible for us to base actions on rationality alone. Simon first pointed this out in his concept of "bounded rationality" (Simon, 1947). Decision makers, in this view, act as *satisfiers*, seeking a satisfactory rather than an optimal solution. But in addition to the limits of our rationality, there are also biological factors that influence our behavior. Just as we humans have a biologically incorporated and evolutionarily developed fear of spiders and snakes or fear of heights (some people have these more than others), we also seem to have developed a kind of default response to authority that leads to obedience.

9.5.3.1 Different Forms of Authority

In this context of ethical leadership, we speak of authority when a person's instructions are followed without regard to the content. It is about the person who gives the instructions. Authority can be divided into personal authority and legitimate authority. In the case of personal authority, the reason for following the instructions is the personal characteristics of the leader.

Legitimate authority exists when instructions are followed because of the position or role that the authority has. People feel obligated to follow instructions because of the position the person holds within an organization. Examples of legitimate authority include the police officer controlling traffic, the teacher in front of the class, or the manager in charge of the department.

Authority is an important prerequisite for compliance within organizations. When rules are stated by people who have a certain authority within the organization, those rules are more likely to be followed by employees. In many organizations, authority is embedded in the organizational structure. All organizations operate to a greater or lesser degree with some form of hierarchy. The hierarchy within the organization assigns authority to individuals. Following an instruction then happens "because the manager says so."

The existence of a hierarchy in which individuals with decision-making authority make decisions is very effective for compliance within an organization. The people with authority can enforce compliance within the organization. At the same time, "authority" also has a downside for compliance: what if the content of the message of authority does not match the (organizational) rules? Will people then follow the rule or command of authority?

9.5.3.2 Obedience to Authority: The Milgram Experiment

History has shown that people can do very bad things. That bad people act negatively is obvious to us. But can good people also do bad things? The idea that there is a clear distinction between good and bad people is a comforting one, as it defines "bad" as a binary entity that is present as a trait in some people and not in others (Zimbardo, 2007, p. 6).

Scientists have studied the effect of authority on human behavior. The best, most famous, and perhaps most extreme example is Stanley Milgram's experiment (Milgram, 1963). This experiment measured the willingness of participants to follow the directions of an authority, even if that direction violated their own conscience.

The Milgram Experiment

Milgram asked subjects to participate in a study of the effect of electric shocks on memory. The subject had to administer electric shocks to another subject. In reality, however, no electric shocks were administered, but the subjects were portrayed by actors. The study wanted to see to what extent the subjects subordinated their own conscience to the authority of the professor who was conducting the experiment. The subject was thus told what to do by the professor. So the experiment was really looking at the relationship between obedience and authority and how people would behave when their own moral judgment was in conflict with the instruction given by authority.

Surprisingly, many people would subject the subject to very high, dangerous, and even lethal electric shocks. Although the psychologists originally anticipated that few sadists would be willing to give the maximum voltage of 450 volts, the results were shocking. In the first series of experiments, more than 66 percent of the participants delivered the maximum shock of 450 volts, even though many felt very uncomfortable doing so.

Thus, the research has shown that when authority is accepted, people are very inclined to follow orders even if it goes against their own judgment and values.

9.5.4 Summary

When people work together, they form organizations. Coordination within organizations is done through people who have some kind of authority. Due to the fact that our development has shown that it is beneficial to follow authority, we as human beings are very prone to do so. One possible risk is that this instinct is so strong that people will even follow the orders of an authority if they disagree or if it goes against their own values. This again shows how important good ethical leadership is to motivate people in the right direction. Therefore, paradoxically, authority is also one of the tools that a mindful ethical leader can use to guide behavior in the right direction.

9.6 Practical Model for Mindful Ethical Leadership: AHRA

9.6.1 Introduction: Combining the Concepts into a Practical Model

In the previous chapters, we have looked at some characteristic elements of a mindful ethical leader. Combining these various elements, we can describe a model that can serve as a guide in explaining (and suggesting) mindful ethical leadership. We use the acronym AHRA to describe the key elements of this model: Authenticity, Hearken (Openness), Reconciliation, and Authority.

Authenticity
The ethical leader begins with a clear set of values that are authentic and provide clear direction. True leadership begins with authentic values and beliefs. The leader sets the direction and provides clarity.

Hearken
The term "openness" is used to summarize the actions that must be taken to avoid organizational silence. A good leader should be open and appreciative of feedback on ideas, goals, and means. The leader should *actively* encourage feedback and the gathering of this information. Listening means paying attention to what is being said, listening with attention.

Reconciliation
A good leader should be able to reconcile the different interests and goals of different people in the best possible way. Reconciliation is the third step in the model, where the different inputs (openness) and the leader's own opinions and values (authenticity) are weighted. Authenticity and reconciliation are in some ways opposites, but both must be present, and the good leader has the ability to balance them.

Authority
Only in the final phase of Mindful Ethical Leadership can the tool of authority be used. When the leader has established the authentic goals and values, been open to feedback and the interest of others, then actively sought to reconcile this in a constructive way for the benefit of the most people, only then can the tool of authority be applied.

In this model, authority is in some ways the opposite of openness, but both are necessary to make things work, because as we learned in the chapter on dilemmas: In reality, there will be no perfect solution. There will always be someone who disagrees or has their interest hurt. But then it is also the responsibility of the leader to make things happen. This is a different way of exercising authority than in the case of leaders who do so solely on the basis of their own interests.

9.6.2 Practical Tips for Developing Authenticity

Authenticity starts with yourself. You need to know what you stand for, what your values are and what you want to achieve. Once you have clarified this for yourself, it is also easier to communicate this more clearly to other members of the organization. A good starting point for articulating your most important values would be the following exercise.

9.6.2.1 Basic Values Exercise

1. Write down three of your core values;
2. For all three values, explain exactly what they mean to you;
3. Describe how these three values are evident in your personal life;
4. Describe how these three values are evident in your work environment;
5. Think of a hypothetical situation that would violate your three core values and explain why this would be difficult for you;

Consider for yourself if there would be a difference in your core values for your personal life and in your professional role.

You can use the results of this exercise as a guide for yourself as to what your most important values are that you want to uphold in your personal and professional life.

9.6.2.2 Communication Tips for Authenticity

As described in the chapter on authenticity, it's not only important to have clarity about your own values, it's also important to communicate this clearly to others. I remember that almost every time I see the results of employee satisfaction surveys, the term "communication" is mentioned as a point of improvement. It's hard for leaders to over-communicate. Most of the time, leaders tend to think they are communicating well, but they don't regularly check it with the people they are addressing. This is another factor that could unintentionally stimulate the effect of "organizational silence." Therefore, some tips for leaders to improve their communication about their authenticity.

1. Clarity: conveying the message in a different form or explaining it in a different way can make it more understandable to different people
2. Repetition: Messages are improved by repetition.
3. Alternatives: Not everyone attended your meeting, read the newsletter, or read the company intranet.
4. Refresh: over time, the memory of the message fades, so repeat it.
5. Specification: When you talk about ethics and values in a general sense, it is hard for people to understand what that would mean to them. Try to give concrete and specific examples of what that would mean to you/all of us in the organization.
6. Honesty: Also explain why it is sometimes difficult to follow your core values. Give examples of dilemmas in the organization. This will also lend credibility to your message as it is current and realistic.

9.6.3 Practical Tips for Promoting Openness

How can you ***actively*** encourage feedback and information gathering? As we have seen, managers' implicit beliefs can influence their perceptiveness to feedback from employees. Some tips for staying open to feedback from employees are listed here:

1. **Ask for feedback after presentations.**
   Get into the habit of asking for feedback directly after you've presented something. This way, you specifically address the possibility of feedback and signal that anyone can speak up. If you do this consistently, it lowers the barrier to comments.
2. **Always ask for feedback after formal performance evaluations.**
   Anyone who has experienced a (negative) employee review meeting where there was no opportunity to respond can confirm what this accomplishes: You are probably no longer very motivated to give feedback to your supervisor on any topic. It is therefore crucial that in formal performance reviews you always give the other person the opportunity to respond and provide feedback on the content, but also on the process of the performance review.
3. **"My door is always open ..." NO! Go out and visit me.**
   It's more effective to invite people inside. Or sit down with your team members in the office garden. Bring coffee to your colleagues. I remember a former CEO waiting in line downstairs at the coffee machine. While waiting, he would chat with other employees. Since this happened frequently, it helped him connect with employees in an informal way. It helped employees to contact him whenever they wanted to address a problem.

   I also remember a human resources manager at another organization who regularly asked her secretary to leave the office and go to a coffee shop two blocks away to get the type of specialty coffee requested by the human resources manager.
4. **Stay in touch with employees who have left your organization or team.**
   Even if we like our colleagues and enjoy staying in touch, our daily work and lives prevent us from staying actively in touch. Try to schedule time to stay in touch with former colleagues on a regular basis. By staying in touch with people, you show that the person is important to you, that your interest is genuine. Since these people know you and your work environment, they may be able to give you very good feedback on situations without holding back because of their hierarchical position.
5. **Listen to employees with more experience.**
   The value of experience is easily underestimated. Employees who have been with the organization or team for a long time can provide a lot of valuable input. Management literature often refers to it as a problem that

(continued)

employees do not want change, but this should not lead to the conclusion that more experienced employees are not positive about change and for this reason only give negative feedback. It is also valuable to learn what the possible reasons for reluctance to change are.

6. **Ask specific questions.**

   Don't just ask for 'feedback'. Be specific! Ask what the benefits of new ideas are. Ask what might be a potential risk. Ask what they would like to see improved further. Ask what employees think of the specific process/ product and why.

9.6.4 Practical Tips for the Creative Dilemma Reconciliation

The ability to reconcile the different interests and goals of different people is something that requires a lot of creativity. As mentioned in the chapter on reconciliation, it will be difficult to find a perfect solution to a real dilemma. Reconciliation in practice means taking a structured approach to dilemma situations and consciously searching for the creative "fifth" answer.

Here we describe a 9-step approach to dealing with a dilemma and finding the best possible alternative.

1. Recognize **a dilemmatic situation and define a problem as a "dilemma" for which there is no direct perfect answer**
2. Define the relevant **facts**: What is the exact situation?
3. List all the **stakeholders** involved: Who is involved?
4. Define the **problem**: Why is this a problem and for whom?
5. Define the problem in the **conflict of values**: which values clash?
6. Formulate **alternative options**: What are all the possible options you can think of?
7. Discuss the dilemma with **others**: What do other people give as possible options?
8. List all **advantages and disadvantages of** the identified alternatives.
9. Choose the best alternative.
10. Dare to implement the alternative you have chosen!

9.6.5 *Practical Tips for Using Authority as a Force for Good*

As described earlier: Authority can be an extremely effective tool in organizations, but it also carries the ethical risk of being abused by bad leaders because people are very susceptible to authority. Therefore, it can only be used as the final step in the Mindful Ethical Leadership model, i.e., only when the leader has established the authentic goals and values, been open to feedback and the interest of others, and then actively and constructively aligned this for the benefit of the largest group of people.

In any case, the ability to use authority is a necessary skill in a leader's toolbox. The leader must be able to set boundaries (authenticity), but this is only effective if there is also the power to enforce it when the boundaries are crossed. Setting goals creates clarity, but is only useful if there are consequences if they are not met. It is a strange paradox that on the one hand people are very receptive to the power of authority, but at the same time many leaders find it difficult to be strict and enforce sanctions. The reason for this is that most people prefer to be led in a coaching style, and therefore prefer this style when leading others. Kaptein uses the example of managing with a "gentle hand" (Kaptein, 2003). Sanctions and punishments are not something that will make you popular as a person.

Authority is certainly not just about sanctioning, but also about demanding and enforcing desired behavior. A good manager therefore dares to take unpopular measures. In the words of Machiavelli: It is better to be feared than loved. The reason for this is that a manager who does not respond to employees who do not perform or does not sanction misconduct loses credibility more quickly than a manager who sanctions too harshly or makes too high demands on his employees.

Therefore, the practical tips provided here focus on how a leader can consciously use his or her authority by developing enforcement and sanctioning skills.

9.6.5.1 Practical Tips for Using Authority as a Tool

1. Be a role model: Authority grows from the fact that your authority is not only based on your hierarchical position, but that you are credible because of your competencies, work ethic and other skills. Therefore, it is important to be confident and also actively show your abilities. For example: you should not be the last one at work and the first to leave ...
2. Reward good behavior: Praise those who do something right. We can call this positive reinforcement.
3. Set high goals for your employees: By high goals, we don't just mean production goals, but these can also be quality, competence and value-related goals.

(continued)

4. Talk about enforcement: make it clear why it is necessary to enforce a certain behavior so it is clear where the boundaries are.
5. Enforce goals: Even when employees have performed well, it is never perfect. Therefore, keep striving for perfectionism and always discuss the improvement points.
6. Let consequences take effect quickly: When something goes wrong, the consequences need to happen quickly so that the context is clear.
7. Stick to a routine: Important things need to stay important. For example, if you set up a weekly team meeting, stick to it and make it known that people who miss the meeting will be sanctioned. Don't forget to give the most boring task to the person who didn't attend the meeting!
8. Establish a distance: you are the leader and therefore some things must remain the leader's area of competence and privilege. Distance in this sense creates authority. Your employees don't have to be your friends and they don't have to be invited to your birthday party. Don't link up with your employees on social media.
9. Don't allow disobedience: Don't be intimidated by anyone who challenges your authority, but act quickly and decisively. There is nothing to be gained by yielding when your authority is challenged.
10. Be fair: don't abuse your authority, as there is a risk that this will have a negative effect on you in the long run. If you use your authority for the right purposes, people will respect your authority even more.

9.6.5.2 Exercising Authority: Dare to Use Your Authority!

As described earlier, many leaders find it difficult to use authority in a negative way to enforce or sanction. Therefore, in this exercise we try to stimulate the use of your authority.

1. Week 1: During a work week, keep a short diary of issues that did not go according to plan.
   (a) Why did this happen?
   (b) Who was responsible?
   (c) What were your first thoughts upon learning the facts?
   (d) How did you actually respond to the person in charge?
   (e) In hindsight, would you say you were too harsh or too lenient with the person?
2. Week 2: Again, keep a journal of things that went wrong, but now review this daily.

(a) Why did this happen?
(b) Who was responsible?
(c) What were your first thoughts upon learning the facts?
(d) How did you actually respond to the person in charge?
(e) In hindsight, would you say you were too harsh or too lenient with the person?
(f) What will you do about this tomorrow and how will you communicate this to the person in charge and other employees?

9.6.6 Summary

The AHRA model is presented as one cycle (see Fig. 9.2), but at the same time there are two equilibria to be found within the cycle. This directly shows why managers always have to make difficult decisions and that reality is not a binary situation but a constant cycle of finding equilibria.

The first balancing act is to be authentic and stick to your values, but also change your values and opinions and balance the different interests. The second is to sometimes be open to feedback and value other opinions and at the same time be dominant and use authority to continue the process and get things done.

There are no clear guidelines for finding these balances; it is always situational. It is a competency that leaders can develop over time as they gain experience in dealing with various challenging dilemmas and as they develop their ability to be authentic, to listen, to reconcile interests, and to use authority to move forward. The mindful ethical leader is aware of these difficulties and knows that this is a continuous improvement process where things are constantly changing. The mindful ethical leader understands this change and sees his leadership as something that needs

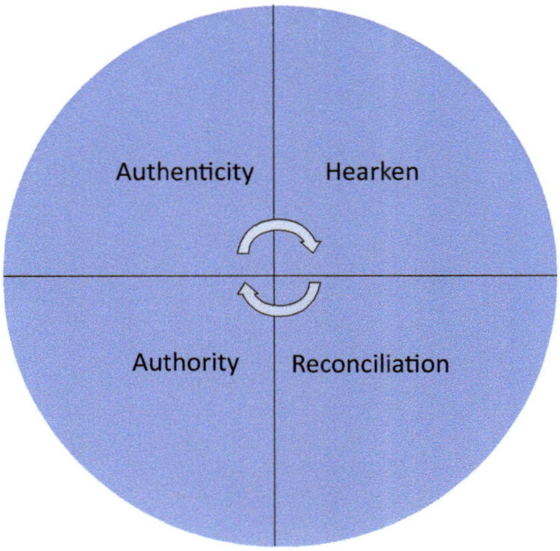

Fig. 9.2 AHRA model for mindful ethical leadership

constant attention and improvement. The Mindful Ethical Leadership model can provide insight and structure to see this personal process more clearly.

References

Argyris, C., & Schön, D. A. (1978). *Learning organizations: A theory of action perspective*. Addison-Wesley.

Bleske-Rechek, A., Nelson, L. A., Baker, J. P., Remiker, M. W., & Brandt, S. J. (2010). Evolution and the trolley problem: People save five over one unless the one is young, genetically related, or a romantic partner. *Journal of Social, Evolutionary, and Cultural Psychology, 4*(3), 115.

Conger, J. A., & Kanungo, R. N. (1987). Toward a behavioral theory of charismatic leadership in organizational settings. *Academy of Management Review, 12*(4), 637–647.

de Waal, F. B. M. (1996). *Van Nature Goed*. Contact.

Foot, P. (1967). The problem of abortion and the doctrine of the double effect. Reprinted in *Virtues and Vices and Other Essays in Moral Philosophy* (1978).

Hampden-Turner, C., & Trompenaars, F. (2000). *Building cross-cultural competence: How to create wealth from conflicting values*. Wiley.

Hauser, M., Cushman, F., Young, L., Kang-Xing Jin, R., & Mikhail, J. (2007). A dissociation between moral judgments and justifications. *Mind & Language, 22*(1), 1–21.

Ilgen, D., Fischer, C., & Taylor, M. (1979). Consequences of individual feedback on behavior in organizations. *Journal of Applied Psychology, 64*, 349–371.

Kaptein, M. (2003). The diamond of managerial integrity. *European Management Journal, 21*, 99–108.

Milgram, S. (1963). Behavioural study of obedience. *Journal of Abnormal Psychology, 67*, 371–378.

Morgan, G. (1997). *Images of organization* (p. 15). Sage.

Morrison, E. W., & Milliken, F. J. (2000). Organizational silence: A barrier to change and development in a pluralistic world. *Academy of Management Review, 25*(4), 706–725.

Simon, H. A. (1947). *Administrative behavior: A study of decision-making processes in administrative organizations* (4th ed.). The Free Press.

Weber, M. (1947). *The theory of social and economic organization*, trans. AM Henderson and Talcott Parsons (New York, 1947).

Zimbardo, P. (2007). *The Lucifer effect*. Rider.

Chapter 10
Digitalization as a Challenge for Mindful Leadership

Kristina Bodrožić-Brnić and Thomas Thiessen

10.1 Introduction

Digital transformation is in its full swing. But it is not purely a technology matter; it must also focus on people. Change management, leadership, innovation and communication are key to the successful digitalization of companies. The following article describes how mindful leadership can support the creation of technology acceptance and design motivation at all hierarchical levels of a company organization.

10.2 Mindful Leadership Between Psycho-Cliché and Agile Transformation Events

The term "mindful leadership" is polarizing. For some, it sounds like the magic word of contemporary leadership; for others, it is a polemically commented cliché of a management understanding which is far removed from reality. After all, mindful leadership has arrived not only semantically in everyday management, but also as the aspiration and goal of a management generation which has left the business schools and now wants to steadily bring its soft skills into the work organization.

Digital transformation reinforces this trend, but it also promotes the further polarization of mindful leadership, because when it comes to digital transformation and the changes that come with it, organizations and companies are often driven into

K. Bodrožić-Brnić (✉)
World Tribe Communications, Potsdam, Germany
e-mail: kristina@worldtribe.de

T. Thiessen
BSP Business and Law School, University for Business and Law Studies, Berlin, Germany

V. Schulte et al. (eds.), *Mindful Leadership in Practice*,
https://doi.org/10.1007/978-3-030-97311-7_10

an experiential maze that is full of unpredictable events. It is not always clear from the outset where the path will lead, what is needed to achieve it, and what challenges those involved will encounter. In the course of digital transformation, companies and institutions must constantly face new framework conditions and be able to react quickly to changes. Digitalization ensures that time is running faster and faster. The pace of innovation is increasing inexorably.

With all this speed and the will to keep up, two important aspects are often neglected: the corporate culture and the associated active integration of employees in the change process. Yet, the real success of digital transformation lies in people and their creative ideas. Without the commitment and acceptance of a company's employees, digital transformation will not succeed. Neither guidelines nor (business) calculations are enough. Three factors though are crucial for the success of digitalization processes in companies: motivation, communication and knowledge.

It all starts with the motivation of managers in their respective departments. With the conviction that digitalization will secure the future of their company, they pass on their willingness to change to the workforce in an exemplary manner. At the same time, targeted internal communication promotes acceptance of digital changes across all hierarchical levels. In addition, a wide range of methods is available to bring managers into a constructive dialog with each other and with the workforce when it comes to digitalization. In this process, expert knowledge significantly reduces scepticism and resistance to digital changes, and digital forms of training also give small and medium-sized companies (SMEs) the opportunity to offer their employees needs-based training courses on digitalization. In the end, all those involved in the digitalization process must be brought along on the path in their respective self-image, whether as entrepreneurs, heads of specialist departments or as operational personnel.

Such a transition process must closely accompany the introduction of technology. Participative leadership, communicative transparency and an open ear for any fears help to reduce resistance. Networked collaboration 4.0 is therefore not just about machines. Without people, sustainable digitalization will not be feasible. These rather "soft" factors of successful change management, which focus on trust, communication, leadership and innovation, promote mindful leadership as a management tool, especially among young managers.

But why does the term "mindful leadership" also meet with strong cliché reservations and sometimes trigger fierce defensive reactions? Apparently, the mindfulness cliché opens up the associative world of a psychotherapeutically backed mainstream for many managers, which stands in blatant contradiction to business success criteria. At the same time, we observe that in many organizations, especially medium-sized ones, the gap between the "mindful" leadership claim and the experienced or lived leadership reality is widening. The topic of digital transformation in particular reinforces this defensive attitude trend in the direction of mindfulness. For many executives, the perceived pressure to find concrete steps geared to the company and to get started with digitalization is at odds with mindful management methods. Day-to-day business must continue. Digital restructuring measures must happen quickly, efficiently and in the background. Information must be easy to understand, easy to find, and tailored to business needs. All this contributes to associating mindful leadership not only with modern, dynamizing change methods, but also with system-inhibiting self-employment.

10.3 Mindful Leadership: What It Is and What It Is Not

For half a century, meditative mindfulness practices have also become established in Western cultural circles. A steadily growing number of managers are applying methods of heightened awareness to get entrepreneurial goals on track. In an average company today, four generations work together, from the so-called "baby boomers" to the so-called "Generation Z." Communication among them is influenced by factors such as educational level, cultural environment, their own experiences and the impact of technological opportunities. The topic of mindful leadership has been gaining increasing attention over the past decade. Apps such as *7Mind* and *Headspace* are increasingly in demand, with the current pandemic situation with its trend toward home offices providing additional momentum.

But what exactly does Mindfulness practice, how does it help against stress, and why is Mindfulness suitable as a leadership tool?

Mindfulness is an increase of one's own perception within the currently lived moment. Everything that appeals to our senses can be perceived by the human brain in context or separately. In the process of perception, according to the philosophy of Mindfulness, what is perceived should not be evaluated. This system of non-judgmental mindfulness is massively influenced by Far Eastern meditation practices. However, meditation does not mean retreating to Buddhist monasteries or relaxing on yoga mats. Instead, meditation takes place in quite complex day-ro-day, mindfulness exercises—for example, when breathing consciously in and out. Sensing one's own body in the interaction of all the senses can create a focused presence in the present moment and help to perceive as many aspects of one's surroundings as possible, which provide information about the current situation.

This is the interface to the idea of mindfulness leadership, because traditional leadership typologies are of little use in the context of digital change processes. The executive floors of many companies are already more diverse than they were years ago in terms of the age, origin, education and gender of their members. What is needed is the ability to shape the future with a view to permanent change, and one of the most important skills in dealing with such challenges is the ability to focus in order to promote calmness in thinking before acting.

10.4 Mindfulness as a Dialogue Tool

Mindfulness practice builds the capacity for heightened attention in the meditation process and then refocuses attention on noticing. Practices associated with mindfulness have been consciously researched since the 1950s (Lenzen et al., 2014).

Numerous studies have documented a range of positive effects on mental and physical health. For example, in 2012, neuroscientist Gaëlle Desbordes used functional magnetic resonance imaging to demonstrate lasting changes in the human brain of meditators after only two months of mediation practice. Desbordes took this research further in studies of altered self-perception in depressed patients, among others. In doing so, she found that mindfulness practice resulted in a longitudinal decrease in right amygdala activation, which in turn was associated with depression reduction (Desbordes et al., 2012). In addition, effects such as stress reduction, improvement of cognitive performance, and significant increase in concentration have been demonstrated in various studies among working subjects (Yong et al., 2011; Tang et al., 2009).

It can be concluded from this that emotional processes in the human brain become individually more controllable through mindfulness practices and can contribute to a higher resilience and performance motivation when transferred to performance requirements intended for business management. Mindfulness can also help managers to carry out their tasks with thoughtfulness, calmness and composure, and to remain capable of making decisions even under high pressure. Against this backdrop, it is hardly surprising that companies such as SAP and BASF, as well as numerous medium-sized enterprises in Germany, have massively promoted internal measures to increase mindfulness over the past 10 years.

In professional exchanges, heightened attentiveness means above all active listening and observation, and the ability to perceive even the smallest details that may be relevant for the successful implementation of (digitalization) projects. A mindful manager puts personal interests in the background when communicating and also pays sensitive attention to the concerns of employees and cooperation partners. The actual needs of the counterpart should be recorded and taken into account in the team process. Such mindful internal dialog systems serve to make an organization resilient and robust, even in the course of challenging change processes. Digitalization is always accompanied by change—both on the "outside" (new rules, work processes and areas of responsibility) and on the "inside" (changed ways of thinking and behaving). Working on the "inside" is the key to sustainable transformation: The more external structures change, the more important it is to maintain internal stability.

In this context, the term "resilience" is also becoming increasingly important. As a key competence in change processes, resilience describes the ability to better deal with stressors and strains and the ability to flexibly adapt to new framework conditions and learn new things. Resilience aims to enable individuals and organizations to maintain or redevelop their own health, quality of life and performance, as well as their enjoyment of mastering different tasks, despite pressure to change and uncertainties. This happens preferably on two levels:

- At the *individual level, the* focus is on questions like these: What are my individual needs? What resources do I still have available? Where do my personal limits lie?
- The *organizational level* is responsible for ensuring that the topic of resilience has an impact on the individual level. This requires a leadership culture that is

characterized by transparent communication and that gives sufficient space to an open exchange. This does not work as a "hack" or a switch, but as a development process with a change of attitude and perspective. The mechanisms of mindful leadership serve as an effective dialog tool here.

10.5 Practical Example of Mindful Leadership: The "SparX" Workshop Series

With the *SparX Digitaler Mittelstand* workshop series, an application example is described below which shows how mindful leadership can be used concretely as a management tool within digital transformation. The SparX series addresses managers in particular and was developed by the (former) Mittelstand 4.0 Kompetenzzentrum Kommunikation (Competence Center Communication). Under the motto "People at the center of digitalization," this competence center was initiated by the German Federal Ministry for Economic Affairs and Energy (BMWK) as a nationwide university consortium led by the BSP Business & Law School, as part of the BMWK's Mittelstand-Digital funding priority. Cooperation partner in the development of the workshop series was the VR Business Club. The SparX series follows the conviction that the starting point of any operational digitalization strategy should be the analysis of the requirements and wishes of managers and employees, but also of customers, suppliers and partners. People are at the center of technological innovation—with their visions, but also with their fears and reservations. Motivation and acceptance arise above all when new technologies can be personally tested and experienced, for example when using virtual reality (VR) or augmented reality (AR) applications. These and many other aspects of digital change processes form the thematic context of the workshop series *SparX Digitaler Mittelstand*.

The four successive working meetings focus on the question of which management methods can be used to create an open corporate and an open leadership culture. The focus is set on change management, corporate communications, trust in digital applications and business model innovation. In addition, the participating executives and entrepreneurs have the opportunity to exchange experiences, gather impetus and discuss innovative solutions together. Ideally, the workshops are accompanied by demonstration environments with experts from defined technology fields, such as VR and AR. Together with these partners, participants can be given a clear demonstration of how digital technologies work and how they can be used to meet their needs. This takes place in four workshop modules that build on each other.

10.5.1 Building Block 1: Change Management

The successful implementation of digitalization strategies is also based on a new understanding of leadership. The inner attitude, personality structures and needs of employees, customers and suppliers are the subject of the "Change Management" workshop. Leaders can self-critically reflect on their own attitude with the help of the "mindset check-up" according to Zeichhardt (2018). In this context, traditionally oriented ways of working and thinking are by no means seen as contradictory to the mindset of modern management methods, as "classic" and "agile" approaches usually complement each other in an extremely fruitful way. In order to achieve this and to better understand employees, customers and suppliers, managers can slip into different roles using the "stakeholder analysis" and the so-called "persona method". In this way, profiles for individual "digital types" can be worked out, with each type embodying specific characteristics, wishes and expectations of the digital transformation. This procedure sharpens the view for diverse decision-making and action patterns.

10.5.2 Building Block 2: Communication

Communication is an essential factor for digital change and often decisive for the success of a digitalization strategy. The alpha and omega of positively experienced digitalization processes is to actively involve all stakeholders in implementation and to allow them to help shape necessary changes. The concrete benefits of new technologies and the resulting advantages for the company and its daily work must always be apparent. The following questions must therefore be answered credibly:

- What are the concrete benefits of using digital applications?
- Do I save time and money by using such tools? And if so, how much?
- How can I get my employees excited about the upcoming changes and motivate them to actively support them?

The "World Café" method is ideal for discussing such questions. Here, digital communication tools such as AR and VR applications can be learned about and tried out at individual stations in order to build up a profound understanding of their potential uses. In a World Café, the atmosphere of a coffee house is set up. The spatial design with small tables or seating groups creates an informal atmosphere and facilitates the exchange of changing discussion partners. World Cafés are particularly suitable for introducing a topic. By repeatedly changing discussion constellations, habitual thought patterns are broken up. Participants are invited to talk about predefined topics at different tables in order to discuss different aspects of the benefits of digital applications.

10.5.3 Building Block 3: Trust in Technology

Linked technologies and digital business models place new demands on security. How can we create trust in digital technologies and IT infrastructures within our own company? The focus of the third workshop module lies on the topic of trust, because people are looking for support and orientation, especially in a change process. Traditional values such as respect and appreciation still play a major role here. A healthy approach to mistakes and empathy generally generates both, a positive effect on corporate culture and a positive attitude toward digital technologies and IT infrastructures. The multiplier effect is also at work here: Individual employees with a fundamentally positive attitude toward technology have a considerable influence on the willingness of an entire college to trust them.

To support a trusting corporate culture, the "fishbowl discussion" methodology offers a proven approach. Fishbowl discussions are initially characterized only by the special seating arrangement of the participants: In the center of a room, the discussants place themselves in a circular seating arrangement. Interested observers take their seats in another outer circle and follow the activities inside as if in a goldfish bowl (fishbowl). Talking only takes place in the inner circle discussion group, while here more chairs than participants are being provided. In this way, people from the observer group can move up to the empty seats at any time. Once the "discussion guest" has presented his point of view, he returns to the outer circle to now give others the opportunity to participate. In the inner circle, a moderator leads the discussion. A room is needed that allows for an inner circle of chairs for about 10 people and another 10 to 50 seats in outer circles. The discussion is usually based on existing work products. Fishbowl discussions help to reflect on existing concepts or solution approaches in an extended circle of participants, to defuse emotionally charged decision-making processes, to uncover contradictions and to reduce possible potential for conflict or frustration.

10.5.4 Building Block 4: Innovation Management

In the digital transformation, the importance of (digital) business model innovations is increasing. The fourth workshop module discusses how innovations can be developed and implemented as an essential part of sustainable digitalization strategies in the company. Various methodological tools are also available for effective innovation management. For example, the interactive creative method "Design Dash" supports in-house teams in finding and implementing new ideas and technical innovation concepts. This involves six steps that are carried out in rapid succession:

1. *Getting to know the team:* Each team member briefly introduces themselves.
2. *Observing someone else:* The team jointly interviews an external person about a specific issue and documents the results.

3. *Defining the subject:* The team creates a profile for the person previously interviewed and defines their needs and/or problems.
4. *Concretize an idea:* Based on the insights gained, the team develops an offer/solution for the analyzed challenge.
5. *Testing the idea: The* developed solution is presented to the external interview partner—the team receives immediate feedback.
6. *Finalize the solution:* The team optimizes its approach to the solution based on the feedback received.

The spatial design ideally allows working in different positions (e.g. sitting or standing) and the room can be quickly adapted to group or individual work situations. The spatial atmosphere is also of great importance for successful work with the design dash method and can thus contribute to a comparatively fast finding of concrete approaches to solutions.

10.6 Mindful Leadership also Means: Playing, Traveling, Educating Together

The application of the SparX workshops follows the guiding principle that digitalization should be understood only secondarily as a technology issue and primarily as a mindset issue. The success of operational digitalization processes can be defined by many factors. One of the most important is the inner attitude toward change and transformation. When it comes to the inner attitude—the mindset—of an employee in the context of digitalization, there is no "right" or "wrong". On the contrary, it is often hybrid organizational forms that support companies in implementing sustainable change management. In this context, it is above all the "ambidexterity" which makes it possible to consider different perspectives depending on the situation and to act in an agile manner. This is where methods of mindful leadership can effectively reinforce digital transformation. In addition to the toolbox of methods described above in the context of the SparX series, there are many other management approaches in the context of mindful leadership that lead to greater communication skills and acceptance within organizations. By way of example, we would like to mention two approaches here that primarily address the "playfulness" and "adventurousness" of the actors involved.

10.7 Stakeholder Analysis: Identify Stakeholders and Take a Closer Look at Them

In every company, a wide variety of interest groups come together. These include employees, the company's own customers, and partners. In the context of digitalization, these can be assigned to different "digital types", which can be defined by different competencies, wishes and fears. A good assessment of the interest groups leads to more trust and a successful exchange in collaboration. With knowledge of the different points of view and wishes, but also of possible hurdles and fears, the individual stakeholders in a change process can be addressed in a much more targeted manner and motivated to participate actively. In a workshop lasting about two hours, the participants (managers, employees and/or external partners) develop personality descriptions for four exemplary "digital types". Specific characteristics and traits are collected on flipcharts on the criteria of interests, attitude toward technology, fears, desires and communication behavior. After the moderator has presented the exemplary "digital types," the participants add further personality traits from their own experience and look for approaches to the best way to address them (tonality, media, topics).

10.8 LEGO® SERIOUS PLAY®: Playfully Developing Digital Strategies

LEGO ® SERIOUS PLAY® describes a facilitated process that combines the joy of modeling with business issues. The method helps to develop new ideas, improve communication and design solutions to problems. Using a variety of different LEGO® building blocks, workshop participants develop detailed models in successive building phases that objectify different aspects of given questions. In a moderated work process, the individual components are finally assembled into a common model. In this way, a partnership-based exchange between different interest groups succeeds as they jointly search for solutions to an overarching issue—for example, an upcoming digitalization process. The LEGO® elements also include various animal figures that are assigned to specific associations in a business context (for example, the lion is usually associated with leadership positions, while an elephant is more likely to be associated with resilient employees), as well as human figures that can be assigned specific roles. Following each building phase, participants explain their design intentions. Beyond the working materials from the "LEGO® SERIOUS PLAY®" series, workstations for modeling and a flipchart or metaplan wall are needed. The workshops should be supervised by methodologically experienced facilitators.

10.9 Digitalization Journey: Identifying Your Own Innovation Potential and Developing Digital Innovations

The digitalization journey is an intuitive method for quickly identifying innovation potential. It describes a simple but effective method for finding suitable starting points for a digital transformation within the organization. It helps to break down barriers to thinking, get people talking to each other, and get ideas for business model innovations bubbling away. The digitalization journey clarifies points of contact with the customer and starting points for innovation from different perspectives (customer, product, time horizon, and many more). First, a time horizon and one of the various possible perspectives are defined. Employees, customers as well as products can be mapped. Through free brainstorming in as diverse a team as possible (within the company or in external workshop situations), the current state is depicted in a cycle. There are basically no "wrong" impulses. In a second round, this "journey" can be used to find interfaces with customers and concrete starting points for different needs. That also involves identifying threats to the company's own business, e.g., competitors from other industries. This creates new starting points for innovation.

10.10 Online Seminars: Sustainable and Effective Qualification

Knowledge creates (self-)trust and (new) motivation to help shape digital transformation processes. In this respect, the establishment of a structured internal qualification culture in the company is an essential instrument of mindful leadership. Online seminars in particular are always excellently suited when low-threshold communication offerings are to be implemented for customers, suppliers and employees as part of mindful leadership. Good online seminars require specific preparation and suitable technical equipment, although the technology is now available at a reasonable price. In any case, content and interaction must be individually tailored and prepared. To this end, technical and didactic information should be collected, prepared and, if possible, tried out in typical practice situations. Webinars are different from offline seminars: It is not enough to transfer experiences and concepts from the analog world to the web. In order to regularly welcome attentive and positively minded participants, the following five questions should always be asked and answered when preparing a webinar:

- What content is suitable for an online seminar?
- Which interaction options should be used in the webinar?
- What technology is necessary to ensure good quality?
- What are the specific requirements for the presentation slides?
- What should I pay attention to during the implementation?

10.11 A Methodical and Managerial Understanding of Mindful Leadership

Again and again, mindfulness is associated with an esoterically intended inwardness that has a strong impact on individual self-perception and is not only alien to the sober business concerns of corporate organization, but even opposes them.

Indeed, the topic of mindfulness is subject to the danger of articulating itself as a self-referential inward-looking system and confirming all reservations as a fashionable topic. However, the transition methods described above also show that mindful leadership can be charged with structured and sustainably effective management tools, especially in the context of digital change processes, and can be developed into an important internal engine. In this sense, we advocate understanding mindful leadership in large as well as in SMEs as an interactive dialog concept in order to create new communication architectures and use them as innovation drivers. Only in this way will Mindfulness be accepted even by more "conventionally" oriented leaders and can be implemented as an important new impulse in one's own understanding of leadership.

This is all the more important because the much-described developments of a digitalized "VUCA World" in all their innovative power and agility do not lead to the business management criteria of a "healthy" company being invalidated. On the contrary, digitalization is subject in a special way to the requirement to serve traditional key performance indicator systems via efficiency increases, market development dynamics and business innovation models. The economic goals of a company have by no means changed even in the so-called "Fourth Industrial Revolution" with its implementation of self-controlling cyber-physical systems, the Internet of Things, Deep Machine Learning and virtual production environments. They are subject to the identical economic logics as in Henry Ford's time.

But precisely because this is the case, mindfulness must become a stronger focus of management action. What was true in the past—the insight that innovations are thought and made by people—is even more true in the age of digital transformation. Managers are jugglers who keep an eye on many different issues, keep the balls of different projects in the air at the same time and have to constantly adapt to new dynamic starting conditions. They are also challenged to deal with high complexity and very contradictory areas of tension: "preserving tradition" and "driving innovation". Digital change management is demanding, and a forward-looking digitalization strategy must not only focus on organizational structures and processes, but must always keep an eye on changes in the company's own corporate culture. Digital change can only succeed if it is actively embraced and shaped by the people within a company. Managers have a special role to play here—in the best case, they shape the "digital mindset" and exemplify the change through their own positive attitude.

Let us therefore say goodbye to the romantic notion of "mindful leadership" as mindful, soft and "uneconomic" management action. Mindful leadership is an approach to change: Used correctly and backed by motivating methods, mindfulness can act as a powerful leadership tool in the context of "hard" economic goal achievement, which considers, accepts and strengthens people in their entirety.

For every company in the digital transformation process, it is therefore advisable to establish a mindful communication and dialog structure both internally and externally. The described design approaches from the SparX workshop series and many other tools could be used in mindful leadership as impulses to identify and practically apply the appropriate approach for each specific situation. In our view, an important step on the right path.

References

Desbordes, G., Negi, L. T., Pace, T. W., Wallace, B. A., Raison, C. L., & Schwartz, E. L. (2012). Effects of mindful-attention and compassion meditation training on amygdala response to emotional stimuli in an ordinary, non-meditative state. *Frontiers in Human Neuroscience, 6*, 292.

Lenzen, M., Geschke, A., Wiedmann, T., Lane, J., Anderson, N., Baynes, T., & Hadjikakou, M. (2014). Compiling and using input-output frameworks through collaborative virtual laboratories. *Science of the Total Environment, 485*, 241–251.

Tang, Y. Y., Ma, Y., Fan, Y., Feng, H., Wang, J., Feng, S., & Zhang, Y. (2009). Central and autonomic nervous system interaction is altered by short-term meditation. *Proceedings of the National Academy of Sciences, 106*(22), 8865–8870.

Yong, J., Kim, J., Park, J., Seo, I., & Swinton, J. (2011). Effects of a spirituality training program on the spiritual and psychosocial well-being of hospital middle manager nurses in Korea. *The Journal of Continuing Education in Nursing, 42*(6), 280–288.

Zeichhardt, R. (2018). E-Leader, CDOs & Digital Fools – eine Führungstypologie für den digitalen Wandel. In *Disruption und transformation management* (pp. 3–21). Springer Gabler.

Chapter 11
Mental Training as a Self-Management Practice at Work

Marc Aeschbacher and Valeria Legena

11.1 Introduction

This essay is dedicated to a topic that is slowly finding its way into professional health management: mental training. The fact that the dissemination of this kind of refocusing took and still takes so much time, suggests that here also certain reservations or resistances were (and are) to be overcome. This essay aims to investigate the reasons for this delay in acceptance and at the same time to take a step beyond it by examining two questions:

(a) What are the (socio-historical) reasons why mental training techniques are not an integral part of corporate health management programs?
(b) How can mental training be used in everyday professional life?

By linking these questions, an attempt is made to couple an analytical, reasoned approach to the topic with a practical utility value for the reader.

11.2 Sociohistorical Reasons for the Absence of Mental Training Techniques from Occupational Health Management Programs

During sports broadcasts, when the cameras capture images of athletes preparing for competition, the viewers in front of the TV sets often see how the athletes are preoccupied in their thoughts with their upcoming action. Some turn their focus

M. Aeschbacher (✉) · V. Legena
School of Business, University of Applied Sciences Northwestern Switzerland, Windisch, Switzerland
e-mail: marc.aeschbacher@fhnw.ch

V. Schulte et al. (eds.), *Mindful Leadership in Practice*,
https://doi.org/10.1007/978-3-030-97311-7_11

inward, blocking out everything and being completely with themselves; others are exalted in these moments, cheering themselves on and prompting the audience to clap rhythmically; thirds, in turn, perform a strict ritual; in exact, irrevocable order, they make their preparations for the ensuing part of the competition; still others stand out with a rehearsed goal celebration. For athletes, these mental acts of preparation and conclusion are a natural part of competition; they are an eminently important part of the process of action, without which success is much less likely.

What seems to spectators in stadiums or at their TV sets to be a natural part of sport and to give it meaning is—just as unquestioningly—not part of their daily professional practice. It therefore appears that what is perceived and recognized as an integral part of enhancing performance in a sub-area of human activity is not considered by most people (and especially by the management literature) to be performance-enhancing and health-promoting when it comes to (one's own) performance at work. This is surprising not least because the so-called mental training already has a long tradition. As early as "the 1920s, a sports psychology research laboratory was established at the Prussian University of Physical Education in Berlin" (Schweikle, 2006). Thus, the belief that the performance and capability of athletes has a direct connection to their mental state is almost a hundred years old. The scientific examination of this relationship led just as directly to the realization that targeted promotion of mental strength results in superiority over competitors, increases the ability of athletes to perform at their best and to better deal with inhibiting factors such as fear and nervousness, as well as to cope better with defeats.

One can now indulge in speculations as to why these practices for performance enhancement and potential retrieval established in sports are not applied in everyday life; one (as obvious as superficial) answer may be: In contrast to the permanent, rather uniform effort, characterized by fewer peaks, that constitutes professional activity, sport is perceived (at least in the part that the public witnesses) as a compression of performance. This circumstance seems to justify, in the eyes of many, the discrepancy of the accompanying phenomena related to performance.

If one digs a little deeper, however, it becomes obvious that in the case of this gap, different aspects must play their decisive role; it cannot be solely a matter of the social distinction between sport and the professional world. It is precisely the logic of a general economization of lifestyle, as analyzed by Max Weber ("The Protestant Ethic and the Spirit of Capitalism", translated by the authors), that would suggest that the actors of a capitalist system would benefit from an increase in performance at work. So why reject what has been proven to work in sports for everyday professional life?

The answer will focus on two aspects that are interwoven in socio-historical and philosophical history: of great importance is, on the one hand, dualism, and on the other hand, the development in the history of medicine.

If one realizes that there is a separation of these spheres, then an association with the so-called dualism is obvious. The substance dualism finds its beginning in the argument about the connection of body and spirit and with it the question about the different levels of consciousness and their coupling to a body. Today's understanding of this question, following the mind-body problem that already preoccupied the ancient philosophers, has been strongly influenced by René Descartes (1596–1650). "For Descartes, all life phenomena, up to and including the ability of animals to perceive and move, can be explained mechanically. For him, plants and animals are machines whose properties and capacities result mechanically from the structure and arrangement of their physical parts in the same way that the behavior of a clock results from the properties and arrangement of the gears, springs, and weights of which it is composed. Only thought is an exception for Descartes. For him, thinking is inseparable from being conscious and having ideas, and machines, according to Descartes, can neither be conscious in this sense nor have ideas. Thinking is thus for Descartes the essential characteristic of the soul. The soul is a res cogitans. Physical things, on the other hand, do not think; their essential characteristic is their extensionality; physical things are res extensae. For Descartes, there are two kinds of substances: thinking and extended things" (Beckermann, 1999, p. 767f, translated by the authors).

For Descartes, this clear separation of mental and physical spheres was important in order to be able to define thinking as a confirmation of being; a purely physical existence could consequently not be the same as the human being making sure of himself through a thinking process. How far into our time this way of thinking was formative is shown for example by the fact that only since the amendment of the Swiss Civil Code of October 4, 2002, which came into force on April 1, 2003, animals are no longer considered as objects (Art. 641a para. 1 ZGB), thus the new criminal offense of cruelty to animals was created, because previously these offenses were punished as damage to property.

For a long time, everything physical was secondary and interaction, such as that postulated by the Portuguese neuroscientist António Damásio, who investigates the connections between language and cognition as well as the interplay between feeling and reason, was unthinkable for a long time. In his books, Damásio speaks of an indissoluble connection between body and mind, which constantly influence each other. His Austrian colleague Thomas Fuchs, holder of the Karl Jaspers Professorship for Philosophical Foundations of Psychiatry and Psychotherapy at the University of Heidelberg, goes even further than Damásio's positions: "Centrally necessary for the emergence of consciousness is the brain, because in it all circular processes converge and are linked, just like the tracks in a main train station. If this is destroyed, then the train traffic breaks down. But, to continue the comparison, the train traffic is neither generated by the station nor is it to be localized there. Rather, it makes use of the track system with its many switches, crossings and, of course, its central coordination point in the main station so that the transport processes run as smoothly as possible. So even if a high degree of track networking and train density can undoubtedly be determined in the main station (this would correspond to the neuronal activations measurable in the brain during certain activities)—train traffic remains bound to the entire track system. Analogously, consciousness activity represents the integral of the entire, ever-present relationships between brain, organism, and environment" (Fuchs, 2018, translated by the authors).

The shattering of the substance-dualistic approach that goes hand in hand with these research results enables us today to take a more liberated view of the connections between body and mind, and in this way also clears the way for the introduction of a way of thinking that brings together physical and mental aspects in the form of a mental influence, and thinks about the connection of both in a mental training in everyday working life.

This brings us to the second reason for the acceptance delay. This is a sociohistorical reason that is also related to a dichotomous distinction that began in the late Middle Ages.

In fact, the late Middle Ages began to emphasize the distinction of academically educated physicians from the autodidacts and laymen, and this was also expressed in the so to speak approved methods of treatment, a distinction that had not been made before. The High Middle Ages did not adhere to a rigid demarcation of treatment methods in terms of physiological or in terms of psychological health. Moses Maimonides, Hebrew Moshe ben Maimon, one of the most important scholars of the High Middle Ages and mediator of ancient knowledge to the Occident, who referred primarily to Galenos of Pergamon in his writings and in his medical advice, In 1195, he gave the ailing eldest son of Saladin, the Emir of Damascus, Ali al-Malik al-Afdal Nur, medical advice regarding his digestive problems and depression, which included wine and music as remedies.

However, a rational approach was already important to Maimonides, who rejected the use of amulets and incantations and was thus in line with his academic successors.

In the late Middle Ages and early modern period, the academically educated Medici distanced themselves from the laymen of nursing, such as feldsher and bather. The latter usually received their medical training by way of oral tradition, helping to care for the wounded on battlefields or preparing naturopathic remedies.

With the bourgeoisification of society during the Enlightenment, the clear demarcation of academic medical education from naturopathy became even more important, just as the university as a whole, as the institutional allocation of science, began to embody the meritocratic rise of the bourgeoisie as the leading class of society.

The early days of a medicine defined by scientific criteria were, however, still characterized by confusion and problems of demarcation. Thus, quacks and charlatans continued to cavort alongside university physicians, who, measured by today's standards, were ultimately—like their non-academic competitors—only partially successful in saving and preserving human life due to the not yet large horizon of knowledge. Of almost exemplary validity for this situation is the life of Franz Anton Mesmer, who completed his medical studies in Vienna in 1766 with a dissertation on "The Influence of the Planets on the Human Body" (translated by the authors).

His experiments on the "magnetic fluid" linked different common fields of research and made Mesmer internationally famous because of his spectacular healing successes. In France, Mesmer opened 20 medical practices, in the manner of today's franchises, which applied his healing method of animal magnetism throughout the country. The French professionals, alarmed by Mesmer's enormous popularity and consequent financial success, appealed to the king, who in March 1784 set up a commission of inquiry (one of its members was Benjamin Franklin) with the task of thoroughly investigating the healing practices used. Together with the Royal Medical Society, the commission came to a devastating conclusion for Mesmer: it stated that no causality could be established between treatment and healing success. Thus, using scientific methodology, a proof had been provided that rejected the presumed scientificity. Mesmer's popularity with King Louis XVI and Queen Marie Antoinette had already suffered before, however; in today's terminology, one could speak of Mesmer as a jet-set doctor whose position at court was taken over by another. The successor is exciting because he is an impostor who is still known today: Giuseppe Balsamo, who toured all over Europe under the pseudonym Alessandro Count of Cagliostro. Before his time at the French court in 1781, Balsamo had worked in Strasbourg as a teacher of occultism and magical healing arts and—as in all places where he worked—tried to gain the favor of the higher-ups.

Mesmer and Cagliostro, two embodiments of a historical development, which in their simultaneity represent the Janus-faced both/and of an early period, were soon overcome as epochal ciphers by the triumph of bourgeois society and its will to critically rationalize all areas of life. The advancing differentiation was also accompanied by a normative demarcation. In this context, the meticulous struggle for semantic distinction is revealing. Christoph Wilhelm Friedrich Hufeland proposed to call academic medicine "rational medicine". For him, the difference between this and naturopathy consisted in "being founded on reason and rational conclusion". Hufeland's proposal failed to gain acceptance among the ranks of medical orthodoxy, and until well into the second half of the 19th century, the largely value-neutral term "state medicine" was preferred (Jütte, 2005, p. 45f). In this designation, the will to affirm at that time is expressed more sustainably than in the term "school medicine" used today, which is derived from the medieval schola medicinae. Ironically, it was precisely the representatives of homeopathy and naturopathy who in the second half of the nineteenth century again propagated "school medicine" as a pejorative fighting term.

This distinction of a scientifically founded, research-based medicine from a speculative, natural-philosophical homeopathy was at the same time a differentiation of critical science from traditional folk knowledge as well as a social demarcation of the middle class from the lower class in a newly forming social structure.

Those who wanted to belong to this new, leading social class naturally sought to subject their achievements to this normative canon. The reward was recognition and social advancement.

Already at the end of the 19th century, breaks in this phenomenon of social self-referentiality become apparent: Certainly it was not by chance that the founders of psychoanalysis drove a wedge into the unquestioned certainties of the bourgeois scientific model with their ambivalent attitude towards hypnosis.

Sigmund Freud, who, in order to be introduced to the mode of action of hypnotic therapies, undertook two trips to French neurologists—in 1885 to Paris to Jean-Martin Charcot and in 1889 to Nancy to Hippolyte Bernheim, some of whose works he later translated into German—"was among the neurologists of his time who were interested in hypnotism and was co-editor of the Zeitschrift für Hypnotismus until 1895" (Schröter et al., 2013, p 134, translated by the authors).

As a student, Carl Gustav Jung attended séances of mediums and table-backers for years and in 1902—a courageous provocation—wrote his dissertation on the topic "On the psychology and pathology of so-called occult phenomena" (translated by the authors).

The early affinity with the paranormal and with trance states that were difficult to grasp and explain scientifically was lost (more strongly in Freud's case, not entirely in Jung's) when the pioneer status of ridiculed exotics gave way to the first signs of a longed-for recognition of his own fields of research as a legitimate medical discipline. Thus, after a decade of experience with suggestive methods, Freud began to distance himself from hypnosis as a method of treatment by emphasizing the superiority of analysis: "Free association and the art of interpretation, then, now accomplish the same thing as formerly the putting into hypnosis" (Freud, 1998, p. 411, translated by the authors).

At the 5th International Psychoanalytic Congress in Budapest in 1918, Freud said with regard to the multitude of war-related neuroses in the poor civilian population that needed treatment: "We will also very probably be compelled to alloy the pure gold of analysis abundantly with the copper of direct suggestion in the mass application of our therapy, and hypnotic influence could also find a place there again, as in the treatment of war neurotics [...]" (Schröter et al., 2013, translated by the authors).

Carl Gustav Jung's reservations about hypnosis are as exciting as Freud's and very similar to them. Jung did not want the relationship with his patients to be affected: "In the beginning I also used hypnosis in my private practice, but very soon I gave it up, because with it one is groping in the dark. You never know how long a progress or recovery will last, and I always had resistance to working in the unknown. Likewise, I didn't like to decide on my own what the patient should do. I was much more interested in finding out from the patient himself where he would naturally develop. This required careful analysis of dreams and other manifestations of the unconscious" (Jaffé, 1961, p. 126, translated by the authors).

Despite their normative relativization, it is to the credit of the founders of psychoanalysis that they advanced the de-tabooing of mental health practices within the context of institutionalized sciences, paving the way for subsequent researchers who revisited and pursued the early approaches, such as Milton H. Erickson, who developed the so-called hypno(psycho)therapy or clinical hypnotherapy.

11.3 Use of Mental Training in Everyday Professional Life

In the following, five mental training approaches for everyday life are presented here, which give more support, strengthen self-confidence, increase motivation, improve performance and help to reduce stress.

11.3.1 More Support Thanks to Self-Talk

When people feel caught talking to themselves in the presence of others, they often use the phrase: "I was just thinking out loud" (translated by the authors).

Instead of being apologetic for talking to yourself, you should give it much more value, because it helps:

- to organize one's own thoughts;
- master difficult situations with instructions from the inner director;
- to persevere;
- to motivate themselves;
- remembering his goals.

The inventor of autosuggestion, Emil Coué (interestingly, just like Freud, a student of Bernheim), pointed out in his book "La maîtrise de soi-même par l'autosuggestion consciente" ("*Self-mastery through conscious autosuggestion*") of 1905 that one should recite to oneself 20 times a day, half aloud, after awakening and before falling asleep, the sentence: "Every day I feel better and better in every respect!" (translated by the authors) should be recited. Helpful is a knot cord or similar for counting off. Coué recommended to speak the sentence as childlike and unstrained as possible, slowly and monotonously in the manner of a litany or a mantra, without straining the will too much. It is obvious that Coué here consciously refers back to old practices such as the ritualized praying of the rosary or the litanies. All religions know these trance-like states, in which the believers get into other levels of consciousness by permanent repetition, rhythmic sequences and the like more, in order to open themselves for (religious) contents.

Memorization strengthens stamina.

When it comes to mastering difficult situations with the help of the inner director, the decision-making system FORDEC (Facts-Options-Risks and benefits-Decision-Execution-Check) illustrates what this can mean. After a series of serious aviation accidents, studies in the 1980s analyzed that 4 out of 5 serious incidents were due to deficiencies in non-technical skills ("NOTECHS"), mainly the non-functioning of cooperation and communication between pilot and co-pilot was responsible. So, a decision-making procedure called FORDEC was developed, which must become automatic through constant practice, so that the natural behaviors that have come about in the course of evolution are replaced by a systematized, rational one. The second sequence element of FORDEC is "Options" (Question: What options do I/have we? Action: Development of action alternatives), with this process step a conscious monologue begins, in which the pilot thinks aloud, explains his possible actions, and thus lets the co-pilot participate in his thoughts, this self-talk (in some cases also a dialogue) is continued during the two following process steps—"Risks and benefits", "Decision"—, thus ensuring that clarity prevails and no misunderstandings arise, which would have fatal consequences. The self-talk provides support and helps to organize one's thoughts, even in situations that are not as dramatic as incidents on an airplane.

There is one special feature that should be pointed out at this point: Those who use self-talk to set goals for themselves must take care to formulate them positively; instead of "I don't want to give up," the formulation must be "I'm hanging in there," because the negative formulation already contains the negative focus that must be avoided.

11.3.2 Strengthening Self-Confidence

A lack of or limited self-confidence prevents people from fully realizing their potential. Subliminally, people are often held back by an "I'm not good enough" attitude. The consequences of this are devastating: instead of achieving goals, people stand in their own way and prevent and sabotage their own success. As a consequence, many people push their tasks ahead of them like a ship pushes its bow wave. The so-called procrastination, the putting off of tasks, makes one feel even worse because the fear of failure and the stress increase due to the accumulation of tasks. This creates a vicious circle, in psychology it is called a maladaptive coping strategy: procrastination is a behavior that ultimately does not lead to the goal, because it does not eliminate the displeasure in the long term. Usually, most people add the idea that they are not allowed to make mistakes. This further accelerates the downward spiral of lacking self-confidence according to the motto "because it went wrong once, it will go wrong again". Failure in our minds is pre-programmed.

Wanting to do everything perfectly, because failure would be failure in one's own eyes or the eyes of others, is the first step on the road to failure. This can be seen very clearly in team athletes, who for this reason start to avoid any risk, thus reducing their own performance and dragging the team with them into the quagmire of losing out of fear of losing. Only the courage to fail (to embarrass oneself, to make mistakes in front of others) opens up the possibility of winning.

To build self-confidence, it is important:

- to give up the desire to be perfect:

  It is crucial in mental training to be completely in the here and now. This also means accepting developments that you cannot influence and accepting mistakes when they happen. If you focus on the mistakes, you block yourself. What's done is done, you can't undo it, it's more a matter of dealing productively with the new situation.
- to detach from the error:

  A mistake is like a lost stone in a huge mosaic, the picture remains recognizable even if it is not 'perfect'. The point is to see the whole, not the fraction.
- to think in scenarios:

  It is important to take away the horror of the error and thus its blocking effect by consciously considering scenarios from the outset that determine how the situation can be remedied, how the error can be corrected. Viewing one's own fears rationally, placing them in larger contexts, helps to take away their terror.

Seen in this way, mistakes become opportunities on the way to greater self-confidence.

- to keep their own successes in mind:
  Those who give themselves an account with a success diary break the spell of the downward pull of failure and create clarity for themselves about how many positive experiences are actually on the books. This strengthens confidence in one's own abilities and boosts self-confidence.

11.3.3 Increase Motivation

Anyone who is confronted with frustrating and demotivating experiences in their everyday working life, who has negative experiences and experiences disappointments, has to pick themselves up again in order to be able to do their work. When joy and satisfaction at work have been lost, it takes a great deal of effort to become motivated again, as the Gallup Engagement Index of 2018 also proves: "As a rule, most employees join a company highly motivated, but then become increasingly disillusioned by experiences in their work environment, at some point mentally say goodbye to the company altogether and quit internally. The main role in this process is almost always played by the direct supervisor, who has the greatest influence on the working environment. His or her importance can be seen in the fact that 75 percent of the reasons given for involuntary turnover can be directly influenced by the manager. In other words, motivated employees become refusers when they are in a work environment where their core emotional needs at work are ignored for an extended period of time. At first, work becomes a nuisance, then a burden, and finally a torment. In short, internal resignation stems from deficits in personnel management" (Nink, 2018, p. 11, translated by the authors).

The disruption of work attitudes and commitment must be taken very seriously, both from the point of view of the company and the individual employee. Because of demotivation, a lose-lose situation is created whose mutual unspoken acceptance is devastating. On the one hand, this means that a person's potential is not being exploited in his or her work, a loss for the employer; on the other hand, a person is wasting his or her lifetime at a job that means nothing to him or her. This creates frustration, in the worst case aggression, which has just as detrimental an effect on the corporate culture and the working atmosphere as it does on the mood in private life.

What is exciting about Marco Nink's observation is already the opening sentence: "As a rule, most employees join a company highly motivated". We would like to point out here that it might be better for all concerned if the motivation curve at the beginning of a new professional activity were not too high. What seems disillusioned at first glance actually means a reality-oriented setting of priorities. Here, too, we should refer to the example of sports. All athletes have to learn to deal with the rapid succession of victory and defeat, success and failure, without falling into a mental hole. In order to be able to better process these ups and downs and to better cope with them in their entirety, many professionals have created a kind of ‘counter-world’ for themselves, into which they can dive in order to recover and prepare themselves for a new day, where again the uncertainty of victory and defeat will have to be dealt with. This counterworld, as the name suggests, is a sphere in which completely different rules prevail: It may be, for example, that a professional athlete likes to fish in his spare time—an activity in which he can enjoy the peace and quiet and switch off—or that he starts the day with meditation. The counterworld is characterized precisely by the fact that it consciously takes individual preferences into account. We suggest that employees also consciously create a counterworld that helps them counterbalance the nerve-racking exclusivity of the working world.

What are the conditions of such a counterworld?

The Opposite World:

- is not results-oriented, but joy-oriented;
- is not rationally based, but emotional;
- is exclusively under its own command, no one but me is in charge here;
- knows no obligation.

How long the stay in the counterworld lasts is an individual decision. With this method of creating a mental balance, motivation at work is maintained at a high level, setbacks and frustrations are absorbed and processed much more easily, and thus everyone is served.

11.3.4 Increase in Performance

Increasing performance—as in sports—is often a matter of preparing for the tasks at hand; our mindset is just as crucial as the routine we have in accomplishing tasks: To the practice (training) is added the mental approach (mental training, mindset). It is a matter of setting up a kind of schedule, a script, for one’s tasks and dividing the activity ahead into small, manageable intermediate steps. These steps are then played out again and again in the mind. Once the action sequence (the script) has been internalized, one can mentally access the information more quickly, more automatically, because the action pattern is anchored. In this way, tasks that lie ahead are more easily mastered, they lose their terror, such as presentations to customers or job interviews. Just as an athlete mentally runs through the race track until he has it completely under control and knows exactly what he has to do where, a surgeon, for example, behaves by running through her operation in her mind’s eye.

To develop this script, it is important:

- to analyze the upcoming action in detail;
- to divide them into the individual steps;
- to imagine them as a picture and to learn them by heart (“First I do this, then I do ...”);

- then store them as an inner film or mental map (this is the linking of the individual steps into a sequence);
- link them to positive feelings ("I'm looking forward to when step X comes along"); and
- then mentally go through them again and again with regard to the stress or strain situation.

On Day X, right before the real situation, you have to stop the inner movie and consciously say, "Now I'm doing it!"

The automated process works best when it is also simply automatic. The mental map, the inner film must be so strong that it carries us when the decisive moment arrives. That's why linking it to positive feelings is important. Here, too, it is helpful if the individual steps are coupled with positive self-talk; one could speak of a pep talk or a battle cry that underscores the mental cinema.

Interestingly, the script is equally suitable for routine actions as for actions to be newly learned or actions under stress.

11.3.5 Stress Reduction

Many people feel stressed by their professional tasks, they fear that they will not be able to master upcoming tasks, or the amount of duties puts them under pressure. If the amount of tasks is unreasonable, it is important to talk to the employer in order to obtain a reduction.

On the other hand, as far as the feeling of stress is concerned, i.e. how we deal with tasks, we have to distinguish between eustress and dysstress, as Hans Selye (1907–1982), who established the theory of stress in science (Selye et al., 1957). Healthy stress (eustress) has a positive influence on the organism, it is the feeling of happiness we have when we are completely absorbed in something, it does not matter how much time we invest in it. Dysstress, on the other hand, weighs us down because we perceive the associated stress negatively. This is primarily a matter of so-called framing, i.e. the mental classification of a task. If one wants to examine one's own frame, then it is purposeful to determine the perspective under which we view the experiences of everyday (professional) life. The terminology we use to characterize our life and work situations in our minds and in conversation with others expresses our frame and thus the way we ourselves deal with our lives.

When you make a conscious decision to replace negative terms with less negative or even positive ones, your frame brightens, you don't feel as bad, and you find it easier to deal with the situation. Example: If you think "I hate this job," you frame yourself negatively and you find it harder to do the job. In addition, the fact that you have to do this work depresses you more, so it also interferes with your free time, because the negativity affects your mood. As a result, this negative frame determines the coexistence with family and friends and one can no longer get out of the negative spiral.

A so-called reframing helps to break up this negativity by developing a positive counter-position: "Well, there are things in life that I like better". For example, one can also ask oneself, "What is the best way for me to successfully complete/positive/accomplish/bring about a good resolution?" Anyone facing a difficult challenge or fear can use this question to move the focus (and therefore the frame) from the problem to the solution.

In addition, the phrase "the best way" helps to reframe oneself mentally in such a way that one does not perceive oneself in a hopeless situation, but that there are options that one can develop. So here, too, the focus shifts mentally away from the victim role to an active coping optic.

The aim of this essay was on the one hand to show that, due to the socio-historical and philosophical-historical development, a wide field of mental strategies still awaits their integration into corporate health management systems, and on the other hand to describe how mental training could be used in everyday professional life. We are convinced that there is a lot of potential hidden here for individuals as well as for companies.

References

Beckermann, A. (1999). Das Leib-Seele-Problem. In H. J. Sandkühler (Ed.), *Enzyklopädie der Philosophie* (pp. 766–774). Hamburg.

Freud, S. (1998). *Brief outline of psychoanalysis* (pp. 403–427). S. Fischer Verlag.

Fuchs, T. (2018). *Das Gehirn – ein Beziehungsorgan*. Accessed October 21, 2020, from http://www.information-philosophie.de/?a=1&t=4908&n=2&y=1&c=2

Jaffé, A. (Ed.). (1961). *Memories, dreams, thoughts of C. G. Jung*. Walter-Verlag.

Jütte, R. (2005). Alternativmedizin. In W. E. Gerabek, B. D. Haage, G. Keil, & W. Wegner (Eds.), *Enzyklopädie Medizingeschichte*. Walter de Gruyter.

Nink, M. (2018). *Engagement index. The latest data and insights from the Gallup study*. Redline Verlag.

Schröter, J., Burkhard, P. & Helle, M, (2013). *Sigmund Freuds Einstellung zur Hypnose*. Accessed October 21, 2020, from https://www.meg-stiftung.de/index.php/de/component/phocadownload/category/1-artikel?download=109:hypnose-zhh-1310-schroeter-freud

Schweikle, J. (2006, January 18). *Quäl Dich, Körper*. Accessed October 21, 2020, from http://www.zeit.de/zeit-wissen/2006/03/Sportpsychologie.xml

Selye, H., Klärner, P. & Sopp, H. (1957). *Stress beherrscht unser Leben* (The stress of life), dt.-vom Autor überprüfte Übers. v. Helmut Sopp unter Mitarb. v.[Paul] Klärner.

Chapter 12
Leadership and Cooperation: Ethical Considerations and Moral Frameworking

Michael Zirkler, Nikolaus Knoepffler, and Reyk Albrecht

12.1 Introduction

Leadership has been studied for a long time predominantly from a perspective of the dyad, operating with the designated difference between the leader and the follower or the leader as the powerholder, the subordinate or follower as the «receiver» of influence or governance (Ko et al., 2018). "Traditional leadership theory is oriented toward dyadic processes that occur at low levels of the organization (...) most researchers still define leadership as a micro-organizational phenomenon occurring between a leader and a follower, while ignoring multiple stakeholders and competing demands on leaders". (Gordon & Yukl, 2004, p. 361). Another study comes to the conclusion that "leadership and ethics research (is) too CEO-centric and focused on the top hierarchies;" and, "it is centered more on declarations than on results or on ideas rather than on real implementations" (Bachmann, 2017, p. 61).

More recently, the understanding of leadership has been expanding and opening for multiple models of leadership (see Chemers, 2000 for a historical review).

Nowadays people should *voluntarily* do what is being demanded and what is generally considered necessary for being successful in the work process and not because a leader or manager is giving instructions or orders as once suggested by Taylor's idea of separating head and hand (Taylor, 2012). More entrepreneurship is asked for, more self-leadership is expected, more governance is taking place, which has its source either in the individual or in the group.

M. Zirkler (✉)
School of Applied Psychology, University of Applied Sciences (ZHAW), Zurich, Switzerland
e-mail: zirm@zhaw.ch

N. Knoepffler
Faculty of Social and Behavioural Sciences, Friedrich-Schiller-University, Jena, Germany

R. Albrecht
Faculty of Social and Behavioural Sciences, Friedrich-Schiller-University, Jena, Germany

V. Schulte et al. (eds.), *Mindful Leadership in Practice*,
https://doi.org/10.1007/978-3-030-97311-7_12

A shift from traditional hierarchical leadership models towards more autonomy of individuals and groups is obvious in practice (Zirkler, M., Power Shift: Transitions from Hierarchy to Holacracy, oral conference contribution). Where previously hierarchy (ranked order) was seen as the mechanism to reduce complexity and to give orientation, now lateral leadership and networks of leadership impulses are more and more enfolding. However, the drifts towards a multiplicity in leadership forces is occurring *although* the hierarchy is still operating, at least on a formal and official level. This results in a variety of leadership models which are operating in a social system at the same time. We propose that the sources as well as the quality of processes leading to order and orientation within a social system become more diverse.

The less power and dominance are forcing people to action, the less hierarchy is the only option of aligning, the more «real» cooperation as a deliberate and voluntary act is becoming necessary.

Cooperation comes in two versions, it reveals a «weak» form (obedience, followership) and a «strong» form (equity, partnership, egalitarian mutuality). Although the two represent rather two ends on a continuum and many mixed forms will be found in between, we will only discuss the extremes for reasons of simplification. We will present findings on the drifts in the concepts and practices of leadership, discuss the theory of cooperation and will present an understanding of an ethics of leadership as facilitating and maintaining cooperation.

This will be done in the context of labor and work as well as against the background of work related productivity.

12.2 Drifts in the Concepts and Practices of Leadership

12.2.1 What Is Leadership?

Leadership is basically and first of all a *function* in a social system. Human's basic social orientation assumed, it's one of the forces to counterbalance a social entropy, the "natural" tendency of social systems to fall apart (Aya, 1978; Deutsch, 2011; p. 253; Elias, 2000). The main objective of this function is to reduce complexity which origins from human's contingency, i.e. people usually have options to decide differently and to do different things. This way, leadership provides orientation, limits potential actions and focusses toward intentional plans, thus alignment is established. These may be plans of individuals who need others to implement them or collective plans that are developed and pursued jointly. When leadership takes place psychological and social influence is used to execute a limitation and set focus towards something which is desired at a given moment: «Leadership today is seen as an *extraordinary* influence that is found in a person or group» (Praszkier, 2018, p. 10).

On the basis of a basic model of "distributing influence", leadership research has been looking for the characteristics of (a) the leader, (b) the follower and (c) the process which explains the relationship, particularly distribution of influence and (d) the outcome of different forms or leadership for (a) and (b) as well as performance indicators such as productivity, quality, but also innovation etc. Another stream of research has been dealing with a variety of ideas, concepts, theories, practices etc. on how leadership is being or could be done.

One of the well-known forms of leadership comes as «hierarchy» (ranked order, literally from Ancient Greek: authority of the priests). Rank has been attached to individuals and symbolized for the sake of "usability", e.g. as the chief, the boss, the king etc. However, rank is only working if most if not all actors in a system accept the principle of rank. Its basis is rooted in the «rule of force», which means the stronger, the one who has more resources, will prevail at the end. The strongest could just take what he wants (Tufts, 1918, p. 29), however we will show that it would be shortsighted to act in this manner, at least under conditions that require the solution of complex tasks, as is often the case today.

Extreme forms of hierarchy would be either Autocracy, where just one person holds the ultimate power or Oligarchy, where a group of people are acting as they want.

Ironically though, these individuals, necessarily need to be replaceable if the *principle* should survive. It's not crucial if Smith or Muller holding the position of a leader, although the person is not completely neglectable due to his personal capacities etc., which will have an impact on the way this person is acting in the leadership role (which is, by the way, itself subject to contingency).

The framework of hierarchical leadership sets a ranked order where the power is situated in the respective person (leader), who gets a "mandate" and obtains the right to use power. Leadership is seen as exercising the leader's will (which is itself often a representation of an "idea" or an organization's will or ends) upon «followers» using power as the main means. The leader's function is to command people do to what he wants them to do, or based on the leader's understanding of what ought to be done. The leader's job has been to align people towards a common goal.

In the light of anthropology and the history, hierarchy seems to be the «natural» way, the way human systems are most used to and the way, which is most elaborate of organizing a social system and structuring leadership. Without going into the related historical, anthropological and sociological discussion, we see many other forms of doing leadership in recent times. Some authors call those «post-heroic» forms of leadership (Sobral & Furtado, 2019).

Heterarchy is the umbrella term for such other forms of leadership (which then might be better called governance). Heterachical systems are network systems with (more or less) equally distributed power or «voice»: "The addition of the term heterarchy to the vocabulary of power relations reminds us that forms of order exist that are not exclusively hierarchical and that interactive elements in complex systems need not be permanently ranked relative to one another. In fact, it may be in attempts to maintain a permanent ranking that flexibility and adaptive fitness is lost" (Crumley, 1995, p. 3).

One line of arguments sees hierarchy reasonably working if the conditions in the environment of a social system are not changing too fast. According to Ashby's law of requisite variety the complexity of a (social) system needs to be sufficiently high to manage external (environmental) complexity (Boisot & Mckelvey, 2011). Hierarchy is not working properly any more when processes need to be accelerated or if more knowledge is required than the top down approach can provide. However, the other reason for a crisis of hierarchy is rooted in the change of society towards a «society of singularities» (Reckwitz, 2019). The emphasis of individuality leads to a pressure "using" individuality, just following and subordination is less and less an option.

This drift goes hand in hand with what Peter Drucker called the «next society» (Drucker, 2012), which is a knowledge society. Digitalization (Neufeind et al., 2018; Schwab, 2019) and its social consequences have accelerated the process of multiplying options (Gross, 2002; Rosa, 2014) for solving work related challenges. Hence new concepts of leadership have been developed by researchers.

12.2.2 Expansion of Leadership Perspectives

Laloux's book «reinventing organizations» (Laloux, 2014) was a milestone from a management practice' point of view. The book displays evolutionary steps of organization development towards a «teal organization». One main feature would be «self-management» (Laloux, 2014, p. 61 ff.): «Teal Organizations have found the key to operate effectively, even at large scale, with a system based on peer relationships, without the need for either hierarchy or consensus» (Laloux, 2014, p. 56).

A growing body of research and literature has evolved focusing on leadership concepts and theories transcending hierarchical models (cf. Praszkier, 2018 for an overview), such as «shared leadership» (Hoch, 2013; Hoch & Kozlowski, 2014), «distributed leadership» (Spillane, 2010), «servant leadership» (Greenleaf, 2002), relational leadership» (Uhl-Bien, 2006). Related issues have been discussed, such as «Holacracy» (Bauer et al., 2019; Robertson, 2016; Heifetz, 1994). Holocracy sees leadership as «mobilizing people to tackle tough problems» (Heifetz, 1994, p. 15). Holocracy (holos = whole, kratein = to govern) literally means that everybody is included in decision making. It is a shared decision making process, where the leader mobilizes the whole group.

However, the situation is more confusing, at least in practice (Zirkler, 2019). Despite the fact, that still much hierarchical leadership is formally seen in organizations, leadership functions are more and more distributed among multiple actors in the social system (Zirkler et al., 2020; Zirkler & Herzog, 2021). Currently we find more patchwork than pure leadership philosophies or styles within a given system.

This conceded, the situation is paradoxical in many cases: while formal and hierarchical leadership is still prevailing and operating officially, many other forms of leadership are present. They are often working inofficially in a given social system *at the same time*. Sometimes this leads to confusion and problems or even tensions and conflicts, sometimes these different forms of leadership are coexisting peacefully side by side, but just few organizations have explicitly integrated different forms of leadership (Kotter, 2012, 2014).

Heifetz (1994) sees an evolution of leadership concepts in business and the corporate world: «For decades, the term leadership referred to the people who hold the top management positions and the functions they serve. In our common usage, it still does. Recently, however, business people have drawn a distinction between leadership and management, and exercising leadership has also come to mean providing a vision and influencing others to realize it *through noncoercive means*» (Heifetz, 1994, p. 15, our emphasize).

Leadership is not just the place where interests and wants are being negotiated and managed, leadership nowadays also means stimulating and maintaining «possibilities» and potentials, in the sense of aspirations, ambitions, dreams, purpose etc. People's talents, capacities and inspirations are waiting to be harnessed for the benefit of their self-fulfilling as well as for the benevolence of the community they belong to (Zirkler & Herzog, 2021).

One particular aspect needs to be addressed when discussing expanded forms of leadership, i.e. responsibility and accountability. The leader is an agent, who is adopting and carrying a specific form of responsibility. Hence, the role of leadership includes «care taking» in the sense of vitalizing, transferring energy to persons or processes. Therefore, leadership is strongly connected with emotions. At the same time, he will often be made (legally) accountable. Unlike in earlier times where blind obedience was socially and legally acceptable or even a virtue, nowadays everyone in an organization could be held accountable for their actions or failures. Since the leader could be hold accountable for what he is doing and neglecting a, it is in his own interest to tact responsibly.

It's still questionable how the acquisition of a person's responsibility and caretaking can be distributed or shared in a group. Accountability can more easily attached to different roles, but a perceived responsibility is not transferable easily. Responsibility has an intrinsic and an extrinsic aspect. Intrinsic responsibility, in the sense of "ethical caring" (Nicholson & Kurucz, 2019) is a very personal thing, whereas extrinsic caretaking could be more easily attached to job descriptions and task lists.

12.2.3 Leadership and Ethics

Leadership and ethics have become of major interest in the recent years (Brown et al., 2005; Brown & Treviño, 2006; Ahmad et al., 2017; Pietersen, 2018). The research field started «from a research context looking at individual traits and virtues before becoming integrated into steward, authentic, and transformational leadership research. Later studies turned to looking at social context and collective leadership behaviour. The most recent focus is on how ethical leadership can change the organisational culture, or how it can be utilised for OD interventions» (Bachmann, 2017, p. 42).

A well accepted definition of ethical leadership was given by Brown et al. (2005): "We define ethical leadership here as the demonstration of normatively appropriate conduct through personal actions and interpersonal relationships, and the promotion of such conduct to followers through two-way communication, reinforcement, and decision-making." (Brown et al., 2005, p. 120).

We see a clear distinction between "ethical leadership" and "moral leadership". Where the former refers to ethically reflected leadership against the background of ethics (moral philosophy), the latter means values and norms for good leadership.

A recent empirical study (Bachmann, 2017) comes to the conclusion that «In the broadest sense, the absence of unethical behaviour can already be seen as bearing positive leadership characteristics (. . .)» (Bachmann, 2017, p. 141).

Wart (2014) presents a compilation of «types of ethical leadership» and assigned concepts, concerns and emphasis». However, he argues that the six major leadership perspectives he could identify are expressions of three classical approaches: the virtue approach, the deontological approach and the teleological approach.

«The view that leadership should be based on values and ethics blossomed in Burns' (1978) [(Burns, 1978)] seminal book, *Leadership*, which is recognized by many as pivotal in the perceptual shift from leadership as vested in an individual to leadership as a process. Understanding leadership as Burns proposed called for transforming relationships among followers and leaders that would result in achieving greater purpose and developing followers into being leaders themselves» (Komives et al., 2016, p. 7).

The consequences for leadership ethics are a related shift from virtue ethics of the leader to an ethics of cooperation. We argue that leader's virtues are still important and have meaning, notably at the limits of compliance (Bachmann, 2017, p. 29 ff.). Where compliance ends, virtues of the leader are coming into place. Since leadership is expanding into networks and relations, virtues of the leader are still of relevance, though an ethical framework for cooperating in a system of changing leadership functions is also required. Hierarchy as a means to reduce complexity and create (social) order could be then seen as one extreme form and special case of distributed leadership, where the distribution is extremely concentrated at one place, i.e. the leader.

In the following sections we will introduce into the theory and practice of cooperation and will elaborate an ethics of leadership as a «service» (function) for the social system: making sure that the interests of all are sufficiently considered (Rescher, 1989a).

12.3 Theory and Concepts of Cooperation

For cooperation within a social system coordination will be required. The elements of the system must be related to each other in a target-oriented manner. Thus, cooperation requires leadership.

Cooperation as co-operation (lat. operari = to work; lat. opus = work) is fundamentally linked to relations. Cooperation requires at least two units or systems, which are distinguishable, operating according to their respective structure and processes (their respective auto-logic), and are related to each other in some way by the same time. Focusing on human or social systems in the following considerations, cooperation indicates a specific *quality of relations* between human beings. This is in contrast to mechanical systems, which can be related purely structurally: «In a two-party relationship, while trust and cooperation can be broken down because of the actions of either party, they can be created or maintained only by the actions of *both* parties» (Bunker & Deutsch, 1995, p. 254). Cooperation points towards surplus values (emergence of values, 1 + 1 equals more than 2, non-zero sum games), whereas its opposite refers to zero sum games (the gain of one is the loss of the other). And we propose that the actors are basically free to make decisions and behave differently in any given case.

On the basis of Martin Buber's ideas on dialog, Rothenberg favors a concept where the partners can exist side by side: "In the «I-Thou» relationship, the «I» and «Thou» remain intact and are not swallowed up in a dialectical process that must and in «I *or* Thou», that is, in a new entity that nullifies the previous one. " (Rothenberg, 2015, p. 9).

Morton Deutsch's «theory of cooperation and competition», an early developed psychological theory on social interdependence (Bunker & Deutsch, 1995; Deutsch, 1985, 2011; Johnson & Johnson, 2011; Tjosvold & Johnson, 2000) and since its inception constantly expanded, is built on a fundamental distinction of positive and negative joining goal attainment: «I identify two basic types of goal interdependence: positive (where the goals are linked in such a way that the amount or probability of a person's goal attainment is positively correlated with the amount or probability of another obtaining his goal) and negative (where the goals are linked in such a way that the amount or probability of goal attainment is negatively correlated with the amount or probability of the other's goal attainment). To put it colloquially, if you're positively linked with another, then you sink or swim together; with negative linkage, if the other sinks, you swim, and if the other swims, you sink» (Deutsch, 2011, p. 24).

Group members can believe that their goals are cooperatively or competitively related or unrelated:

> I. In cooperation, individuals' goal achievements are positively correlated; individuals perceive that they can reach their goals if and only if the others in the group also reach their goals. Thus, individuals seek outcomes that are beneficial to all those with whom they are cooperatively linked.
>
> 2. In competition, individuals work against each other to achieve a goal that only one or a few can attain. Individuals' goal achievements are negatively correlated; each individual perceives that when one person achieves his or her goal, all others with whom he or she is competitively linked fail to achieve their goals. Thus, individuals seek an outcome that is personally beneficial but detrimental to all others in the situation.
>
> 3. In independence, there is no correlation among participants' goal attainments. Each individual perceives that he or she can reach his or her goal regardless of whether other individuals attain or do not attain their goals. Thus, individuals seek an outcome that is

> personally beneficial without concern for the outcomes of others. Of course, most situations are mixes of these pure forms. (Tjosvold & Johnson, 2000, pp. 133–134).

Interdependence leads to three psychological processes: substitutability, attitude (cathexis) and inducibility (Johnson & Johnson, 2011, p. 42). Substitutability means the extent to which actions of one individual can be substituted for actions of another one. Deutsch's definition goes as follows: «how a person's actions can satisfy another person's intentions» (Deutsch, 2011, p. 25), e.g. building a house will need the support of many people with specific expertise, without cooperation one might only build, if at all, a simple hut.

Attitude (cathexis) is defined by a natural tendency to react positively or negatively, respectively on stimuli given by the environment:

> This inborn tendency to act positively toward the beneficial and negatively toward the harmful is the foundation on which the human potentials for cooperation and love as well as for competition and hate develop. The basic psychological orientation of cooperation implies the positive attitude that 'we are for each other,' 'we benefit one another'; competition, by contrast, implies the negative attitude that 'we are against one another,' and in its extreme form, 'you are out to harm me.' (Deutsch, 2011, p. 25).

Inducibility refers to the capacity to influence and being influenced by others. Deutsch talks about the «readiness to accept» influence from others (Deutsch, 2011, p. 25). It is assumed that in a cooperative setting individuals will be able to manage mutual influence by persuasion (argument) rather than by force. Openness should mitigate communication problems and create an atmosphere of positive attitude among the actors.

Bateson's concept of «schismogenesis» (Bateson, 1936) fits Deutsch's ideas on the dynamics of cooperation and competition. Bateson postulates two forms of schismogenesis, symmetrical and non-symmetrical relationships. A symmetrical schismogenesis is a pattern of behavior which can be called competitive. Competition comes in the form of armament. While reacting on an opponent's move, one escalates the rivalry further. The more A is doing the more B is doing, which causes A to do even more. Complementary schismogenesis is indicated by a behavioral pattern where one part is showing dominance, the other submission. The more A is getting assertive, the more B will become submissive. If B has the role of the leader, submissiveness of the leader has unwanted consequences. If A embodies the role of the leader, the result is the old hierarchical form of leadership. Shared decision-making with different roles (leader, team) prevents schismogenesis.

The basic dynamics of positive and negative relationships, respectively, is clearly linked to the prisoner's dilemma paradigm, particularly zero-sum games. Those are characterized by a strategical situation where «rational» «players» aim to realize the best result for themselves, which is maximum pay off (utility maximization) (Rescher, 1989b). However, they are limited in their options to behave. No direct communication is possible, not coercive power can be executed on the other, just lone reasoning, anticipating and decision making exists. By the same time the «players» are connected, dependent in the way that what one decides has an impact on the other as well, and vice versa. The massive research on this issue clearly shows that one, as a «rational» actor, has to consider the other to opt for a move which could mean massive loss (Pies et al., 2009). In this situation it's rational to choose a «solution» which is less than optimal for both actors, but, and this is an advantage, they can avoid the risk of a big loss. The research also shows that trust can be quickly destroyed if one of the actors decides to defect (Bunker & Deutsch, 1995, p. 133). Thus, the prisoner's dilemma paradigm leads into the midst of moral issues. One could argue that from a virtue ethics' point of view an individual does not necessarily need to follow the "rational" strategy as suggested by economic theory, because it's not a natural law. Studies in experimental psychology (Kahnemann & Tversky, 2000) show that the "rational" strategy is not followed as strictly as economic theory seems to postulate. Rather individuals very often decide to give trust in advance. From a philosophical point of view there are good reasons to question the paradigm of "rational" strategy by practical reasoning (Nida-Rümelin, 2020). Cooperative leadership is required to prevent prisoner's dilemmas for the team.

A connecting pattern of cooperation and competition so far is the fact of two (at least) having a relationship of interdependence. Hence, we need to focus on the relationship's quality, which is crucial for justifying if it shows characteristics and effects of productivity for both (cooperation) or just for one (competition).

Based on the theory presented, we posit two forms of cooperation: a weak and a strong form of cooperation. The weak form of cooperation forces a joint mutual operation and the relationship will always be asymmetric in the sense of Bateson or competitive in the sense of Deutsch. A prerequisite for the strong form of cooperation is the principally free independent individual, which has the choice to engage in mutually operations or not. One of the main prerequisites of cooperation as interdependence is independence. Cooperation is driven by the insight, that joint goal attainment makes sense to meet one's own needs and wants; at the same time, it is an admission that the other has the same legitimate intention and a fair process of considering all interests is required. In this latter case the individual chooses deliberately and is a full-fledged partner. The less formal or factual power systems force cooperation (in its weak form), the stronger forms of cooperation are possible and in need. We also see weak forms of cooperation as compliance (individuals are more or less behaving according to the rules given), strong forms as partnership (two or more actors who are «free» to make decisions) (Ulrich, 1988; Nida-Rümelin, 2020).

There is a conceptual connection to trust. Lewicki und Bunker (Bunker & Deutsch, 1995, p. 133 ff.) distinguish three forms of trust in professional relationships: deterrence-based trust, knowledge-based trust and identification-based trust. Deterrence-based trust implies that people do what they ought to do due to their fear of negative consequences if they don't behave according to the rules set. Knowledge-based trust is rooted in predictability of another person's behavior. Identification-based trust is characterized by fully internalizing the others desires and intentions: «At this level, trust exists because each party effectively understands, agrees with, emphasizes with, and endorses what the other wants, and can act fort the other. Identification-based trust permits one to act as an agent for the other, substituting for the other in interpersonal transactions» (Bunker & Deutsch, 1995, p. 143 f.).

In the following section we aim to clarify the ethical foundations for cooperation as well as the role of leadership in cooperative relationships amongst individuals.

12.4 Ethics of Cooperation and the Role of Leadership

12.4.1 Ethics of Cooperation

Cooperation as co-operation as we have defined it above is a relationship of (at least) two independent (free) humans who are operating jointly (Ulrich, 1988). Joint operation means making things (ideas, services, resources etc.) available to each other of which one can dispose of (knowledge, goods etc.). Cooperation manifests itself in different forms and versions:

> Early in this great process of social organization three divergent types emerged, which still contend for supremacy in the worlds of action and of valuation: dominance, competition, and coöperation.[1] All mean a meeting of human forces. They rest respectively on power, rivalry, and sympathetic interchange. Each may contribute to human welfare. On the other hand, each may be taken so abstractly as to threaten human values. I hope to point out that the greatest of these is coöperation, and that it is largely the touchstone for the others. (Tufts, 1918, p. 4 f.).

According to Tufts dominance means inequality, cooperation "implies some sort of equality, some mutual relation" (Tufts, 1918, p. 5 f.). Tufts distinguishes two forms of competition, viz. a social and an unsocial form. The best example for a social form of competition would be sports. Sports is rivalry where the participants agreed to act according to rules given (see also Caillois, 1979). Tufts sees a common purpose in sports, which is "the zest of contest" (Tufts, 1918, p. 8 f.): "The contending rivals are in reality uniting to stimulate each other. Without the coöperation there would be no competition, and the competition is so conducted as to continue the relation" (Tufts, 1918, p. 9). An unsocial form of competition is characterized by not having a common purpose: "to contests in which there is no intention to continue or repeat the match, and in which no rules control" (Tufts, 1918, p. 10). An example would be the illegal use of doping substances in sports and the competition about which loopholes in the rules on the use of doping can be still discovered. Competition in those cases is, according to Tufts, wasteful and rather destructive.What are the ethical aspects of Tuft's concept of cooperation? Unlike competition, where one needs the others to play one's own games, cooperation builds on mutuality and common ends for "playing together". Mutuality implies more than mere transactions (exchange of things), mutuality means partly or temporarily becoming a unit, although the actors remain basically isolated and independent.

[1] Please don't be irritated by the outdated spelling due to a former indication in the English language: The diaeresis signifies that the second vowel forms a separate syllable.

> The purpose in cooperation is joint. Whether originally suggested by some leader of thought or action, or whether a composite of many suggestions in the give and take of discussion or in experiences of common need, it is weighed and adopted as a common end. It is not the work or possession of leaders alone, but embodies in varying degrees the work and active interest of all. (Tufts, 1918, p. 7)

To see this form of dependency from one to another leads to acceptance and respect of respective basic freedom and independence as well as all interests as equally significant:

> A cooperating group has two working principles: first, common purpose and common good; second, that men can achieve by common effort what they cannot accomplish singly. The first, reinforced by the actual interchange of ideas and services, tends to favor equality. It implies mutual respect, confidence, and good-will. The second favors a constructive and progressive attitude, which will find standards neither in nature nor in humanity's past, since it conceives man able to change conditions to a considerable extent and thus to realize new goods. These principles tend toward a type of liberty different from those just mentioned. As contrasted with the liberty of a dominant group, cooperation favors a liberty for all, a liberty of live and let live, a tolerance and welcome for variation in type, provided only this is willing to make its contribution to the common weal. Instead of imitation or passive acceptance of patterns on the part of the majority, it stimulates active construction. As contrasted with the liberty favored in competing groups, cooperation would emphasize positive control over natural forces, over health conditions, over poverty and fear. It would make each person share as fully as possible in the knowledge and strength due to combined effort, and thus liberate him from many of the limitations which have hitherto hampered him. (Tufts, 1918, p. 19–21).

The last sentence in above's quote reminds us, by the way, of Seligman's and Csikszentmihalyi's central pillar of Positive Psychology: to make regular people stronger and to include the perspective of what could be, rather than what just currently is Seligman and Csikszentmihalyi (2000). Thereby, it refers to a potential which is not yet fully tapped.Mutuality, communality, reciprocity are important terms which are in the center of Tufts' ethical concept of cooperation. Cooperation is the basis for innovation and progress within a group of people:

> Similarly with justice. Cooperation's ethics of distribution is not rigidly set by the actual interest and rights of the past on the one hand, nor by hitherto available resources on the other. Neither natural rights nor present ability and present service form a complete measure. Since cooperation evokes new interests and new capacities, it is hospitable to new claims and new rights; since it makes new sources of supply available, it has in view the possibility at least of doing better for all than can an abstract insistence upon old claims. It may often avoid the deadlock of a rigid system. It is better to grow two blades of grass than to dispute who shall have the larger fraction of the one which has previously been the yield. It is better, not merely because there is more grass, but also because men's attitude becomes forward-looking and constructive, not pugnacious and rigid. (Tufts, 1918, p. 21 f.)

> Power is likewise a value in a cooperating group, but it must be power not merely used for the good of all, but to some extent controlled by all and thus actually shared. Only as so controlled and so shared is power attended by the responsibility which makes it safe for its possessors. Only on this basis does power over other men permit the free choices on their part which are essential to full moral life. (Tufts, 1918, p. 22 f.).

> As regards the actual efficiency of a cooperating group, it may be granted that its powers are not so rapidly mobilized. In small, homogeneous groups, the loss of time is small; in large

> groups the formation of public opinion and the conversion of this into action is still largely a problem rather than an achievement. New techniques have to be developed, and it may be that for certain military tasks the military technique will always be more efficient. To the cooperative group, however, this test will not be the ultimate ethical test. It will rather consider the possibilities of substituting for war other activities in which cooperation is superior. And if the advocate of war insists that war as such is the most glorious and desirable type of life, cooperation may perhaps fail to convert him. But it may hope to create a new order whose excellence shall be justified of her children. (Tufts, 1918, p. 23 f.)

Tufts is fully aware of the problem of the size of a system. His remark points towards a practical challenge, i.e. the systems' size, which could be handled productively without too much corrosive effects, a challenge we will later discuss in the pragmatic's section.

An ethics of cooperation must illuminate the question of why and how human actors decide to solve problems jointly. We want to expand our proposal of seeing cooperation on a continuum from "weak" to "strong". A weak form of cooperation would be given when the actors are forced to act according to somebody's intentions. A strong form of cooperation would be characterized by a deliberate act of decision making, coming to an agreement and eventually work on joint problem solving.

In the middle there is a form of cooperation, where the leader listens to the suggestions of the group/others, but decides at the end. The group has only a socalled votum consultativum (only consultancy), not a votum deliberativum (right to decide by majority or other established rules).

Even a strong form of cooperation could be in the rational interest of both actors, therefore we do not need any driving force like altruism. What we need conceptually is a sufficient overlap of the perception, that the outcome and the way of joint action is considering the interest of both. This is what usually is expressed by the term "trust". Trust is an expression for the assumption that outcome and means of doing things jointly will be (sufficiently) beneficial to all involved actors. "Cooperative action (...) unlocks options through trust by reducing complexity for actions that would have remained unlikely and unattractive without trust, i.e. would not have found favor" (Luhmann, 1979, our translation from the German edition p. 30).

If weak and strong forms of cooperation are situated on a continuum, many "blends" of cooperative qualities in between are conceivable. There might be settings where we find weak forms of cooperation in a traditional setup of hierarchy in an organization and, by the same time, strong forms within a team. However mixed forms of cooperation will cause some problems, e.g. the need for specific boundaries which can protect the system against pressure from outside (Vanderslice, 1995).

Nicholas Recher's "hierarchy for moral norms" is a useful model for further study of cooperation because it combines fundamental ethical aspects with a very pragmatic perspective (Kellerwessel, 2014).

Rescher starts with the basic proposition that "at the heart of morality lies *benevolence*—a due care for the interests of people-in-general" (Rescher, 1989a, p. 6). Thereby he clearly expresses his conviction that no moral relativism exists and that variability of behavior (more or less, sometimes against moral norms) does not undermine moral absolutism (see also Gabriel, 2020).

THE STRATIFICATION LEVELS OF THE IMPLEMENTATION HIERARCHY FOR MORAL NORMS

Level 1	CHARACTERIZING AIMS	"due care for the best interest of others"
Level 2	BASIC PRINCIPLES AND VALUES	"honesty"
Level 3	GOVERNING RULES	"Do not lie"
Level 4	OPERATING DIRECTIVES (GROUNDRULES OF PROCEDURE)	"Say plainly what you believe (to be so)"
Level 5	PARTICULAR RULINGS	"Answer Jones truthfully (as best you can)"

Fig. 12.1 Rescher's Levels of moral norms (Rescher, 1989a, p. 50)

His model posits 5 levels of abstraction, from a universal and "absolute moral principle" (Rescher, 1989a, p. 48) to the "individual resolutions with respect to the specific issues arising in concrete cases" (Rescher, 1989a, p. 52) (Fig. 12.1).

He sees a variety of ways of being moral, without questioning the higher-level norms: "Different 'moralities' are simply diverse implementations of uniform moral principles" (Rescher, 1989a, p. 48).

At the top level of Rescher's model we find the proposition for the aims of morality, when it comes to cooperation to "act with a view to safeguarding the valid interests of others" (Rescher, 1989a, p. 50). Basic principles and values (level 2) must support in a way, that "such values define the salient norms that link the abstract characterizing aims to an operating morality of specific rules" (Rescher, 1989a, p. 51). It's important for Rescher to make clear that on the two topmost levels "there is simply no room for any 'disagreement about morality'" (Rescher, 1989a, p. 51).

Level 3 contains "controlling do's and don'ts of the moral practice of a community, providing us with general guidance in moral conduct" (Rescher, 1989a, p. 51). However, those guidances are still sometimes abstract and too much disconnected from currently prevailing circumstances. On level 4 context comes on stage and exceptions from the norm are possible under certain conditions (killing is legitimate if done in cases of self-defense). Level 5 incorporates action plans for all concrete real cases one could encounter.

Some more illustrative examples are displayed in Fig. 12.2.

Since the notion of "interest" is pivotal in Rescher's concept we aim to discuss the question of "what is a 'real' or 'best' interest" briefly.

People certainly have different understandings of their respective interest. And they may vary in time and culture. "Morality is concerned with furthering (. . .) particular interests only insofar as they reflect the universal interest that all people have" (Rescher, 1989a, p. 17). This would be met by gaining "one's livelihood in an way that suits one's abilities and enables one to derive some personal satisfaction" (Rescher, 1989a, p. 17).[2]

[2] See also the debate on individual merit and achievement and advantageous conditions, respectively, initiated by Michael Sandel with his latest book (Sandel, 2020).

ILLUSTRATIONS FROM THE IMPLEMENTATION HIERARCHY OF MORALITY

Level 1: *Characterizing Aims*

- Support the interests of people.
  - -Avoid injury to the interests of people
  - -Act to advance the interests of people

Level 2: *Basic Principles (Controlling Values)*

- Do not cause people needless pain (GENTLENESS)
- Do not endanger people's lives or their well being unnecessarily (CARE FOR SAFETY)
- Honor your genuine commitments to people; in dealing with people give them their just due (PROBITY)
- Help others when you reasonably can (GENEROSITY)
- Don't take improper advantage of others (FAIRNESS)

Level 3: *Operating Rules*

- Don't hurt people
- Don't lie; tell the truth
- Don't cheat

Level 4: *Operating Directives*

- Use anesthetics when operating on people
- Be candid when asked questions
- Play with fair dice

Level 5: *Concrete Rulings*

- Return the money you borrowed from Smith
- Don't pollute this river, dispose of your sewage elsewhere
- Don't let these children play with those matches

Fig. 12.2 Exemplary illustration of Rescher's hierarchy of norms (Rescher, 1989a, p. 53)

"What is at issue with *real* interests are those things that are *worthy* of being wanted, preferred, pursued because their attainment would be better for us—would enable us actually to improve our condition and circumstances. It is on the things we should want and prize that our best (or real) interests turn—and it is these that determine morality" (Rescher, 1989a, p. 17). Hence, to act heedfully (nowadays we may say in a reflective way) and in an awareness of mutual interests is essential for acting morally.

12.4.2 The Role of Leadership

Coming back to our definition of leadership as a function in a social system which reduces complexity and gives orientation, we can restate leadership to asking (and answering) the significant question: what shall we do? From a moral point of view we need to add: what would be good to do? And how can we do the things well?

"Analysing ethical leadership involves the interpretation of values and various assumptions about how influence is exercised" (Bachmann, 2017, p. 31).

Leadership is a joint task with shared responsibilities in a social system. The sources of leadership are manifold and stem from rank (hierarchy), team (distributed, shared leadership) as well as from the individual itself (self leadership) (Zirkler et al., 2020). Leadership can be executed in the field of norms (deontic leadership) or in the field of expertise (epistemic leadership) (see Bocheński, 1974). Pure hierarchy is one extreme and special form of leadership, e. g. the epistemic leadership of a schoolteacher. But by no means the only one. However, it might be the form we are most used to, which is familiar and seems to have proofed its functionality for a long time.

An ethics of leadership has to embrace threefold responsibilities: economic, ecological and social sustainability (Knoepffler & Albrecht, 2009): "The principle of sustainability should be regarded as a fundamental ethical principle also guiding ethical leadership behavior" (Knoepffler & Albrecht, 2009, p. 468, our translation).

Based on the work of Peter Ulrich (1988, 1998, 2016, 2017) an ethics of leadership needs to discuss issues of leadership in an normative-reflexive way, covering the relationship between the leader and followers, the legitimization of leadership (what may one do, what should one do) and its limits (what one must not do). All this has to be discussed against the background of inalienable human and personal rights (Knoepffler, 2006, p. 65 ff.).

Leadership ethics as applied ethics must be placed in a superordinate framework that is "not an uncorrectable system of rules" (Knoepffler, 2006, p. 15, our translation). "This framework of a good world must then be concretized for the different ranges of the ethics. (...) Each concretion of the ethics on a special sector of options of human action must orient itself so to speak at the 'rules of the game', which apply in it" (Knoepffler, 2006, p. 15 f., our translation).

While leadership in weak cooperations represents the one-sided exercise of power, it is different in strong cooperations. Here leadership is the expanded function of moderating the moral norm of care for the interests of all. It raises the questions of level 3 to 5 guidances (according to Rescher (1989a)) and ensures that the moral norm becomes feasible in practice. While doing so, leadership is fully aware of the fact that "feasibility" could be misused. Taking the context for implementing a norm into account does not mean that the context justifies any behavior. Feasibility rather means do to the best to meet the norm and considering that certain context factors may work as hinderances and obstacles in fully meeting the norm and acknowledging that there may be different ways to meet the norm best (equifinality).

The role of leadership can be illustrated by the Drucker's idea of "social ecology" (Drucker, 1992). The social ecologist cares for his system and provides conditions in which the system can flourish. However, this needs to be done without maintaining one's own comfort on the costs of others. This suggests a moral understanding in which fair relationships are significant.

A leadership ethics that wants to meet the demand for strong cooperation must express a specific moral leadership. Moral leadership related to strong cooperation takes care of creating a special environment. «The major challenge for leaders of cooperatives is to provide strong leadership for the organization while at the same time encouraging the development of leadership and responsibility throughout the organization. Leaders must provide a clear vision of cooperation at the framework for organizational functioning and yet nurture the development of an evolving organizational vision that is shared by all organizational members» (Bunker & Deutsch, 1995, p. 195).

Therefore, it aims at:

1. Establishing a purpose quest in the organization, expressing the organization's purpose explicitly, reflecting and adjusting the organization's purpose from time to time, keeping a joint and mutual vision vivid and attractive for all people involved
2. Transparency: providing and stimulating exchange of information, giving access to information, preventing information asymmetry as best as possible
3. Maintaining a culture of "non-coersive discourse" (Habermas, 2009); this requires psychological safe spaces and error friendliness
4. Inquiring how the interest of all can best be met within the group or system, differentiating frequent interests and single interests, since frequent interest have more urge to be met; documenting and (internally) publish the commitments made
5. Finding solutions as best as possible to solve individual issues (interests) if they are in conflict with the joint interests
6. Prophylactic conflict management, perceiving the "weak" signals at the passage from difference to conflict (Deutsch, 1985; Zirkler, 2014).
7. Frequent reflections on the principles of the game, adapting the rules if required, reflecting on the processes which lead to specific rules, adapting the rule making process, if required, inviting outside observers who can help to mitigate blind spots
8. Accepting the fact, that not every issue (conflict) can be solved to the satisfaction of all, giving solace if required, preventing people to fall into a pattern of "learned helplessness" (Peterson, 1993).

It is certainly helpful if the person who has the leadership role (however long and intensive) is virtuous, i.e. has developed a set of habits, which are "prescription for action in accordance with a good plan of life. The actions which express moral virtue will, Aristotle tells us, avoid excess and defect" (Kenny, 2010, S. 213; Nass, 2018, S. 33 f.). Virtue ethics is particularly of meaning in strong forms of cooperation. The person represents the entire idea of the way actors agreed to jointly operate (if they cooperate strongly), "walk the talk" is supporting the idea, role models promote the idea, they signal integrity. Virtues are particularly of relevance where a person in its leadership role cannot invoke on rules and regulations, i.e. beyond compliance, where the person has to act according to the idea behind the rule, not following the rule literally. Moreover, a leadership position can be seducible. The person holding the position needs a good inner compass to not exploit the position for the sake of her singular interests. He may gain some personal profit while serving as a leader, however she must by no means take full advantage.

Beyond compliance is also the realm of organizing processes which allows a social system to come to agreements and doable solutions of how the can and how they want to be productive together.

12.5 Pragmatics of an Ethics of Leadership as Facilitating Cooperation (How to Do «It»)

It's one thing to claim an ethics of leadership which ought to facilitate (strong) cooperation and envision reason why this should be good and beneficial. But it's another thing to implement such an approach in real life. According to modern thinkers in business ethics like Ulrich (1988), Homann and Suchanek (2005), and Lütge and Uhl (2018) it would be naïve and quixotic to implement an ethics of leadership and cooperation against the predominant logic of "modern" organizations, particularly their calling for efficiency and effectiveness.

However, we can basically distinguish between a logic of maximization and optimization. The logic of maximization would mean to be as much as possible effective and efficient by all means (Tufts would speak of "cut-throat competition" (Tufts, 1918, passim)), whereby maximation is restricted to the well-being of the respective organisation without caring for external effects Optimization, instead, gives room to other aspects as well, e.g. ecological and social sustainability, which may be of consideration with good reasons as well (e.g. human rights). The distinction refers to the ethical discussion about what a "good" life consists in and to the question whether business is restricted to business only (are means of "productivity" according to capitalist ideas) or business is there for improving our common well-being.

Rescher's level model is in itself a recommendation how to come from abstract norms to everyday activities. A group or any other social system does not necessarily need to do this on their own, although they may and some actually do. Instead, a lot of ethically functional practices are already available and can serve as "templates" or blueprints. Leadership should make sure that the discourse on a practical level is continuously, we are not saying all the time, keep on going. Templates are also available on a management level as "operating systems" such as Holacracy (Robertson, 2016) and as documented experience (Bauer et al., 2019). From Holacracy we derive the idea to distinguish between settings which are determined to clarify operative issues and such where it is about reflecting the (cooperative) processes on a meta level.

Those templates, blueprints and experiences need to be customized and adjusted to the respective conditions. This is possible by discourse, decision making and implementation of whatever was decided. Facilitating and maintaining a non-coersive discourse (as much as possible) will be one of the most important tasks for leadership functions if strong cooperation is desired. This will be prerequisite on a personal level, and is a specific virtue of the respective leader. Some degree of moral and personal development will certainly be required from every member of the group. It's the leaders' task to support and foster the process of individual maturation as a joint task.

For managing the discourse and mutual sense making processes (Weick, 2009) some methods and means have been turned out to be helpful, such as "nonviolent communication" (Rosenberg, 2015), "sociocracy" (Buck & Villines, 2017), "Warm Data Lab" (Bateson, n.d.), "appreciative inquiry" (Cooperrider, 2005). Schein's concept of levels of relationships (Schein, 2018) helps to better understand the consequences of carefully listening and being interested in the other, rather than just utilize the other to meet my needs because I may have the power to do so. We must not forget that "my needs" often are representations of interests of others (the boss, the organization, the nation etc.; introjects in psychoanalytic language), for whom people feel obliged.

Another pivotal aspect of the pragmatics of an ethics of leadership refers to conflict management. Leadership in cooperative social systems has to carefully observe and "manage" differences prior to them getting real conflicts. We see the various differences in social groups as an inevitable part of social life and the basis of progress and development. However, if differences are being expressed as conflicts there is an increasing risk of acceleration and "widening the gap" which would be an amplification of potential negative aspects within a relationship. Prophylactic conflict management would be an important competence for those who function as care takers, i.e. leaders in a social system. Since differences are inevitable and productive within a range of quantity and quality, leadership should be sensitive to induct differences into a discourse, before they become "hot" (Pastoors & Ebert, 2019, p. 25 ff.).

In some cases hot conflicts cannot be prevented of evolving. The way those in leadership function manage the process of conflict resolution will be a crucial signal for all actors on how much trust, justice, equity etc. is really existent in the system (see also Deutsch, 1985, p. 72 ff.).

For conflict management, too, many tools, methods and frameworks exist, such as the "principled negotiation" (Harvard Negotiation Project) (Fisher, 1983).

The inclusive leadership model (Zirkler & Herzog, 2021) with its continuum of uniqueness and belonging seems to be a useful framework to create a social space allowing to express individuality and addressing the need of social affiliation at the same time.

However, most of the "tools" depicted can be abused for fueling, self-interest, unfair power execution etc. if they are not utilized in a spirit of and based on an ethics of cooperation. Therefore, an agreement of all people involved is required to adhere to the principles of an ethics of cooperation while being fully aware of the risk of abusiveness (sometimes, someone, somewhere). Abusing the principles not necessarily puts them into question. Abuse could be understood as a form of "violating" the principles at their margins and limits. Crucial will be the way a social system and their leaders handles "violations".

Insight in the benefit of cooperation is rooted in rationality plus positive emotions. The more encounter people have they perceive as positive, the more trust will be built, the more cooperation we can expect. Leadership can stimulate positive emotions in "really" engaging with the individuals involved (Schein's level-2-relationships (Schein, 2018)). This is in accordance to Deutsch's "crude law of social relations": "the characteristic processes and effects elicited by a given type of social relationship also tend to elicit that type of social relationship" (Deutsch, 1985, p. 69).

For shared leadership responsibilities we need commitment and obligation, i.e. a system of clearly defining and describing roles as well as attached accountabilities. It must be clear who is taking care of what and whom. And the person adopting a role must clarify itself. Once tensions are observable about a misfit or a vagueness of roles, whoever has adopted this part of the leadership role should pick up the "weak signals" and induct them into to social system in an appropriate way (i.e. not always and not any time). Clarity, in turn, is an ongoing process of clarification that will never be completed and will never be finished.

People are different, they have diverse competencies and capabilities, different aspirations, hopes, desires etc. It might be useful to think about the question which characteristics of individuals are more or less useful for a leadership position. An evaluation of the deep-rooted traits of a person (Knoepffler, 2009, p. 147 ff.) would address the question with whom best to engage in cooperation and who is best qualified for leadership positions. The ethical principal which applies is the request for self-clarification; leadership can and should help to improve and professionalize the associated social processes.

On the basis of his theory of cooperation and competition, cooperative groups will show some positive characteristics, which are good operationalizations and measures for the extent to which the social system is cooperative. We summarize and order those as follows:

1. More communication (quantity) will be going on and the quality of communication is better (listening, trying to understand what other's mean). More ideas will be expressed.
2. More kindness, more support and less destructive expression will be found in the communicative exchange of ideas. Group members will be more satisfied with the group and feel better (save) in the group. They will be more attentive to each other. See the concepts and methods of "Positive Psychology" for practical usage (Seligman, 2011).
3. More feelings of (psychological) safety, more confidence, a higher rate of similarities in believes, values etc. are perceived among group members
4. More division of labor, more coordination of problem-solving tasks, more orientation to task achievement, more discipline in discussions will be shown. More productivity will be seen in such groups.
5. Differences and conflicts in such groups are seen as a joint problem, which needs joint effort to resolve it. The interests of all actors are considered as important and equally legitim, thus solutions would need to address those interests as best as possible.

If a social system wants to increase its capacity to cooperate, the issue of justice will be central to succeed. Deutsch (1985) raises the central question: "Under what conditions are people with conflicting interests able to work out an agreement (that is, a system of justice defining what each shall give and receive in the transaction between them) that is stable and mutually satisfying?" (Deutsch, 1985, p. 6). He broadly understands the associated values as those values "that foster effective social cooperation to promote individual well-being" (Deutsch, 1985, p. 37). More in details Deutsch proposes several principles, such as:

1. In cooperative relations in which economic productivity is a primary goal, equity rather than equality or need will be the dominant principle of distributive justice
2. In cooperative relations in which the fostering or maintenance of enjoyable social relations is the common goal, quality will be the dominant principle of distributive justice
3. In cooperative relations in which the fostering of personal development and personal welfare is the common goal, need will be the dominant principle of distributive justice (Deutsch, 1985, p. 38)

We derive from (Deutsch, 1985) a typology of social relations, admittedly an oversimplification of what's going on in reality, but a good starting point. In the cooperative section we find a variety of productive relations in contrast to the competitive part of his overview. Interestingly hierarchy is also subsumed in the cooperative category. However, it is said, that hierarchy as a superordinate-subordinate relationship if not fully legitimized by those in the subordinate position, is often a cause of conflict and competition, "this type of relation is rarely free of strong competitive elements. It follows then that some superordinate-subordinate relations in hierarchically organized systems will have the character of power struggles, and these would be more appropriately classified as belonging to cell 16" ("regulated power struggle") (Deutsch, 1985, p. 78).

For cooperation, whether formal or informal, we find a range of ways to create productive relationships that can be alternatives to top-down relationships, such as "problem solving", "organized cooperation", "caring", "protecting" and even "educational". All those approaches would fit into an understanding of leadership of establishing, fostering and maintaining cooperation (see also Schein, 2018). They can be outlined as distributed leadership roles within a social system and strongly support cooperation as caring for the interest of all as a joint challenge (Fig. 12.3).

12.6 Does Cooperation Pay Off?

Weak forms of cooperation (transactionally operating according to the rules and principles set, thus to comply) are in any case inevitable in today's highly specialized and labor-divided world.

The more we rely on the creativity, power for innovation and communication skills (presenting ideas, freely speaking up, listening to others, adding ideas etc.) the more strong forms of cooperation are needed. If a social system in total wants to benefit from the innovative power of its "human resources" it needs to create the

Sixteen Types of Social Relations

		SOCIAL-EMOTIONAL		TASK-ORIENTED	
		Informal	*Formal*	*Informal*	*Formal*
COOPERATIVE	*Equal*	1 a. "intimate" b. (lovers) c. love-making	5 a. "fraternal" b. (club members) C. social party	9 a. "problem-solving" b. (colleagues) c. staff meeting	13 a. "organized cooperation" b. (members of a task force) c. working together with differentiated responsibilities to solve a problem
COOPERATIVE	*Unequal*	2 a. "caring" b. (mother child) c. nursing	6 a. "protecting" b. (policeman-child) c. helping	10 a. "educational b. (professor-graduate student) c. working together informally on a research project under professor's direction	14 a. "hierarchical organization" b. (superviso-employee) c. supervisor assigning employee to a certain task
COMPETITIVE	*Equal*	3 a. "antagonistic" b. (personal enemies) c. fighting	7 a. "rivalry" b. (divorced couple) c. contesting for child's attention	11 a. "competition" b. (contestants in an informal game) c. trying to score points against the other	15 a. "regulated competition" b. (business rivals) c. bidding against each other for a contract
COMPETITIVE	*Unequal*	4 a. "sadomasochistic" b. (bully-victim) c. tormenting	8 a. "dominating" b. (expert-novice) c. intimidating	12 a. "power struggle" b. (authority-rebel) c. guerrilla warfare	16 a. "regulated power struggle" b. (guard-prisoner) c. ordering the prisoner to keep in step

Each type of social relation is: (a) given a label; (b) illustrated in terms of people who might be in such a relationship; and (c) illustrated in terms of a kind of activity might occur in such a relationship.

Fig. 12.3 Sixteen Types of social relations according to Deutsch (1985, p. 78)

conditions where creativity, innovation, productivity etc. is more likely. Strong forms of cooperation have some social prerequisites.

The strong form of cooperation is a way of life and the conviction that ethics matter. Paradise is hard to reach, and it's not even clear if the state of paradise should be aspired, but with cooperation you can get a little closer to a life which deserves to be called humane, as, for instance, indicated in the declaration of independence: "We hold these truths to be self-evident, that all men are created equal, that they are endowed by their Creator with certain unalienable Rights, that among these are Life, Liberty and the pursuit of Happiness" (*Declaration of Independence*, 2015).

However, we can identify some more sturdy and hands-on reasons, why cooperation pays off.

A study by Espedal et al. (2012) shows that cooperation pays off in terms of organizational performance, i.e. invested capital. Ehnert (2009) connects cooperation to sustainability: "Sustainable HRM is the pattern of planned or emerging human resource strategies and practices intended to enable organizational goal achievement while simultaneously reproducing the HR base over a long-lasting calendar time" (Ehnert, 2009, p. 74). Bachmann found positive impact of ethical leadership on motivation and climate: "It is noticeable, at least in the plant researched here, how much the absence of criteria like normative conduct, integrity, trust or fair treatment of employees, which are typically associated with ethical leadership, can contribute to a low employee motivation and a bad climate" (Bachmann, 2017, p. 142).

Though, the answer to the question of pay off depends largely on the value system in which it is raised. However, cooperation in the way outlined here will pay off in the long run not only ethically, but economically, too.

Acknowledgments The authors wish to thank Jan Müller for his support and help in preparing the manuscript for this publication.

References

Ahmad, I., Gao, Y., & Hali, S. M. (2017). A review of ethical leadership and other ethics-related leadership theories. *European Scientific Journal, 13*(29). https://doi.org/10.19044/esj.2017.v13n29p10

Aya, R. (1978). Norbert Elias and "the civilizing process". *Theory and Society, 5*(2), 219–228.

Bachmann, B. (2017). *Ethical leadership in organizations*. Springer.

Bateson, G. (1936). *Naven: A survey of the problems suggested by a composite picture of the culture of a New Guinea tribe drawn from three points of view*. University Press.

Bateson, N. (n.d.). *Warm data*. Accessed from https://batesoninstitute.org/warm-data/

Bauer, C., Hohl, E., & Zirkler, M. (2019). Der lange Weg zur Holakratie. *Zeitschrift Organisationsentwicklung, 2*(2019), 37–44.

Bocheński, J. M. (1974). *Was ist Autorität? Einführung in die Logik der Autorität* ([Orig.-Ausg.]). Verlag Herder.

Boisot, M., & Mckelvey, B. (2011). *Complexity and organization–environment relations: Revisiting Ashby's law of requisite variety* (pp. 279–298). Sage. https://doi.org/10.4135/9781446201084.n16

Brown, M. E., & Treviño, L. K. (2006). Ethical leadership: A review and future directions. *The Leadership Quarterly, 17*(6), 595–616. https://doi.org/10.1016/j.leaqua.2006.10.004

Brown, M. E., Treviño, L. K., & Harrison, D. A. (2005). Ethical leadership: A social learning perspective for construct development and testing. *Organizational Behavior and Human Decision Processes, 97*(2), 117–134. https://doi.org/10.1016/j.obhdp.2005.03.002

Buck, J., & Villines, S. (2017). *We the people: Consenting to a deeper democracy* (2nd). Accessed from Sociocracy.info.

Bunker, B. B., & Deutsch, M. (1995). *Conflict, cooperation, and justice: Essays inspired by the work of Morton Deutsch*. Jossey-Bass.

Burns, J. M. (1978). *Leadership*. Harper & Row.

Caillois, R. (1979). *Man, play, and games* (Repr.). Schocken Books.
Chemers, M. M. (2000). Leadership research and theory: A functional integration. *Group Dynamics: Theory, Research, and Practice, 4*(1), 27–43. https://doi.org/10.1037/1089-2699.4.1.27
Cooperrider, D. L. (2005). *Appreciative inquiry*. Berrett-Koehler Publishers.
Crumley, C. L. (1995). Heterarchy and the analysis of complex societies. *Archaeological Papers of the American Anthropological Association, 6*(1), 1–5. https://doi.org/10.1525/ap3a.1995.6.1.1
Declaration of Independence: A Transcription. (2015, November 1). National Archives. Accessed from https://www.archives.gov/founding-docs/declaration-transcript
Deutsch, M. (1985). *Distributive justice: A social-psychological perspective*. Yale University Press.
Deutsch, M. (2011). Cooperation and competition. In P. T. Coleman (Ed.), *Conflict, interdependence, and justice: The intellectual legacy of Morton Deutsch* (pp. 23–40). Springer. https://doi.org/10.1007/978-1-4419-9994-8_2
Drucker, P. F. (1992). Reflections of a social ecologist. *Society, 29*(4), 57–64. https://doi.org/10.1007/BF02695313
Drucker, P. F. (2012). *Managing in the next society*. Taylor & Francis.
Ehnert, I. (2009). *Sustainable human resource management: A conceptual and exploratory analysis from a paradox perspective*. Physica-Verlag.
Elias, N. (2000). *The civilizing process*. Wiley-Blackwell.
Espedal, B., Kvitastein, O., & Grønhaug, K. (2012). When cooperation is the norm of appropriateness: How does CEO cooperative behaviour affect organizational performance?: When cooperation is the norm of appropriateness. *British Journal of Management, 23*(2), 257–271. https://doi.org/10.1111/j.1467-8551.2011.00737.x
Fisher, R. (1983). *Getting to yes*. Hutchinson.
Gabriel, M. (2020). *Moralischer Fortschritt in dunklen Zeiten: Universale Werte für das 21. Jahrhundert*. Ullstein.
Gordon, A., & Yukl, G. (2004). The future of leadership research: Challenges and opportunities. *German Journal of Human Resource Management, 18*(3), 359–365. https://doi.org/10.1177/239700220401800307
Greenleaf, R. (2002). *Servant leadership: A journey into the nature of legitimate power and greatness*. Paulist Press.
Gross, P. (2002). *Die Multioptionsgesellschaft* (9. Druck, Bd. 1917). Suhrkamp.
Habermas, J. (2009). *Theorie des kommunikativen Handelns* ([7. Aufl.], Bde. 1175, Ed. 7). Suhrkamp.
Heifetz, R. A. (1994). *Leadership without easy answers*. Harvard University Press.
Hoch, J. E. (2013). Shared leadership and innovation: The role of vertical leadership and employee integrity. *Journal of Business and Psychology, 28*(2), 159–174. https://doi.org/10.1007/s10869-012-9273-6
Hoch, J. E., & Kozlowski, S. W. J. (2014). Leading virtual teams: Hierarchical leadership, structural supports, and shared team leadership. *Journal of Applied Psychology, 99*(3), 390–403. https://doi.org/10.1037/a0030264
Homann, K., & Suchanek, A. (2005). *Ökonomik eine Einführung* (2., überarb. Aufl.). Mohr Siebeck.
Johnson, D. W., & Johnson, R. T. (2011). Intellectual legacy: Cooperation and competition. In P. T. Coleman (Ed.), *Conflict, interdependence, and justice: The intellectual legacy of Morton Deutsch* (pp. 41–63). Springer. https://doi.org/10.1007/978-1-4419-9994-8_3
Kahnemann, D., & Tversky, A. (2000). *Choices, values, and frames*. Cambridge University Press.
Kellerwessel, W. (2014). *Nicholas Rescher—Das philosophische System: Einführung—Überblick—Diskussionen: Bd* (Vol. 5). De Gruyter.
Kenny, A. (2010). *A new history of Western philosophy*. Oxford University Press.
Knoepffler, N. (2006). *Einführung in die angewandte Ethik: Bd. Band 1* (Originalausg.). Alber.
Knoepffler, N. (2009). *Angewandte Ethik: Ein systematischer Leitfaden* (Vol. 3293). Böhlau.

Knoepffler, N., & Albrecht, R. (2009). Entwurf einer Führungsethik—Ein Weg zu einem nachhaltigen unternehmerischen Wirken. In *Betriebswirtschaftliche Forschung und Praxis: BFuP* (Vol. 61). NWB-Verlag.

Ko, C., Ma, J., Bartnik, R., Haney, M. H., & Kang, M. (2018). Ethical leadership: An integrative review and future research agenda. *Ethics & Behavior, 28*(2), 104–132. https://doi.org/10.1080/10508422.2017.1318069

Komives, W., Susan, R., & Wagner. (2016). *Leadership for a better world*. Jossey-Bass.

Kotter, J. (2012). Accelerate! *Harvard Business Review, 90*, 44–54.

Kotter, J. (2014). *Accelerate: Building strategic agility for a faster-moving world*. Harvard Business Review Press.

Laloux, F. (2014). *Reinventing organizations: A guide to creating organizations inspired by the next stage of human consciousness* (1st ed.). Nelson Parker.

Luhmann, N. (1979). *Trust and power*. Polity Press.

Lütge, C., & Uhl, M. (2018). *Wirtschaftsethik*. Verlag Franz Vahlen.

Nass, E. (2018). *Handbuch Führungsethik Teil 1 Systematik und maßgebliche Denkrichtungen*. Verlag W. Kohlhammer.

Neufeind, M., O'Reilly, J., Ranft, F., Network, P., & Zentrum, D. P. (2018). *Work in the digital age: Challenges of the fourth industrial revolution*. Rowman & Littlefield International.

Nicholson, J., & Kurucz, E. (2019). Relational leadership for sustainability: Building an ethical framework from the moral theory of 'ethics of care'. *Journal of Business Ethics, 156*(1), 25–43. https://doi.org/10.1007/s10551-017-3593-4

Nida-Rümelin, J. (2020). *Eine Theorie praktischer Vernunft*. De Gruyter.

Pastoors, S., & Ebert, H. (2019). *Psychologische Grundlagen zwischenmenschlicher Kooperation*. Springer Fachmedien Wiesbaden.

Peterson, C. (1993). *Learned helplessness: A theory for the age of personal control*. Oxford University Press.

Pies, I., Hielscher, S., & Beckmann, M. (2009). Moral commitments and the societal role of business: An Ordonomic approach to corporate citizenship. *Business Ethics Quarterly, 19*, 375–401. https://doi.org/10.5840/beq200919322

Pietersen, C. (2018). A typology for the categorisation of ethical leadership research. *African Journal of Business Ethics, 12*(2). https://doi.org/10.15249/12-2-153

Praszkier, R. (2018). *Empowering leadership of tomorrow*. Cambridge University Press.

Reckwitz, A. (2019). *Die Gesellschaft der Singularitäten: Zum Strukturwandel der Moderne* (Wissenschaftliche Sonderausgabe, Erste Auflage). Suhrkamp.

Rescher, N. (1989a). *Moral absolutes: An essay on the nature and rationale of morality* (Vol. 2). P. Lang.

Rescher, N. (1989b). *Rationality: A philosophical inquiry into the nature and the rationale of reason*. Clarendon Press.

Robertson, B. (2016). *Holacracy: The revolutionary management system that abolishes hierarchy*. Portfolio Penguin.

Rosa, H. (2014). *Beschleunigung: Die Veränderung der Zeitstrukturen in der Moderne* (10. Auflage, Bd. 1760). Suhrkamp.

Rosenberg, M. B. (2015). *Nonviolent communication: A language of life* (3rd ed.). Puddle Dancer Press.

Rothenberg, M. (2015). *The psychology of Tzimtzum*. Maggid Books.

Sandel, M. J. (2020). *The tyranny of merit*. Farrar, Straus and Giroux.

Schein, E. H. (2018). *Humble leadership*. Berrett-Koehler Publishers.

Schwab, K. (2019). *Die Zukunft der Vierten Industriellen Revolution: Wie wir den digitalen Wandel gestalten*. Deutsche Verlags-Anstalt.

Seligman, M. E. P. (2011). *Flourish—A new understanding of happiness and well-being – and how to achieve them*.

Seligman, M. E. P., & Csikszentmihalyi, M. (2000). Positive psychology. *American Psychologist, 55*(1), 5–14.

Sobral, F., & Furtado, L. (2019). Post-heroic leadership: Current trends and challenges in leadership education. *Revista de Administração de Empresas, 59*, 209–214.

Spillane, J. P. (2010). *Distributed leadership*. Jossey-Bass.

Taylor, F. W. (2012). *The principles of scientific management*. The Floating Press.

Tjosvold, D., & Johnson, D. (2000). Deutsch's theory of cooperation and competition. In M. M. Beyerlein (Ed.), *Work teams: Past, present and future* (pp. 131–155). Springer. https://doi.org/10.1007/978-94-015-9492-9_8

Tufts, J. H. (1918). *The ethics of cooperation: Bd. [5]*. Houghton Mifflin. Accessed from https://archive.org/details/ethicsofcopera00tuftuoft/page/n11/mode/2up

Uhl-Bien, M. (2006). Relational leadership theory: Exploring the social processes of leadership and organizing. *The Leadership Quarterly, 17*(6), 654–676. https://doi.org/10.1016/j.leaqua.2006.10.007

Ulrich, P. (1988). Zur Ethik der Kooperation in Organisationen. In *Forschungsstelle für Wirtschaftsethik an der Hochschule St. Gallen für Wirtschafts- und Sozialwissenschaften* (Vol. 21). University of St. Gallen.

Ulrich, P. (1998). *Führungsethik: Ein grundrechteorientierter Ansatz* (2., vollst. überarb. und erw. Aufl., Bd. 68, ed.2). Institut für Wirtschaftsethik.

Ulrich, P. (2016). *Integrative Wirtschaftsethik: Grundlagen einer lebensdienlichen Ökonomie* (5., durchgesehene Auflage). Haupt Verlag.

Ulrich, P. (2017, November 3). *Grundzüge der Führungsethik. Forum Wirtschaftsethik*. Accessed from https://www.forum-wirtschaftsethik.de/grundzuege-der-fuehrungsethik/

Vanderslice, V. J. (1995). Cooperation within a competitive context: Lessons from worker cooperations. In *Conflict, cooperation & justice* (pp. 175–204). Jossey-Bass.

Wart, M. V. (2014). Contemporary varieties of ethical leadership in organizations. *International Journal of Business Administration, 5*(5), p27. https://doi.org/10.5430/ijba.v5n5p27

Weick, K. E. (2009). *Making sense of the organization*. Wiley.

Zirkler, M. (2014). Reconciliation in der postmodernen Arbeitswelt. In U. Mäder, B. Schürch, & S. Mugier (Eds.), *Reconciliation: Vergeben ohne zu vergessen?* (pp. 165–177). edition gesowip.

Zirkler, M. (2019, September 26). *Power shift—Transitions from hierarchy to Holacracy*. Holacracy Forum, Amsterdam. Retrieved from https://www.holacracyforum.com/

Zirkler, M., & Herzog, J. (2021). Inclusive leadership: Die Gestaltung von Zusammengehörigkeit als zentrale Herausforderung in der digitalen Arbeitswelt. *Wirtschaftspsychologie, 23*(3), 6–31.

Zirkler, M., Scheidegger, N., & Bargetzi, A. I. (2020). *Führung auf Distanz. Eine Untersuchung zur Distanzführung während des Corona-bedingten Lockdowns 2020 an der ZHAW [Forschungsbericht]*. Zürcher Hochschule für Angewandte Wissenschaften.

Chapter 13
Mindfulness and Technology

Jan Willem de Graaf

13.1 Introduction

This chapter discusses the relationship between mindfulness and technology. Especially in today's world, where technology has so naturally invaded the smallest details of our existence, the need for distance and reflection is vital. Mindfulness can play an important role in achieving this distance and reflecting on what we know and do.

13.2 Man and Technology

13.2.1 Technology: Expanding the Possibilities on a Collective Level

On average, on an individual level life has become more monotonous with each revolution in civilization: from nomadic hunter-gatherers to the first sedentary farmers (the Neolithic Revolution began about 15,000 years ago), from farmers to workers in the Industrial Revolution of the eighteenth century, and more recently from workers to computer workers in the information technology revolution. For the species as a whole, however, there is a tremendous increase in opportunity after each revolution. The availability of fire, for example, moved our prehistoric ancestors from a middle position to the absolute top of the food chain. Virtually any hunter could start a fire quickly and accurately to use for warmth, hunting (strategy), food preparation, or tool making. On the individual level, almost no one has this

J. W. de Graaf (✉)
Man & Labour, Saxion University of Applied Sciences, Enschede, The Netherlands
e-mail: j.w.degraaf@saxion.nl

V. Schulte et al. (eds.), *Mindful Leadership in Practice*,
https://doi.org/10.1007/978-3-030-97311-7_13

competence today, but on our collective level, we all have access to energy through internal combustion engines and central heating systems where fire is controlled very precisely, efficiently and accurately.

During the Industrial Revolution in the eighteenth and nineteenth centuries, it quickly became clear that what was good for a machine was not necessarily good for humans. For many factory workers, life became monotonous, while on a collective level, great innovations emerged, such as mobility by train, car and airplane, radio, television and household appliances, and—on an abstract level—leisure. Information and communication technology in the twentieth century brought unprecedented opportunities to society. It is a paradox that the loss of a diverse and rich life at the level of the average individual produced new opportunities at the collective level. Our 200,000-year-old biological systems provide a hardware system, an "emulator," on which we have enormous latitude to develop and play various "cultural" systems-religions, theories, arts, concepts, stereotypes, forms of government, NGOs, and multinational corporations. It is indeed cultural software on biological hardware. Incongruence or even disruption is the force of progress or development, although we prefer to keep the clashes between different views and cultures manageable. Yet there are biologists who believe that our brains have been getting smaller and smaller since the first Homo sapiens. Apparently, we need less brain volume today than our hunting and gathering ancestors. If this development continues, it will be another 200,000 years or so before we return to the brain of our closest living relative, the chimpanzee.

We contrast the concept of mindfulness with that of thoughtlessness, of thinking and behaving in a rigid and automated (machine) way, regardless of actual circumstances. The increasingly monotonous life described above can produce this very thoughtlessness. But time and again, individuals break free from the yoke that a revolution initially imposed on them. Reflection on automated existence—mindfulness—plays a role in this escape, which in the past was often stimulated by religion. Mindfulness then means being open to surprise and sensitive to the specific context, freeing oneself from the tyranny of the old mindset. As a result of their ongoing reflection on an increasingly machine-based existence, some farmers, machine workers, and later computer workers were able to free themselves from it on an individual level. Later, they cleared the way for many others. Mindfulness plays an important role in two different ways. First, reflection is required to be able to distance oneself and stay connected to others as well as the larger cultural or religious narratives. This kind of collective knowledge forms the basis of human society and cooperation and, more importantly, meaning. Second, mindfulness is necessary to optimize the use of new technologies from each individual's unique situation. Humans are not machines, but they are capable of learning mechanics at a very high level. After much practice and thought, a top pianist, for example, adjusts the mechanics of keys, hammers, pedals, and strings according to his or her own needs and control. From people's sense of technology and from their own influence, new uses and interventions kept emerging. Mindfulness is a powerful mediator for both—the maintenance of solidarity and the control of machines. Through mindfulness and meditation, the experience of meaning in a technologically monotonous existence can be restored because one's biases—automated responding and thinking—can be experienced and possibly dismantled so that the image of one's unique experience of life is not constantly obstructed.

13.2.2 Brain and Technology

It is an automatic and timely response to equate the great merits of scientific thought with progress. We speak of the Enlightenment for good reason. One of the great insights of mindfulness is the shift out of automatic responses. How is this shift from individuality to an increasingly global scale psychologically possible?

Many of the cognitive processes that are part of our daily functioning relate not only to our brains themselves, but also (and often especially) to the tools and devices we use every day. These are not just devices such as household appliances, transportation, kitchen, plumbing, and multimedia devices. In fact, we "build" these tools into our overall organic and cognitive functioning. Consequently, our cognition is not "brain-bound" but "organization-bound."

As a result, we learn how to make devices so much a part of the way we function that we actually think of them as part of ourselves. A number of interesting psychological phenomena are the result of this. One of them is the *illusion of knowledge*. People believe that they understand a device that is part of their functioning, even if they understand it only at the procedural automatic level. That is, as part of their repertoire of actions, how to work with it. When asked, we often do not understand even seemingly simple devices such as a water closet. This is also true, for example, of understanding the mechanism of an office chair or—even more so—of understanding complicated concepts such as electricity or politics. Many people see electric light only as a light bulb in a socket and with a light switch. People believe they have adequate knowledge of these devices and concepts. The less knowledge we have about a device that is nevertheless part of our daily functioning, the more likely we are to overestimate it. Things are often even more complicated when it comes to social constructs (policy matters, rules and procedures). Since our daily functioning depends heavily on building all mechanisms into our cognitive schemas—and as we know the world, we think we understand the world as well.

Overload is a particular case of the illusion of control that is innate but reinforced by technology. Human actions, feelings and thoughts are much less rational than we assume. Moreover, coincidence always has the final say. However, our illusion of control is deeply rooted in our genetic makeup. We tend to attribute success to our competence, while we attribute failure to bad luck. Technologization contributes to the illusion of a feasible world in which chance no longer seems to matter. Fortunately, we tend to perceive ourselves as having above-average intelligence, talent, and competence. Patients with depression, however, seem to have a more realistic type of attribution, but their chance of survival is reduced, thus making it clear that our irrationality, our "technological illusionism," offers evolutionary advantages.

Individually, we have little "trouble" with our irrationality, our attributional errors and mistakes, but collectively the attitude is leading us to ecological disaster.

Children—symbolized by Greta Thunberg—are fighting back against this at the UN in New York, where in 2019 she pointed an accusing finger at country leaders who were invited precisely because their countries were reasonably busy implementing the agreements of a previous climate treaty. But with accusations back and forth, the same attribution error is made. No one brought about this state of affairs in a controlled way; it is a consequence of the extensive interdependencies that characterize large-scale patterns. And these large-scale patterns have emerged from the bottom up. To blame one person—or one occupational group—is again evidence of the attribution error already mentioned. What we need to do is clear: back to smaller scales, but the fact that this can only be done if it is addressed on a large scale (i.e., technologically) immediately reveals the irreconcilable controversy.

Another way is to regain respect for *coincidence,* but this requires a radical change in our mindset, even against our nature. Through mindfulness, we are able to recognize that technology, by definition, does not make our lives better, and that the profit numbers of high-tech giants do not simply increase our global sustainability. Above all, we need to recognize that making life seemingly easier does not make it better. The higher our position, the more likely we are to check off entry after entry in our schedule, to always be short on time, and that chance will always have the last word anyway. How long we live, how much recognition we receive—coincidence plays a much bigger role everywhere than our ingrained illusion of control and rationality would have us believe. The only thing we have to counter coincidence is our dignity: neither blame nor fame harms me. Mindfulness can play a role in changing this mindset.

Mindfulness is a necessity to break through technological influence. Self-awareness is crucial in a fast-changing world where you have to reinvent yourself again and again. Are my feelings and thoughts "authentic," or does Netflix determine what I see, or Google what I feel? Mindfulness is necessary to recognize serendipity. Investing in mindfulness helps prevent choosing the easiest path by default or automatically running away or looking the other way. It helps to look at oneself and the products of one's thoughts, feelings and actions on a meta-level, to recognize what was necessary for the progress of our cultural being. As individuals, as we have seen, we can live increasingly mechanized or automated (mindless) lives, losing diversity, while society as a whole becomes more diverse in its cultural "products." Above all, mindfulness can help the individual to contrast diversity with uniformity by organizing their own feedback!

13.2.3 Energy and Technology

Besides material technology, there is also *abstract* technology. Language and religion can be interpreted as man-made techniques, as can mindfulness.

If sufficient measurements are made, almost everything, no matter how arbitrary, is normally distributed: the length of trees, blades of grass, people, or the age of the inhabitants of a given city, etc. Above one standard deviation, one is intelligent or obese, for example. The image of the normal (healthy) person is produced at the expense of all who deviate from it. And it is this power that surrounds us, in lifestyle magazines, in education, in psychology, in preschool ratings, and in insurance premiums, like Orwell's Big Brother (Dr. Psych) from the novel 1984, helping us to become "normal" (opaque, but ever-present) again. From birth, we are in different ranks (distributions). Fortunately, we usually end up somewhere in the 68% margin around the average. We are either normal or disturbed or gifted. It is precisely because we have all internalized normal distributions individually that we are subject to the distributions without resistance. We have become jailers and big brothers to ourselves and others: We can always be seen, but we never know when we are being observed.

Nowadays, we are constantly monitored digitally (assigned to virtual distributions), including by advertisers and service providers. This is inevitable. But the psychology and psychiatry that create their own disorders and services through normal distributions are not much more scientific than the shamans of yesterday! We often struggle to free ourselves from the implicit power that the normal distribution imposes on us. Again, mindfulness can be used in two ways, as a form of meditation to free ourselves from constant influence and locate ourselves in the present, making stress or negative feelings manageable, and as a step in awareness of being fundamentally influenced by technology.

13.2.4 Technology and Organic Life: Entropy Versus Negative Entropy

Our relationship with (intelligent) technology is still young. Technology is lifeless and always evolves entropically. That is, a device that comes out of the factory does not simply develop additional functionalities. In addition to the internal combustion engine that a car comes out of the factory with, for example, another powertrain (electric motor) will not simply develop spontaneously. Entropy means that the degree of complexity (ordered structure) decreases, e.g. because (partial) functions fail or parts are broken.

Everything that lives, including humans, develops exactly the other way round: negatively entropic. In the development of plants and animals, there are countless moments of switching, of new formation, e.g. from stem to branch in a plant or from one-word sentence to complex sentence structure (syntax) in humans. Sometimes we literally grow out of our skin, fur, or trunk. Growth is a prerequisite for entering the new phase. A condition that no longer fits—imperfection—stimulates transformation. Although every single technical device is entropic, the development of "things" in general is negatively entropic. In 130 years, cars evolved from horseless carriages to autonomous driving meeting rooms. But the evolution (negative entropy) of "things" is always based on people (organic life), partly conscious, partly random, guided by need and supply. For example, to keep up with our changing needs, we evolve our house through renovations. Technology is alive because we lend it our lives. So is smart technology, even on a large scale.

Life is change. Sometimes we forget that nothing is permanent. In our 24-h economy, everything seems to be available around the clock: energy (heat, light), entertainment (Internet, TV radio) and food (long store hours). We are significantly depriving ourselves of the natural cycles of nature and the seasons. At most, summer vegetables are a little more expensive in winter, or the heating system has to work a little harder on winter nights, but climate and nature have been reduced to mood-setters in the background. Technology plays a crucial role in realizing and organizing such a continuously available reality around us; information technologies and services contribute to the illusion that we humans are as continuous as the artificial—denaturalized—world around us. This makes it easy to forget that our psychological and biological reality is completely cyclical, just like nature and climates. Mindfulness can help us focus on our own mutability, on our continuous growth and development. Especially in a world so dominated by technology (entropy), it is important to be mindful of our own negative entropy. We are not devices that can be easily "displaced" by others. By coming to terms with our own mutability, we can only remain (or become) ourselves. What do we feel beyond the immediate automatic responses to the technological world around us? What do we really want, beyond what we should or should not want? In our relationship to other natural life ("negative entropy"), we need to make space for constant evolution/change. Technology also changes, but always discontinuously, from one device to another. Again, our relationships with ourselves and each other can easily lead to the illusion of immutability. Through mindfulness, we can free ourselves from this illusion. Moreover, instead of fleeing, we can learn to recognize and use the power that remains with us in less desirable circumstances.

13.2.5 The Simpler, the Better?

As mentioned earlier, there is an implicit assumption that the Enlightenment brought us progress and that new technologies by definition bring progress. In higher education, we can observe a transition from learning from printed copy to learning on a screen. About three decades ago, a similar transition occurred from writing (pen and pencil) to typing (and to computers), from manuscript to typescript. However, recent research suggests that our understanding (comprehension) is at stake. Students who took notes with pen and paper were better able to answer questions about the lecture than students who took notes on a keyboard. This was the case both immediately after the lecture and several weeks later. The better understanding with pen and paper was notable because the written notes were full of half-sentences, arrows, and sometimes drawings that appeared to have nothing to do with the content. However, students who were not present at the lecture did much better after studying the typed rather than the written notes.

Recently, some studies (Singer & Alexander, 2017; Singer Trakhman et al., 2019) showed that students learn much better on paper than on screens such as e-readers, tablets, or laptops when the length of the text exceeds one A4. Again, this proved to be contrary to students' expectations (the "digital generation" preferred to learn from the screen in advance). The learning effort involved seems to be the decisive factor. The main idea was grasped just as well from the screen as from print (one learns faster from the screen), but the processing of other relevant contexts was much worse when learning from the screen.

Is the digital world making us more superficial? We often judge things to be more valuable when we have to invest a lot of effort instead of acquiring them effortlessly. Sometimes we can't see the value of things until we lose them. Many studies show that rapid scrolling has a disruptive effect on our understanding. Why do educators who can base their knowledge and insights on 2500 years of research in didactics and development change everything because IT provides a new resource?

13.3 Mindfulness and Human Development

We have seen that our thoughts and actions are largely "mechanized" in the technological world in which we are developing. In order to be able to let go, one must first hold on to something. Practicing mindfulness in dealing with one's being in the—technological—context leads to getting in touch with one's inner experience. The value here is not to reflexively run away, not to react directly in automatisms, to feel, experience and act, but to learn to look at oneself on a meta-level. What does the situation evoke, what do you feel, what do you think, what do you tend to do "instinctively"? Further on, we focus on how brain pathways—automatic reactions and learned skills and thought patterns—emerge so that we learn to let go of them or even break them.

13.3.1 Constructions in the Brain

Our brain forms traces (memory) through repetition. Not that anything ever repeats in our world; reality is a continuous stream with infinite variance. But, for example, every time it gets dark again, our brain starts to construct the pattern as repetition. The more often events like "same" (invariant) end up in such a constructed brain trajectory, the deeper the trajectory in question is worn out. Repetition is thus a construction of our brain and not a reality; patterns and patterns of patterns etc. are brain structures. Every brain learns to automatically use invariants from small details to interpret events (just like Sherlock Holmes)—automatically, because in the infinitely variable world, our brain focuses attention as quickly as possible on the unexpected, which is always lurking. Therefore, "decoded" patterns are processed automatically as much as possible. Automatic responses are retrieved quickly and with low energy costs. But they are not prepared for completely new situations. Sometimes our whole life runs automatically! This is not a problem until stability turns into stagnation and we doze off. When our automated life no longer sufficiently meets the demands of the environment, this can lead to burn-out or bore-out!

13.3.2 The Advantage of the Illiterate

It is sometimes noted that, for example, Elvis Presley impersonators almost without exception sing technically better than Elvis. Yet we all miss the magic. Swap Elvis for any other groundbreaking star, thinker, writer or scientist, and the findings remain the same: technically better performers, less magic. What's the deal with that?

Every child comes into the world illiterate. The beginning of the acquisition of our first language starts when our brain begins to construct invariants from an endless stream of sound variants. Your brain constructs traces based on the sounds of the voices of mom (high voice) and dad (low voice), among others. Pitch is still variable, but it also includes regularities and repetitions that can be recognized and thus constructed into additional invariant brain sounds. Neurons network. Slowly but steadily, from the bottom up, each child constructs the native language. However, when learning a second language at a later age (e.g., high school or elderly), the circumstances are completely different. The person is no longer helpless in the cradle and, moreover, has already developed an instrument of understanding, the mother tongue. The new language is learned in large part through the first language, through a kind of top-down shortcut. This is a disadvantage. In newborns, the first contact with the world is on a sensorimotor basis, by tasting and touching, by bringing things to the mouth. The first words bring about this sensorimotor understanding and later replace it. In this way, words replace grasping, becoming abstract grasping—understanding. In this sense, first language acquisition is about abstract understanding (grasping) of things, events, and situations, all the way from the bottom up. However, second or third language learning is not primarily based on bottom-up features. Top-down aspects (pre-existing language, knowledge of the world, etc.) prevent the emergence and thus the bottom-up acquisition of the new language. Moreover, there is much less synesthesia (connection between different modalities, e.g., sound/hearing and form/vision, for example) in second language acquisition, both because second language acquisition depends heavily on top-down processes and because the brain is already divided into specialties/modularities. Knowing this provides opportunities for education. A good language teaching method should inhibit logical thinking and allow for the bottom-up aspects of first language acquisition.

What does this have to do with Elvis? Often a first generation artist, scientist, or writer is especially busy discovering new art, technology, or science from the bottom up. They invent themselves, quite illiterate in terms of their goals to be achieved. The second generation is literate, uses top-down acronyms, and knows what has become successful. Often this leads to stereotypes, exaggerations, only when people aspire to more than imitation—transformation—can this lead to redevelopment. Then again, this second generation becomes a new first generation (from the bottom up) and goes exploring: New language variation, theories, music styles can be born!

After all, virtually all great inventions are made simultaneously in several places, often independently of each other. The name that later becomes known everywhere is the one that got to the patent office first, or the artist who was in the right place at the right time. History—both individual and collective—emerges from the bottom up. Illiteracy means searching from the bottom up, not yet fully grasped by reason, as opposed to literacy (from the top down with reason). Sometimes new things emerge more easily from illiteracy than from literacy. In the second language we have learned to trust our eyes, our reason, our literacy. We have forgotten to listen to our hearts, our inner selves, and still perceive the magic. The benefits of illiteracy elude us. In the course of any development, it is important to create space for exploration starting from relative illiteracy. In education, more attention should be paid to this path. In the words of the fox from Saint-Exupéry's "The Little Prince": "This is my secret, it is very simple: one can only see well with the heart. The essential is invisible to the eyes" (Antoine de Saint-Exupéry, 2015).

By the way, for first generation stars like Elvis, it often also becomes more difficult over time not to become a copy of themselves (an increasingly "smaller" section of their original originality). For them, transformation is definitely also a necessity. Mindfulness offers the possibility to face the situation or reality as if it were the first time. As will be explained, it is important to step out of the track of repetition and to reinvent oneself, so to speak, so that one does not become a weaker and weaker—automated—repetition of oneself. Mindfulness, then, is the link with which you can potentially maintain or regain your originality. But again, you must first grasp something in order to let go. Since many brain traces, knowledge, and skills have already been automated, the main issue is letting go. The purpose of mindfulness is to temporarily regain illiteracy, to feel like a child, to be fascinated, and to completely reinvent yourself.

13.3.3 Two Systems

Nobel Prize-winning psychologist Daniel Kahneman describes in his best-selling book "Thinking fast and slow" (2011) that we have two systems of thinking. The first system is an autopilot based on intuitions, wordless understanding, and first impressions. The second system always requires a cognitive effort: to think and consciously pay attention to something. The first system is automatic (therefore requires relatively little energy) and works in parallel: many processes are processed simultaneously. The second system works serially. That is, only one aspect can be paid attention to at a time. Central attention costs relatively much energy. After a lot of training, the system can eventually be used to check the first system, so that we have to rely less on first impressions and gut feelings. This is again a prerequisite for (re)development. But both systems are crucial for our development.

13.3.4 The Power of Emotions

Art appeals to emotions. Art that appeals to the broad masses often expresses new collective emotions, as the Beatles did in the 1960s. More recently, "Je suis Charlie" expressed a sense of peaceful yet militant outrage against terrorism by millions of Europeans. How does that work?

According to psychologist Paul Ekman (1992), six universal expressions of emotions can be distinguished: Anger, disgust, fear, joy, sadness, and surprise. Precisely because the facial expressions in these emotions seem to be culture-independent, it is assumed that the underlying emotions are firmly anchored in evolutionary terms. The direct link to (neuro-)physiological processes is then considered to be the cause of the expression, such as the dilation of the pupils and an increase in blood pressure due to the corticosteroid response (HPA axis).

Of course, we experience many more emotions, such as indeterminacy, homesickness, coziness, etc. Such *complex* (i.e. composite) emotions form the link between our biological origin and cultural processes. In the course of life, each person forms the second nature, which is much more important because it is changeable. Starting from the basic emotions, which are the fuel or motivator, we form our second nature, our culturally integrated personality. The virtues, such as courage and justice, serve as a guide. If we want to be courageous, we can make courage our second nature step by step by transforming fear through thought and practice. This gives rise to many new compound emotions/feelings, such as honor, respect and awe. The six basic emotions thus form a basic alphabet with which we can compose a variety of emotions in interaction with our thinking and cultural processes. Aristotle thus established the role of education.

From our biologically hard-wired basic emotions, we develop and unfold complex emotions, just like language, art or science. Complex emotions are a living "language," a cultural phenomenon. To return to the introduction: They gave rise to Beatlemania and #je-suis-Charlie, for example. At the beginning of the twentieth century, feelings of insecurity and despair emerged in the industrialized modern world, as expressed, for example, in the 1920 opera "Die tote Stadt" (Erich Korngold) as an unreal, machine-like feeling. Later in the twentieth century, in the art of Basjan Ader and still later in the music of the metal band Rammstein, these emotions return, now combined with a new emotion of ambiguity between having control and losing control.

Of course, new emotions can also cause new suffering. In psychiatry, diagnoses come and go, coupled with emotions that arise, become important, and lose relevance again. In the nineteenth century, for example, hysteria was a common reaction of women from the wealthy Viennese bourgeoisie, who had to function in a kind of

Victorian straitjacket. In the clinic, patients were sometimes completely paralyzed and diagnosed with conversion hysteria. But when there was a fire in the clinic, for example, the patients were usually able to move again very quickly. Today, this clinical picture is no longer encountered, although somatoform disorder seems to be a contemporary variant of it. Just as art originates (in part) in the expression of emotions, clinical psychology/psychiatry consists in part in treating (or shutting down) too strong effects of developing emotions.

13.4 Mindful Leadership

In summary, it can be said so far: Technology creates frameworks, but also limits our degrees of freedom. Our brains create contingent patterns of responses, feelings, and knowledge, but can prevent desired adaptations or new patterns from being automated. Technology creates space for mindfulness and restricts it almost equally (Valorinta, 2009). Mindfulness presupposes development and thus contingent patterns in a (technological) world. After all, you can't let go if you haven't reached for something first. It is important for leaders to achieve a certain level of autonomy and authenticity. This requires finding one's own voice, determining one's own position, discovering what a particular situation evokes in oneself and thus triggering the automatic reactions. Mindfulness is a possible path to authenticity in leadership.

As a technique, mindfulness-based cognitive therapy has a wide range of applications. When mindfulness is followed by intense virtual reality experiences (immersive virtual environments, IVEs), the effects of 8 weeks of mindfulness training appear to be evident in responses to virtual reality (Crescentini et al., 2016): decreased heart rate, less muscle activity in the frontal area, and decreased anxiety levels when confronted with IVEs compared to a control group. As an exposure therapy, VR appears to have been successfully addressed by mindfulness for some time (Difede & Hoffman, 2002). My team is currently exploring the opposite: the possibility of first experiencing a salient VR experience in a burnout situation so that mindfulness training can be started afterwards, because especially in severe burnout it is sometimes difficult to free oneself from the (stressful) here and now *in order* to be able to open up for training.

To learn to look at entrenched routines in a new way, mindfulness offers many opportunities, according to the scientific literature (for a review, see Luken & Sammons, 2016). For managers, there are particular challenges. They examine equity and reciprocity. Equity considers the principle of equal rules for all. In practice, this means that for the manager, each individual belongs to the abstract category of workers. A (procedural) response to this abstraction has been mapped out in advance from the manager-worker relationship. But a mindfulness response can mean not doing something or allowing someone freedom in a particular situation. When possible, giving people priority over procedures can make a difference. To this end, the manager must learn to control his or her automated responses to the actual situation in which the employee is subject to his or her own subject and in which natural fluctuations occur.

"Natural" fluctuations are most easily observed in our relationships with family and friends or with a new job. Our willingness to invest in a workplace (relationships) depends on a variety of factors, but they differ depending on the phase. In the initial phase of a work relationship, for example—the growth phase—it is often necessary to invest a lot in order to adjust to aspects and tasks that are still new to the employee. To do this, it is important that the experienced compensation is properly aligned with these investments. The processes here are not always psychologically linear. For example, a high investment at a moderate but appropriate compensation has proven to be much better than a generous compensation with a lower investment. The theory of cognitive dissonance plays a role here. Because we want to keep the image we have of ourselves consistent, someone who invests a lot and receives relatively little in return will be inclined to take the investment for its own (internal) account (motivation): We work hard because we care!

After the *first* (growth) phase in a new (working) relationship, we enter a *second* phase of more stability. In this phase, we can focus on things other than the new relationship, even though it is not until the *third* phase, the routine phase, that we can fully rely on autopilot. But of course, things always change at work (a new boss, a new colleague, or new procedures). Where it is relatively easy to adapt to change in the stability phase, it is again difficult in the *third,* routine phase. Ingrained patterns are often difficult to break. When it is really necessary to break the patterns, one can easily enter a *fourth* phase, the phase of renewed choice or transformation. In this phase, everything is possible again. Breaking or, on the contrary, growing into a deeper or different level is more feasible here than in the other three phases. After a break (job-hop, burn-out, advancement in the organizational hierarchy, etc.) or a more positive "choice," the cycle repeats: growth, stabilization, routine, and transformation/choice.

Mindfulness allows a supervisor to subtly learn about the employee's situation and process and act accordingly. In the choice phase, for example, a little nudge may be all it takes to get someone to initiate development or growth again. But changing something in the routine phase requires much more energy (and possibly more resistance) from an employee than from one who is still in the midst of the growth phase. The entire employee team also goes through a dynamic cycle, and again, different opportunities and challenges can be identified for each phase. Through mindfulness, a supervisor can orient to what is going on where and when. A response can be mindfully adapted that goes beyond protocols and procedures, even though the aforementioned biodeterminism and the great emphasis on procedures and protocols (and lean management) may give the false impression that supervisors can act mechanically and thoughtlessly (Fichman, 2004).

Another example concerns reciprocity. People need people. No one can survive completely independently. For example, trying to survive in the jungle will soon lead to threatening disruption. The pursuit of autonomy is illusory; we need each other all the time. In a rural society, "one another" consists of a group of acquaintances (the butcher, carpenter, doctor, teacher, etc.). In the city, "each other" has (largely) become an abstraction. The abstraction of our social network results from both urbanization and automation. Both factors contribute significantly to our illusion of autonomy. Finally, we have become anonymous in cities. Sometimes we share the same front door with more than 1000 fellow citizens, to be able to choose from a range of stores within a mile to satisfy the basic needs of life.

In the real world, in order to survive, we have to pay special attention to almost no one. We can do whatever we want at our own pace. Stores are open 7 days a week (so there's no continuity on the staff side anymore), and web stores and Internet banking have made the disconnect between necessary physical connection and the ability to satisfy needs even more apparent. In contrast to the real world, it is the virtual world that we can no longer ignore. Thanks to automation, some of us work at home, and our colleagues are increasingly becoming remote abstractions. We tend to bury ourselves in anonymity and live in the illusion that we are autonomous, because the other has become nothing more than a virtual reflection, an ambiguous address, and an ambiguous face. We are no longer dependent on anyone in particular, but on everyone in general.

One problem is that we approach the outside world via (information) technology and social networks. We can get in touch with others via social media, and so making contacts in our real lives has once again become less necessary.

However, pretending is much easier in the virtual world than in the physical world. Beautifully designed, carefully edited, as bloggers or vloggers, home workers or "just" Facebook users, we wave to each other from our illusory perfect lives. We live up to the impression that we are perfect and hide our loneliness and sadness. The first "official" psychological syndromes have been named, e.g., selfitis (someone who takes multiple selfies a day, Balakrishnan & Griffiths, 2017), and bloggers and vloggers are at increased risk of burnout! Imperfection in technology is irritating or even dangerous and therefore forbidden. But humans evolve through mistakes, through trial and error, and thus through imperfection. By mirroring our technical tools—technology is perfect and so are we—we close ourselves off more and more from development.

We channel feelings of indecision by pointing the finger at imperfections that are far beyond us. When talented soccer player Abdelhak Nouri goes into cardiac arrest in 2017 due to a heart defect, someone has to be blamed. Was Nouri warned by his cardiologist 15 years ago that playing soccer was a risk? This question was investigated in serious newspapers in the case of Nouri, followed by the demand for more rules so that such "abuses" can be avoided. The demand for rules and regulations goes on and on. Are we on our way to a risk-free "brave new world"? We can only evolve by taking risks. Most of the time this goes well, but unlike technology, there is no guarantee certificate for people or their behavior.

People need each other—not just virtually. We need each other especially when we are scared, insecure or sick. Then we need physical instead of virtual support, attention from person to person. But the delusion of perfection not only leads us astray, it also tempts us to exclude any kind of imperfection through rules and regulations. In doing so, we exclude a part of ourselves that is necessary for development. Technology and our lives are so intertwined that we can no longer see that, unlike technology, we grow and develop in imperfection. What seems wrong today may turn out to be very good later, and vice versa. If we demand perfection, we exclude life. If the neighbor is only allowed to give advice when she is accredited to do so, we may miss the chance to make a valuable contribution to our problem. When human relationships are regulated down to the last detail, our autonomy is only an illusion.

References

Balakrishnan, J., & Griffiths, M. D. (2017). An exploratory study of "Selfitis" and the development of the Selfitis behavior scale. *International Journal of Mental Health and Addiction*, 1–15.

Crescentini, C., Capurso, V., Furlan, S., & Fabbro, F. (2016). Mindfulness-oriented meditation for primary school children: Effects on attention and psychological well-being. *Frontiers in Psychology, 7*, 805.

de Saint-Exupéry, A. (2015). *The little prince*. eBook original edition, CloudShip.

Difede, J., & Hoffman, H. G. (2002). Virtual reality exposure therapy for World Trade Center post-traumatic stress disorder: A case report. *Cyberpsychology & Behavior, 5*(6), 529–535.

Ekman, P. (1992). An argument for basic emotions. *Cognition & Emotion, 6*(3–4), 169–200.

Fichman, R. G. (2004). Going beyond the dominant paradigm for information technology innovation research: Emerging concepts and methods. *Journal of the Association for Information Systems, 5*(8), 11.

Luken, M., & Sammons, A. (2016). Systematic review of mindfulness practice for reducing job burnout. *American Journal of Occupational Therapy, 70*(2), 1–10.

Singer, L. M., & Alexander, P. A. (2017). Reading across mediums: Effects of reading digital and print texts on comprehension and calibration. *The Journal of Experimental Education, 85*(1), 155–172.

Singer Trakhman, L. M., Alexander, P. A., & Berkowitz, L. E. (2019). Effects of processing time on comprehension and calibration in print and digital mediums. *The Journal of Experimental Education, 87*(1), 101–115.

Valorinta, M. (2009). Information technology and mindfulness in organizations. *Industrial and Corporate Change, 18*(5), 963–997.

Chapter 14
Outlooks: A Plea for a Humane Society

Volker Schulte, Christoph Steinebach, and Klaske N. Veth

The authors have described blueprints for mindful leadership in the last 260X pages. Indeed, good people leadership is the noblest and most important task for developing humane work cultures. Meanwhile, there are several other reasons why we need to create a paradigm shift in leadership.

14.1 New Social Capital in the Network Society

The new generations are our most important social capital. By social capital, the editors mean the willingness of individuals in a society to contribute to it with their own resources and opportunities. Today, we live in network societies to an even greater extent than in the past. These result from the strong links via social media and platforms, which create both knowledge and political knowledge formation at lightning speed and with high scaling. Network-like organizational structures can be formed in a very short time, with regional, national and transnational nodes and links. The consequences for traditional organizational structures at the corporate and governmental levels are not yet even foreseeable.

V. Schulte (✉)
School of Business, University of Applied Sciences Northwestern Switzerland, Windisch, Switzerland
e-mail: volker.schulte@fhnw.ch

C. Steinebach
ZHAW School of Applied Psychology, Universities of Applied Sciences Zurich, Zurich, Switzerland

K. N. Veth
Hanze University of Applied Sciences Groningen, Groningen, The Netherlands

V. Schulte et al. (eds.), *Mindful Leadership in Practice*,
https://doi.org/10.1007/978-3-030-97311-7_14

These networking approaches have a completely different dynamic than traditional network formation via training, professions, industries or associations. Frederic Vester foresaw this trend almost 50 years ago (Vester, 1974). He derived systemic networked thinking from biocybernetics. In such a system, there are strong effects and wave movements that take place through respective feedbacks, because there is mutual interaction in these dynamically self-regulating networks.

The important thing here is that these networks each contribute to added value for society as a whole. The core insight here is that each generation wants to bring its own innovations into the world. The history of mankind is characterized by steady, albeit not linear, progress. It is therefore absolutely essential that the players in and between these networks cooperate with each other and create social trust. This requires and at the same time promotes strong social cohesion in the few remaining democratic societies.

We depend on innovations, whether from individuals, charismatics or via networks. Innovations are irreplaceable if we want to solve the major challenges facing humanity, such as the climate crisis, hunger or armed conflicts. In our post-industrial societies, it is only through innovations that we can succeed and contribute to keeping this planet viable.

14.2 The Imperative of Demography

We have too few descendants. Those we do have no longer live in family clusters, are highly individualized and independent. Frank Schirrmacher already put this in a nutshell 15 years ago and pointed out the consequences (Schirrmacher, 2006). According to figures from the Swiss Federal Statistical Office, at the end of 2018 a good third of the approximately 3.8 million private households were one-person households. Two people lived in just under another third of households. The average household size was 2.23 persons. This fragmentation of traditional forms of living in families and larger communities will sooner or later lead to new forms of living that will have to do without the traditional social nucleus, the family (Bundesamt für Statistik, 2020).

One can welcome or reject this development, it remains a fact. Social responsibility must therefore redefine itself. How will trust be created via the networks mentioned above? How will sociality, which is already genetically ingrained in people, develop in the coming years, what are its characteristics? A priority social goal must therefore be to train the few people in the current cohorts to become mindful leaders.

The fact that there will be a severe shortage of skilled workers once the COVID 19 crisis is over means that we will have to do everything in our power to provide these people with the best possible leadership training. Good leadership requires two things above all: empathy and trust. What happens when trust is lost within an organization or a company? Transaction costs increase. The lower the level of trust, the more contract, negotiation and control costs will increase at all levels of society.

Only through education—and more specifically—good leadership education, will we be able to build cultures of trust, which are also and especially necessary in virtual yet real worlds. Approaches to this are available. Generation Greta wants to create a better world—and in all radicality of peaceful coexistence. It is incumbent on the older ones among us to support this generation and to share with it our experience of how to deal with each other in a resource-oriented manner.

References

Bundesamt für Statistik. (2020). *Haushalte. Neuchâtel.* Accessed October 21, 2020, from https://www.bfs.admin.ch/bfs/de/home/statistiken/bevoelkerung/stand-entwicklung/. . .

Schirrmacher, F. (2006). *Minimum. Vom Vergehen und Neuentstehen unserer Gesellschaft*. Karl Blessing Verlag.

Vester, F. (1974). *Das kybernetische Zeitalter*. S. Fischer.

MIX
Papier aus verantwortungsvollen Quellen
Paper from responsible sources
FSC® C105338

If you have any concerns about our products,
you can contact us on
ProductSafety@springernature.com

In case Publisher is established outside the EU,
the EU authorized representative is:
Springer Nature Customer Service Center GmbH
Europaplatz 3, 69115 Heidelberg, Germany

Printed by Libri Plureos GmbH
in Hamburg, Germany